D1432362

# Mark Twain's West

*The author's memoirs about his boyhood,
riverboats and western adventures*

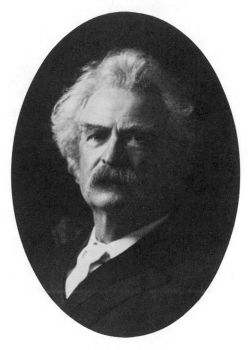

*Samuel Langhorne Clemens at age 64.*
*About the time he wrote the reminiscences included in this book.*
Courtesy of the Mark Twain Papers, The Bancroft Library

The Lakeside Classics

# MARK TWAIN'S WEST

*The author's memoirs about his boyhood,
riverboats and western adventures.*

EDITED BY
WALTER BLAIR

The Lakeside Press

R. R. DONNELLEY & SONS COMPANY
CHICAGO
*Christmas,* 1983

Grateful acknowledgement is made to Harper & Row Publishers, Inc. for permission to reprint selections from the following volumes by and about Mark Twain.

MARK TWAIN A BIOGRAPHY by A. B. Paine.
Copyright 1912 by Harper & Row, Publishers, Inc.
Copyright 1940 by Dora L. Paine.

MARK TWAIN IN ERUPTION by Mark Twain.
Copyright 1922 by Harper & Row, Publishers, Inc.

THE FAMILY MARK TWAIN (LIFE ON THE MISSISSIPPI) by Mark Twain.
Compilation Copyright 1972 by Harper & Row, Publishers, Inc.

THE INNOCENTS ABROAD by Mark Twain.
Copyright 1869, 1897, 1899 by The American Publishing Co.

ROUGHING IT by Mark Twain.
Copyright 1871, 1899 by The American Publishing Co.

SKETCHES NEW AND OLD by Mark Twain.
Copyright 1875 by Samuel L. Clemens.

HOW TO TELL A STORY AND OTHER ESSAYS by Mark Twain.
Copyright 1897, 1898, 1899 by Harper & Row, Publishers, Inc.

A TRAMP ABROAD by Mark Twain.
Copyright 1907 by Samuel L. Clemens.

The selections from *Villagers of 1840-3* were first published in MARK TWAIN'S HANNIBAL, HUCK & TOM edited by Walter Blair, University of California Press, 1969. They are copyright 1969 by the Mark Twain Company - now the Mark Twain Foundation - which reserves all reproduction or dramatization rights in every medium. Permission to reprint has been obtained from the University of California Press and Robert H. Hirst, General Editor of the Mark Twain Project, The Bancroft Library, University of California, Berkeley.

# PUBLISHERS' PREFACE

A QUICK check of the previous *Lakeside Classic* selections (which are listed at the back of this book) will reveal a broad spectrum of titles, all of which concern "the coming of age of America." One will also note a similarly broad spectrum of authors, many of whom can be quickly recognized because of their reputations in politics, exploration, military service and adventure. Others, whose names are not familiar, might be classified as ordinary Americans who were thoughtful enough to record their experiences. Collectively, they have given us valuable insights into American life and life styles just a relatively short time ago.

Such an investigation will also reveal that none of these authors had attained any sort of literary reputation. So, with this thought in mind, we have spent a portion of the past several years searching for an autobiography of an American author. To be sure, we had already become acquainted with several when, quite by chance, we ran across a two-volume set of books with the rather confusing title: *Mark Twain's Autobiography* by Albert Bigelow Paine. We became intrigued and investigated further.

We found that Samuel Langhorne Clemens, who used the pen name of Mark Twain, had never organized an autobiography. Yet, because so much of his material could be classified as autobiographical, three literary personalities have, at different times, put together in book form various selections from Twain's previously published accounts and personal reminiscences.

The first occurred in 1924, when Albert Bigelow Paine, who was appointed by Twain to be his biographer, edited various Twain material into the two-volume set previously mentioned.

In 1940, Bernard DeVoto edited a book titled *Mark Twain in Eruption* which drew upon some new and also some of the same selections chosen by Paine. Then in 1959, Charles Neider prepared *The Autobiography of Mark Twain* in similar fashion. All three chose from a wide selection of Twain's work. There was some overlap, yet each was edited to conform to different objectives.

And so, the idea of a *Lakeside Classic* containing a collection of Mark Twain's reminiscences took hold—not only as our selection for Christmas 1983, but also as a prelude to the 100th anniversary celebration of Twain's renowned *Huckleberry Finn* in 1984, and Twain's 150th birthday in 1985.

What appeared to be an idea of some merit was brought into full fruition when Dr. Walter Blair, Emeritus Professor of English at The University of Chicago, accepted our offer of editorship. Dr. Blair, a scholar of American humor for 50 years, is recognized as the nation's foremost authority on Mark Twain. He, too, is a prolific author—his latest book, *The Mirth of a Nation* was released earlier this year—

and he has received the Hubbell Award denoting top recognition by the American Literature Section of the Modern Language Association. It has been our pleasure to work with him.

In order for the proposed Mark Twain volume to best fit the *Lakeside Classic* mold, it was decided to include reminiscences from Twain's boyhood days in Missouri; the time he spent learning to be a Mississippi riverboat pilot; his overland trip across the plains to Nevada; his silver mining exploits; and his jobs as a young newspaper reporter and editor in Nevada, California and Hawaii. These events, arranged in chronological order, highlight Twain's first 31 years. They also represent the time he spent in what was then "the American West." The selections chosen by Dr. Blair have appeared in other Mark Twain books but never in the particular organization and sequence represented in this book which we have named *Mark Twain's West*. The book is further enriched by a most interesting Historical Introduction by Dr. Blair plus an occasional footnote to "keep the record straight" or to provide a fuller meaning to Twain's text. All-in-all, we believe our readers will gain a deeper knowledge and broader understanding of a portion of the life of the man whom many consider to be America's most revered and still most popular author.

This book, like the eighty that have preceded, adheres to the same objectives that were set forth when the series was conceived in 1903, that being to produce a book of highest quality standards using the most modern production methods.

Computer generated typesetting was furnished by our Electronic Graphics Central Division. Their work also included composing pages to the established *Classic* style as well as accurate proofreading. All aspects of book manufacture and distribution were performed by our Crawfordsville (Indiana) Manufacturing Division. This year, for the first time, several illustrations were converted to film for printing plates by the use of an electronic scanner. We have used this procedure for quite some time in the production process for catalogs and magazines, however just recently, we have expanded its use into book production. Other facets of work done in Crawfordsville include high-speed web offset printing using fast make-ready book presses especially designed for short runs, and a continuous binding system that begins with the gathering of signatures and ends with individually cartoned books with labels affixed, sacked and ready for mailing. Design services were handled as they have been for many years by our creative services subsidiary, Mobium Corporation for Design and Communication.

1983 has been a good year for R. R. Donnelley & Sons Company, and we would like to present some of the significant happenings and aspects.

Net sales are expected to reach a new high, continuing an uninterrupted rise of twenty-five years.

The same holds true for profits except for the year the LIFO method of accounting for inventories was adopted. The first half of the year was exceptionally good, due to lower start up costs, and the results of past planning, increased sales effort, improved productivity, and cost control. In face of much open capacity in our industry resulting in severe competitive price pressures, and open time in some categories of our own, we were able to maintain margins reasonably well, for the reasons mentioned above. Our growth represented real volume rather than higher prices. We do not pursue projects where the return on investment is expected to be abnormally low. Throughout the history of our company and our industry there has always been account turnover; usually more in periods of recession. Many of our accounts grew, and fine new ones were added.

Since all we produce is preceded by a sale, our sales effort and organization are all important. Our representatives are specialized, just as the products they sell and the customers they serve. We expect them to know thoroughly our skills, abilities, and capacities as well as to understand our customers' needs and desires. When both of these are done well, we are able to serve our customers in unique ways that enhance the value of the customer's products and increase his marketing effectiveness. This, in turn, helps us.

Because of our conservative financial policies and practices, the quality of our earnings is high and our liquidity has prepared us well to meet the challenges and opportunities of the future. Capital expenditures for 1983 will approximate 180 million dollars, mostly generated from internal financing, depreciation, and retained earnings equaling roughly two-thirds of net income. Our directors voted an increased dividend at the beginning of the year, and even with the realization that the unusually favorable circumstances of the first half were not expected to continue, they voted to increase the dividend again at midyear. Also, our stock was split 2-for-1, to give more smaller investors the opportunity to hold round lots of shares.

The past may not be the prologue of the future and we certainly are not going to rest on our laurels. However, we do take some pride in our accomplishments over the years. In current dollars from 1956 when the Company went public through 1982, our net sales have increased approximately 1400%, net income up 1300%, gross property, plant and equipment up 1400%, while the average number of employees only 112%. Investment per employee increased 700%, showing the value of productivity gains, as well as the importance of invested capital to employment and opportunities for promotion. In constant dollars, the increase of course is not as dramatic but still substantial. During the same period, the number of customers increased from 650 to over 2,200, which afforded us an even sounder base for our expanding operations.

While no new manufacturing divisions were established in the United States, modernization and expansion continue apace at the present divisions, as can be inferred from the size of our capital expenditure budget. Much of this will result in renewed start up costs. Last September, the Company announced the agreement by its British subsidiary to purchase Her Majesty's Stationery Office's telephone directory plant at Gateshead, near Newcastle upon Tyne. Under long term agreements with British Telecom, Ben Johnson and Company, Ltd. will print a large share of its directory requirements in its present plant at York and the new one which will be modernized and substantially reequipped.

To serve our many customers more effectively, present sales offices were expanded and additional ones established for a total of 24. New ones are located in Tampa, Florida and Ft. Worth, Texas for books; Philadelphia, Pennsylvania, Tampa, Florida, Bellevue, Washington, and Sherman Oaks, California for general directories; Atlanta, Georgia, Dallas and Ft. Worth, Texas for financial and legal printing. Significantly, a new London headquarters was established for Ben Johnson sales and Donnelley Satellite Graphics at Cutlers Gardens. Part of this is an attractive remodeled old warehouse of the East India Company. It is part of our satellite network which includes several U.S. facilities.

Important to our present and future success is the rapid development of technology in our Company, in almost every area. Use of automation was further employed in the control of manufacturing processes and material handling. Expanded and new uses of information in digital form were applied to design, cartography, color separation, composition, and platemaking, as well as data storage, retrieval, and transmission. Our ability to process a customer's copy at locations convenient to him is important. This, coupled with our ability to transmit by satellite to our decentralized printing centers, can give him the advantage of quick startups in multiple locations. This applies to both gravure and web offset. Additional transmitting and receiving stations were established to enhance communications here and abroad using our dedicated satellite channel. We can create various digital data bases, and from these bases we create printing surfaces. These bases will also allow us to create other forms of text and tone copy desired by our customers.

Selectronic binding was used by many more of our customers to tailor magazines and catalogs to the individual interests of their readers and customers. A Merge/Purge service was initiated to eliminate duplication of names when two or more lists are combined for mailings, thereby reducing cost of printing and postage and annoyance to recipients from duplicate (and more) mailings. Also helping to reduce mailing costs is our Entry Point Mailing Service. Quick Type Access (QTA) is designed to reduce the time span between receipt of copy and finished product. In order for our Digital Group to concentrate on this aspect of business, its former financial and legal printing operations were established separately as the Financial Printing Group.

Major changes occurred at the Director and General Management levels: David B. Meeker resigned in late 1982, and Harold J. Berry and Gaylord Donnelley retired as Directors at the Annual Meeting in March in accordance with established policy. The latter was elected Honorary Director and later Honorary Chairman. Charles W. Lake, Jr., who served the Company as President and Chairman for a total of 19 years, retired in accordance with Company policy, but continues as Director and was elected Chairman of the Executive Committee. The growth of our Company over the past two decades stands as unambiguous testimony to Mr. Lake's foresight and the strength of his leadership. Equally important has been his absolute dedication to quality and integrity in all aspects of his business and personal relationships. Mr. Lake's successor as Chairman is John B. Schwemm, who also continues as President.

Robert H. Smith joined our Company as Executive Vice President, Finance, while John C. Dennis continues as Executive Vice President, Operations. Robert C. Fields, Vice Chairman, chose early retirement at the end of 1982, as did Robert W. Crowe, Vice President and Secretary, in March of 1983. Charles C. Haffner, III succeeded Mr. Fields as Vice Chairman, and continues as Treasurer.

While 1983 might be considered a year of revolutionary transition because of the above mentioned developments, we hold steadfast to our well established philosophies, principles, policies and practices, our "four P's". We are committed to high standards of integrity, quality, reliability, and service to our customers. While maintaining a strong, liquid financial condition, we have not hesitated in investing in plant, advanced technology, and people to keep us in the forefront of our industry. Our dedication to people is real and no recent phenomenon, nor a self-serving claim. Our fine benefit programs for current employees and retirees alike, and the preference of our people to deal directly with management on a person-to-person basis, are some evidence of this. Our dedication to our "four P's" is firm because we are convinced that these, judiciously applied to the ever changing scene and with the support of many dedicated skilled people, form the basis of our past success and will for our future.

For this success we owe much to many—customers, suppliers, our own "Donnelley family", now over 16,000 strong, and others. To them our deep felt gratitude, and our very best wishes for a Merry Christmas and a Happy New Year.

THE PUBLISHERS

Christmas 1983

# CONTENTS

xviii                    *Contents*

# ILLUSTRATIONS

# HISTORICAL INTRODUCTION

A LTHOUGH *Mark Twain's West* is 99.9% pure Mark Twain, it never before was issued as a book. In it, the editor has put together chronologically a great author's reminiscences, separately published, about his eventful life in pre-Civil War Missouri, on the Mississippi riverboats, and in the Far West between his birth in 1835 and his move to the East in 1866. It proves that Samuel Langhorne Clemens (who beginning January 31, 1863, used the pen-name Mark Twain) was a superb historian.

Recognition of his skill is by no means new. Every now and then for many years, critics have asserted that, although he was chiefly famous for other achievements, he also was a pre-eminent chronicler. As far back as 1872, William Dean Howells predicted in the *Atlantic Monthly* that the readers of Twain's recently published *Roughing It* would find "at the end . . . that, while he has been merely enjoying himself, as he supposes, he has been surreptitiously acquiring a better idea of those flush times in Nevada, and of the adventurous life generally of the recent West, than he could possibly have got elsewhere."[1] In 1897, another *Atlantic* critic, Charles Miner Thompson, wrote of Twain: "He has recorded the life of certain southwestern portions of

[1]*Atlantic Monthly*, June, 1872, quoted in William Dean Howells, *My Mark Twain* (New York, 1910), p. 113.

our country, in one fleeting stage of their development, better than it is possible it will ever be done again."[2] In 1902, George Bernard Shaw remarked to Twain that "I am persuaded that the future historian of America will find your works as indispensable to him as a French historian finds the political tracts of Voltaire."[3]

In 1932, Bernard DeVoto, himself an outstanding historian, buttressed a similar claim with an interesting justification:

There is more of America in Mark Twain's books than in any others. *Roughing It* and *Life on the Mississippi* record their part of that experience: nothing will ever take their place. . . . More widely and deeply than anyone else who ever wrote books, he shared the life of America. . . . He, more completely than any other writer, took part in the American experience.[4]

Almost fifteen years later, Dixon Wecter agreed with both the claim and its justification:

*By his own participation*, no artist in our literature save Lincoln spans so broad a segment of typical American experience in the last century. . . . *His life* makes those

[2] *Atlantic Monthly*, 79 (April, 1897), 448. As will be shown, Thompson erred when he called Twain's picturings "absolutely accurate," though not when he called them "surprisingly comprehensive."

[3] Albert Bigelow Paine, *Mark Twain, a Biography* (New York, 1912) IV, 1398—hereafter *MTB*. Shaw's reason: "I tell you this because I am the author of a play in which a priest says, 'Telling the truth's the funniest job in the world,' a piece of wisdom which you helped teach me."

[4] *Mark Twain's America*, hereafter *MTA* (Boston, 1932), p. 321.

of literary men in Boston and Concord and New York resemble (in Hawthorne's phrase) the flowering of talents that blossomed in too retired a shade. *He knew* the greatest river of the continent as Melville knew the high seas. *He witnessed* the epic of America, the westward tide at its full, with . . . perception.

Wecter quoted a sentence Twain wrote about a murder he saw in the Hannibal of his youth, "I saw the red life gush from his breast," and contrasted its vividness with scenes Walt Whitman wrote about claiming "I was there." No such thing, said Wecter: "Walt's immediacy was imaginative;" the boy Sam's was "actual."[5]

Everything that Clemens learned about his forbears seemed to show they were the fantastically varied kind tradition held qualified a descendant for a "typical American experience." They included pirates, slave-traders, merchants, yeomen, a regicide judge (who wed a Castilian lady and thereby mingled Spanish with English and Irish blood), commoners, nobles, aristocratic planters, log cabin pioneers who fought red coats and "redskins" and who shot bears for table meat, Anglicans, Quakers, Calvinists and Free-thinkers.[6]

[5]"Mark Twain," in *Literary History of the United States* (New York, 1953), p. 917.

[6]Dixon Wecter, *Sam Clemens of Hannibal* (Boston, 1952), except when another source is indicated, is drawn upon for details about Clemens's ancestry and his Hannibal years. In the essay cited in footnote 5, Wecter says, "In the activities of the external man as well as in character and temperament, Mark Twain was a representative American. . . ."

Moreover if—as the nation's nineteenth-century credo held—a man followed a common American pattern when he started life poor and rose from rags to riches,[7] Clemens's ancestors over centuries made sure he'd get a proper start. When they took part in the great movement from the old world to the new, then westward overland which brought wealth to some and disaster to others, they fell in with the less lucky group. They avoided rich Virginia tidelands and lush old Southwestern farmlands and acquired less fertile uplands, knobs, and hollows. When they moved to new townsites, they hurried past where cities would flourish to those sure to deteriorate.

The humorist's father, John Marshall Clemens (usually called Marshall), had a talent for failure. Forced by poverty to fend for himself at fourteen, he made a move to Columbia, Kentucky, where he met Jane Lampton, whose family fortunes also were in a bad way. They married on May 6, 1823.

Chances that this union would be happy were

[7] A gratifying belief was that opportunities were so ubiquitous that any poor boy who worked hard could succeed. In 1873, Twain or his collaborator, Charles Dudley Warner, wrote, "To the young American . . . the paths to fortune are innumerable and all open; there is . . . success in all his wide horizon."—*The Gilded Age* (Hartford, 1873), p. 114. Howells in 1882, discussing Clemens's "typically American life," wrote, "The average American is the man who has risen; he has known poverty, and privation, and low conditions; . . . and now, in his prosperity, he regards the past with a sort of large, pitying amusement. . . ."—*My Mark Twain*, pp. 139–140.

small. Overly-conscientious, the groom had toiled daytimes to pay family debts; ambitious, he'd studied at night to become a lawyer, thus ruining his health to enter a profession for which he had little talent. Worry-bedeviled and bad-tempered, he became a chilly, frustrated husband and father. Jane was ebullient and warm-hearted, but according to family tradition married less for love than to spite a suitor who had irked her. Whether a blighted romance or Marshall's coldness was responsible, the marital relationship was tepid.[8]

In Columbia, the Clemenses hovered briefly in a house near—but prophetically not on—Fortune Street. As their fortunes waxed and waned—chiefly waned—they moved during the next fifteen years to five other localities where, altogether, they lived in a dozen houses. They did best in Jamestown, where by holding three political offices, practicing law and running a store, Marshall saved $3500. He invested $400 in 70,000 acres of land among the nearby Tennessee Knobs, sure that in time they'd make the family rich. (They never would.) The family was doing poorly in Three Forks on Wolf River when a letter from a relative who'd gone to Missouri persuaded them to move on to a new El Dorado.

Starting in the spring of 1835 they traveled over roads muddied hub-deep a hundred and seventy-five miles across the border into Kentucky, back to

[8] *Mark Twain's Hannibal, Huck & Tom*, ed. Walter Blair (Berkeley, 1969), p. 39.

Columbia, then to Louisville. Packed into the barouche were Marshall, Jane, three children, and personal and household effects. Their slave girl rode a pacing horse, Orion, the nine-year-old son, a trotting horse. From Louisville they went by steamboat down the Ohio to Cairo then up the Mississippi to St. Louis—about five hundred miles. They planned to settle in St. Louis, but a raging cholera epidemic kept them from making an unprecedented halt in a community that would soon flourish. So they moved overland another sixty miles to the minute town of Florida, Missouri. It was from Florida that a relative had announced a prediction that the place would thrive. The Clemens's settlement there, of course, was an omen that the relative's guess was wrong.

So, about June 1, the family's longest journey of more than 700 miles ended the movement Westward of the author's forbears that had started generations earlier. The movers in 1835 carried with them a snatch of song that, long after, Mark Twain would say he never could hear sung without a surge of deep emotion:

> John, John, the piper's son,
> He married me when I was young.
> We journeyed toward the setting sun,
> Over the hills and far away.

Atavism, prenatal memories, or—far more probably—family reminiscences and the author's identification of Jane Clemens with the singer must have evoked the nostalgic response. For the most important fact for him about that strenuous journey was that at some time and somehow during its course he was conceived.

Samuel Langhorne Clemens, only a seven months baby, was born on November 30, 1835, in a rented two-room clapboard, shake-roofed cabin that now is preserved in the Mark Twain Memorial Shrine in Stoutsburg, Missouri. "When I first saw him," his mother remembered, "I could see no promise in him. . . . He was a poor looking object to raise." Family mortality statistics were unfavorable: of seven Clemens children, one died at the age of three months, one lived only nine years, a third, ten. But Sam got through the winter in the ill-heated cabin, lived through frequent illnesses until he was seven, then avoided any serious sickness during the remaining twenty-four years covered by this book.

As he did after each move, Marshall Clemens felt sure that his fortunes were on the mend. He kept store, practiced law, bought land, helped fight for pork barrel appropriations. In 1837, he became a county court judge, salary two dollars a day, and thus acquired the title "Judge" for display during his remaining years.[9] But soon Florida's prospects petered out, the judge's income shrivelled, he saw he'd guessed wrong again, and he began to look for

[9]Roswell P. Henderson and Ralph Gregory, "Judge John Marshall Clemens," *Bulletin of the Missouri Historical Society* (1964), pp. 25–30.

a new town and a new start. He chose Hannibal, on the Mississippi, about thirty miles away. So at the age of four, like his father before him, Sam was carried to a new village.

Except during eight or nine summers when he stayed on his uncle's farm near Florida, Hannibal would be Sam's home until he was seventeen. Once again in Hannibal, the changing Clemens fortunes brought about a series of moves. On two occasions when, briefly, things went well, the family lived in the white frame house now shown to tourists as the author's boyhood home. It was small but it was their most impressive residence. While at a low ebb, they shared a flat above a drugstore with another family, and Jane cooked for both families in lieu of paying rent. Marshall died there in 1847.

## II

IN THE year of Sam's birth, 1835, the Old Southwest was glorying in newly acquired pre-eminence. The president was Andy Jackson of Tennessee—"Old Hickory"—whose two elections had certified the growing power of the common man and also the ascendancy of the region. Davy Crockett, who was also from Tennessee, was the country's second most famous political figure. He was often quoted and kidded in *Crockett Almanacks* and hundreds of newspapers. Davy was on his way to Texas, where he'd win great fame in 1836 by dying in the Alamo—a battle that was destined to become an American legend.

The Missouri of Sam's boyhood and youth, legally a part of the nation only since 1803 and a state only since 1821,[10] was often in the news because it was part of the Old Southwest and because its towns, Independence and St. Joseph, were the chief gateways to what would become the last Far West on the continent.[11]

DeVoto's description of Hannibal helps one to picture that village:

The river was one side of the village; the other three were countryside, prairie, and forest. The actual border had withdrawn almost to the boundaries of Missouri. . . . The frontier, as a line of hazard, was extinct. But as a condition of simplicity, isolation, and noncompetitive society, it existed in Hannibal till after Samuel Clemens had gone elsewhere. The loveliness of prairie and forest was not hidden from boys. Wilderness, tamed past actual menace, nurtured the memories of Samuel Clemens. . . .[12]

So in his reminiscences not only about Hannibal but also about his Uncle John Quarles's farm, even

[10]The Louisiana Purchase of 1803, which doubled the nation's size by adding 828,000 square miles, included what would be eight entire states—Louisiana, Missouri, Arkansas, Iowa, North Dakota, South Dakota, Nebraska, Oklahoma—and most of four others—Kansas, Colorado, Wyoming, and Minnesota. Missouri became a state in 1821 following passage of the Missouri Compromise.

[11]The annexation of the Republic of Texas, the conquest of California, the acquisition of "New Mexico" and the Oregon Treaty during the 1840's added more land than the Louisiana Purchase had—846,400 square miles. The Oregon Trail and the Sante Fe Trail started in Independence.

[12]*MTA*, pp. 29–30.

closer to the wilderness, the author carried readers
back to ways of thinking and living important in
Western history.

A striking instance is what surely is one of Mark
Twain's most eloquent and moving passages, "the
evocation of the Quarles place," as Henry Nash
Smith calls it, which is "a reverie, almost an incan-
tation,"[13] reproduced in Chapter 2 of this book, "A
Heavenly Place for a Boy." Here Twain summons
up memories of "sumptious meals—well, it makes
me cry to think of them," with a long and loving
listing of farm cuisine. "I can see the farm yet, with
perfect clearness," he continues, "all its belongings,
all its details," and he makes good his claim by
describing them at length. There is more: "I can
call back the solemn twilight of the deep woods,
the earth smells, the faint odors of wild flowers . . .
I can call it all back and make it as real as it ever
was, and as blessed." The woods and prairies surrounding the farm are vividly represented. And so
it goes—a hymn of praise in poetic prose: "I can
see. . . . I know the taste. . . . I can feel the thumping rain. . . . I can remember. . . ."

Particularized and personal though they are, the
cataloguing and the expression of delight are characteristic of thousands of passages written over the
centuries about the brave new world. Away back in
1588, Thomas Hariot, in *A Brief and True Report of*

[13] *Mark Twain: The Development of a Writer* (Cambridge,
1962), pp. 156–157.

*the New Found Land of Virginia*, published a pri-
mordial version acclaiming "the excellent temper-
ature of the air" and the "wholesomeness thereof"
that enabled his exploring party to live splendidly
on "the victuals of the country" and huge supplies
of "beasts, fish, and fowl." "The air there," he goes
on, "is so temperate and wholesome, the soil is so
fertile and yielding such commodities" that settlers
are certain to have "victuals that are excellent good
and plenty enough." Another representative enco-
mium for a long time has amused readers of history—Francis Higginson's *New England's Plantation*
(1630), was even more jubilant about the location's
fertility—sixty-fold increases in corn; vegetables
"bigger and sweeter than ordinarily found in England;" prodigious numbers of beasts, fish in the sea
"almost beyond believing;" a climate that makes
New England about the most "healthful place in
the world" and that has completely cured all of
Higginson's very serious illnesses. Why, "a sup of
New-England's air is better than an entire draught
of Old England's ale." The comedy of the passage
for readers, if not the writer, was heightened when,
the very year he wrote this, he sickened and died.[14]

As new areas for settlement opened in the West,
many other writers published laudatory reports and

[14]T. W. Higginson, *Life of Francis Higginson* (New York,
1891), p. 128. Similar tributes occur in the writings of many
contemporaries such as Richard Alsop, George Morton, and
Nathaniel Ward.

promotion tracts and many a Western newspaper "became a weapon and a tool, to conquer the forests and build new communities" by playing up local attractions. So familiar did extravagant paeans become that American humorists got into the habit of burlesquing them. An example is a portion of a comic masterpiece of the antebellum period, T. B. Thorpe's "The Big Bear of Arkansas" in which Jim Doggett is boasting about "Arkansaw—the creation state, the finishing-up country—a state where the *sile* runs down to the centre of the 'arth, and government gives you a title to every inch of it. Then its airs—just breathe them, and they will make you snort like a horse."[15]

Mark Twain's enthusiastic tribute to the Quarles farm, written with no humorous intention, thus is part of a vital tradition hundreds of years old—a product of the settlement of a continent.[16]

Although Mark Twain followed established patterns as he wrote about his early years, he adapted

[15]For a valuable wide-ranging study of this famous piece, see J. A. Leo Lemay, "The Text, Tradition, and Themes of 'The Big Bear of Arkansas,'" *American Literature*, 47 (November, 1975), 321–342.

[16]In 1893, Rollin M. Daggett recalled that Clemens's "bogus Fourth of July oration" of 1861 led him and fellow editor Joe Goodman of the *Territorial Enterprise* to decide "at once that the writer was a man worth cultivating."—"Doggett's Recollections," San Francisco *Examiner*, January 22, 1893. The piece, which hasn't survived, must have followed the tradition concerning Independence Day speeches exaggerating American superiority in every area. The saying was that speakers that day "made the eagle scream."

them so that what he wrote would reveal ways of living and feeling which were characteristic of that era and that area.

In the rhapsodies, for instance, the fruits and vegetables fed by the fertile soil, and the fauna breathing the salubrious air, did belong to that time and place and were harvested and hunted in appropriate ways. The typical culinary treats, as he boasts, were of a sort that had been carried northward and westward by a great cross section of women who had learned to cook in the South.

In another instance: While Missouri was a slave state, slavery there, as Twain makes clear, differed greatly from the servitude of the deep South where huge numbers of blacks toiled under overseers on large plantations.[17] In northern Missouri, the relatively few slaves were workers on small farms and in middle class households. Black and white children were playmates; Uncle Dan'l was a dear friend who told children folktales and inculcated folk wisdom. The huge amount of Negro folklore that finds its unobtrusive way into Twain's writings was impressive enough to inspire studies devoted to it.[18] And

[17] Mark Twain indicated how northern slaves felt about conditions to the south in two novels: Jim in *Huckleberry Finn* runs away when he hears his owner prepare to sell him "down to Orleans," and the most depraved act of the villain in *Pudd'nhead Wilson* is selling his mother as a slave.

[18] Examples: V. R. West, *Folklore in the Works of Mark Twain* (Lincoln, 1930) and Daniel Hoffman, "Jim's Magic: Black or White?" *American Literature*, 32 (1960), 47–54.

though sentimental songs whose titles Twain listed were being sung throughout the country, his life-long passionate affection for spirituals was nurtured by blacks he heard singing them during his impressionable youth.[19]

The Hannibal of the reminiscences is remarkably well populated—by school teachers, pupils, lawyers, religionists, freethinkers, the quality folk, the trash, and so on. These are recognizable as types recurrent in thousands of fictional works and autobiographies. But here, in addition to being shaped by their environment, they are introduced through uniquely detailed biographies made possible by a network we tend to forget in an age when the radio, television and scandal weeklies give us the dirt, not about our neighbors, but about celebrities. The network is conjured up in Chapter 11 of *Tom Sawyer* which tells how news spread in a village that is the spittin' image of Hannibal—news of a murder that took place at midnight: "Close upon the hour of noon [the next day] the whole village was suddenly electrified by the ghastly news. No need of the as yet undreamed-of telegraph; the tale flew from man to man, from group to group, from house to house, with little less than telegraphic speed." Mouth to ear gossip, that, in pre-telegraph Hannibal, was the chief medium. And, as will be seen, startling details in a number of the life histories show how well it passed along scandal even to a youth who left the

[19] *MTA*, pp. 38–40.

place before his eighteenth birthday.[20] Thanks to antebellum Hannibal's news-mongers, Twain pictured a community that isn't completely unlike the later Spoon Rivers, Winesburgs and Peyton Places. His representation—that is mingling sentimentality and brutality, godliness and depravity, the idyllic with the sordid—has a complexity that convinces us that it is historically accurate.

The description of "the House Beautiful"[21] which recreates a good many features of the Quarles farmhouse,[22] shows not only how the folk of Sam's boyhood were domiciled, but also how they amused themselves—the books they read, the art they displayed, the songs they sang or steps they danced to piano or guitar accompaniment, the trips they took and recalled with the aid of souvenirs.

When the author concluded his detailed description of "the residence of the principal citizen" by contrasting it with a splendiferous steamboat, he approached one of Hannibals' most precious assets,

[20]Of course, he worked for a time in a newspaper office, the kind of a place that still teems with detractions, most of them unpublished.

[21]Twain stole the title from a magazine series and a book published in 1878, and used it ironically.

[22]This, despite the fact that Twain located such mansions all along the river between New Orleans and St. Louis. As is indicated in Walter Blair, *Mark Twain and "Huck Finn"* (Berkeley, 1960), pp. 227–230, Huckleberry Finn's description of the same house, somewhat refurnished, shows how Twain's different handling of similar details achieved a very different effect.

the great river that flowed past it. During the boom-time years of river traffic, as one of Mark Twain's descriptive passages shows, ship arrivals day after day awakened the drowsing town to vigorous life. The boats brought the town all of its most exciting entertainment—mesmerists, evangelists, showboats and their melodramas, farces, and Shakespearian plays, as well as minstrel shows such as the one Twain lovingly describes. More important, it may be, travelers of many sorts were part of the endless pageant—Mormons from upstream bound for Utah, hunters, trappers, miners, confidence men, soldiers and pioneers. As one historian puts it, "All the world moved down the Mississippi. And here was Hannibal, at the waterside."[23] Sam Clemens was there to see it, remember it, and tell about it.

Well equipped to write about his home town and his uncle's farm, he was equally well qualified to write about Mississippi steamboat life as he lived it during its finest years.

River commerce was an important part of our nation's history—the chief means of inland transportation from about 1812 until the Civil War brought about an interruption and railroads provided competition that ended its preeminence. The 1850's, Sam's decade, was the decade during which it reached its greatest affluence, with more than two thousand steamboats plying the Ohio and the Mississippi, carrying many tons of essential freight and

[23]*MTA*, p. 52.

about three million passengers every year. First as a cub and later as a licensed pilot along the river from St. Louis to New Orleans between 1857 and 1861, he was an impeccable eye witness.[24]

From the time he got the idea of writing his account until he finished what are chapters numbered 6 through 9 in this book, he had in mind a single aspect that he would treat—"the old days of steamboating glory and grandeur as I saw them (during five years) *from the pilot house.*" The italics were his. "I," he boasted, "am the only man alive that can scribble about the piloting of the day—and no man ever has tried to scribble about it yet. Its newness pleases me all the time. . . ." And when a contemporary, John Hay, who had lived forty miles north of Hannibal, complimented him upon his accuracy "of his own free will & accord," Twain was so delighted that he copied the letter and mailed it immediately to the editor of the magazine publishing *Life on the Mississippi*: Wrote Hay: "It is perfect—no more nor less. . . . I knew all that, every word of it, knew the same crowd; saw the same scenes."[25] Understandably, from the first publication of the

[24]Between his departure from Hannibal and his period on the river, Clemens worked as a journeyman printer in St. Louis, New York, Philadelphia, Keokuk, and Cincinnati. His best account of the life of such a worker, a brief one, is in a speech, *Speeches* (Stormfield Edition), pp. 140-141.

[25]*Mark Twain-Howells Letters*, ed. Henry Nash Smith and William M. Gibson (Cambridge, 1960), I, 34, 47, 55. John Hay wrote a very successful book of dialect poems and, with Nicolay, a biography of Lincoln.

narrative to the present, one historian of Mississippi steamboating after another has cited it as an invaluable source.[26]

Although the humorist did consider writing at least a chapter or possibly a goodly part of a book about his career as a full-fledged pilot, so far as is known, he never wrote at any length about his experiences between April 9, 1859, when he got his license, and April 19, 1861, when he finished the last trip. We can only speculate why. I have thought of two possible reasons: The account of his learning the river had a well-rounded plot that added chapters would damage; and quite possibly those added chapters would have enriched very little his recounting the steamboating days "as he saw them . . . from the pilot house."[27]

His least valuable contribution to American history in the form of personal recollections recounted his inglorious Civil Wartime service as a member of the Marion Rangers not long after he finished piloting. He might well have neglected to reminisce about this except for certain circumstances: In 1877, he was invited to speak to the Ancient and Honor-

[26]Some historians have complained because, except very briefly, Twain failed to treat the abundant disreputable aspects of river life. True, but he treated definitively his subject as he described it.

[27]He wrote himself a note, "Begin with a chapter of my experiences as a pilot?" and he told one interviewer that *Life on the Mississippi*, would deal "altogether" with his early life on the river, though only about two-fifths of it did. See *Mark Twain & Huck Finn*", p. 286.

able Artillery Company of Massachusetts when they had a reunion. Speakers preceding him were emotional and eloquent as they told about the glorious deeds of the company during all the years after its founding in 1638. So the audience was well prepared for the comic relief that it expected he would provide. In contrast with the heroics and the high-falutin' oratory, his deadpan, playful account of his insignificant performance triggered howls of laughter. Years later, when the *Century Magazine* was running a great series of firsthand narratives—"The Battles and Leaders in the Civil War"—the editor urged the very popular humorist to contribute his contrasting account.[28] At the start of his article, he offered a justification for it as history:

> Thousands entered the war, got just a taste of it, and then stepped out of it permanently. These, by their very numbers . . . are therefore entitled to a sort of voice . . . they ought at least to be allowed to state why they didn't do anything, and also to explain the process by which they didn't do anything.

Actually, valid additional claims may be made for the historical value of this book's chapter 10. Admittedly the finest historical novel regarding a phase of the Civil War, Stephen Crane's *The Red Badge of Courage* (1895) recounts a raw rookie's roughly similar experiences, but does so with great

[28] Justin Kaplan, *Mr. Clemens and Mark Twain* (New York, 1966), pp. 207–209, 274–275. Recently Clemens had amused General Grant and his family by contrasting his wartime experiences with the general's.

seriousness. Twain's comparable humorous story about a youth's frightening confrontation that ends, not with a heroic action but with ignominious desertion, adds important dimensions. And moderns well may find it enlightening to be reminded that, like more recent conflicts, the War Between the States had its draft evaders and deserters, and a great author was one of them.[29]

Mark Twain's own "Prefatory" to *Roughing It*, the chief source of the remaining autobiographical chapters in *Mark Twain's West*, amusingly speaks by understatement, for their historical value:

This book is merely a personal narrative, and not a pretentious history or a philosophical dissertion. It is a record of several years of variegated vagabondizing, and its object is rather to help the resting reader while away an idle hour than afflict him with metaphysics, or goad him with science. Still, there is information in this volume . . . concerning an interesting episode in the history of the Far West, about which no books have been written by persons who were on the ground in person, and saw the happenings of the time with their own eyes. I allude to the rise, growth and culmination of the silver-mining fever in Nevada—a curious episode . . . the only one, of its peculiar kind, that has occurred in the land. . . .

Yes, . . . there is a good deal of information in this book. I regret this very much; but really it could not be helped: information appears to stew out of me naturally, like the precious ottar of roses out of the otter.

[29]Other leading American authors who weren't in the services during the Civil War included Herman Melville, William Dean Howells, Henry James, and Henry Adams.

Sweeping though this claim is, it doesn't touch upon several generous contributions these chapters make to our Far Western history. There are, for instance, a vivid re-creation of travel by stagecoach from Missouri to Nevada in 1861, full descriptions of the countryside along the route at that time, a personal introduction to a desperado, Joe Slade, viewed at close quarters at a stage-station, and one of the best sightings extant of a dashing rider in motion as a carrier in the brief-lived but epochal Pony Express. Then there is Mark Twain's tale of a carelessly kindled forest fire near Lake Tahoe, bloodcurdling not only because of its concreteness but also because of its unhorrified objectivity.

Mark Twain summarized other parts of his story in a letter of 1891 telling an unidentifiable correspondent that he wrote fiction about "boy-life on the Mississippi because it had a peculiar charm for me and not because I was not familiar with the other phases of life." Among the other phases he cites some that he dealt with in his reminiscences:

I have shoveled silver tailings in a quartz mill a couple of weeks, and acquired the last possibilities of culture in *that* direction. And I've done "pocket-mining" during three months in the one little patch of ground in the whole globe where Nature conceals gold in pockets—or *did*, before we robbed all of those pockets. . . . There are not thirty men left alive who, being told there was a pocket hidden on the broad slope of a mountain, would know how to go and find it or have even the faintest idea of how to set about it—but I am one. . . .

And I've been a prospector and know pay rock from poor when I find it—just with a touch of the tongue. And I've been a silver *miner* and know how to dig and shovel and drill, and put in a blast. . . .

And I was a newspaper reporter four years in cities, and so saw the inside of many things; and was reporter in a legislature two sessions . . . and thus learned to know personally . . . sample bodies of the smallest minds and the selfishest souls and the cowardliest hearts that God makes. . . .

And I have been an author for twenty years and an ass for fifty-five.[30]

The chronology involved in the self-depreciating closing sentence is worth considering, since in it Mark Twain implies that he didn't become "an author" until 1871, just a couple of years after *Mark Twain's West* ends its autobiographical account. By that time, however, he had become famous as a writer—first in the Far West for his newspaper hoaxes and feature stories, later nationwide for his "Jumping Frog" story and still later even beyond the Atlantic for a bestselling travel book, *The Innocents Abroad*. My best guess is that, if asked, he would have defended his claim by arguing that up to that time he was not an author but a journalist.[31]

True enough, he was a newspaper man on the

[30] *The Portable Mark Twain*, ed. Bernard DeVoto (New York, 1946), pp. 773-775.

[31] Both books he had published before 1871 might have been considered collections of newspaper pieces. As late as 1871, he was an editor and part-owner of the Buffalo *Express*, and he completed *Roughing It*, the first book that he wrote "from scratch"—almost—in 1871.

Virginia City *Territorial Enterprise*, later on the San Francisco *Call*, and finally as travel reporter for the Sacramento *Union* during his time in the West. It was for the *Union* that he wrote about his exploration of our nation's Pacific outpost more than eight decades before it became our fiftieth state.[32]

Regardless of how he classified his Far Western writings, there can be no doubt that they were tremendously important for his literary development. The wild hoaxes of chapter 17, for instance, one of which seems to show he honed his skill by imitating Rabelais,[33] taught him—as he himself says—a valuable lesson. More important, a convincing case can be made for the claim that the Winter of 1864–1865 visit he paid to the California mining territory (chapters 20 and 21) brought a crucial turning point in his artistic development. For it enabled him to discover his happiest style of writing, and its yarn-spinning sessions were germinal to at least eight of the best stretches of writing in all his books. Three of them are included hereafter in chapters 20–22, and one of them, "Baker's Blue-Jay Yarn," is in my opinion the best short narrative he ever wrote.[34]

[32] As chapters 23 and 24 will show, at the time of his visit it still was called the Sandwich Islands.

[33] Walter Blair, "The Petrified Man and His French Ancestor," *Mark Twain Journal*, 19 (Winter 1977–78), 1–3.

[34] Walter Blair, "Mark Twain and the Mind's Ear," in *The American Self*, ed. Sam B. Girgus (Albuquerque, 1981), and *America's Humor*, pp. 333–348. The writing style is that of "Baker's Bluejay Yarn" and *Adventures of Huckleberry Finn*.

### III

NUDGED then, like his ancestors, by adverse fortunes and high hopes for better ones, Clemens during his Western years became highly mobile. And because what he called his "vagabondizing" so often put him where the action was, his personal reminiscences illuminated American history. The accounts also were valuable because along the way he developed great skill as a storyteller. But readers do well to keep in mind that in some ways that very skill, and the memory it exploited, caused the author to deviate quite often from literal accuracy.

A well-documented study by two scholars published in 1981 reflects on that memory at length. Thomas M. Walsh and Thomas D. Zlatic naturally recall the eloquent passages that Twain wrote about mnemonics as river pilots developed them—"Nothing short of perfection would do"—along with his heroic, and victorious, struggle to learn the river "perfectly." And yet, they find, throughout his life, "Clemens had a notoriously poor memory;" he knew that he did; and he ceaselessly worked at improving it.[35] He knew his limitations and frequently joked about them. He praised his mother, for instance, for cultivating the art when he was still a boy of "getting at the jewel of any fact of mine and digging it out of its blue-clay matrix." Her formula:

[35] "Mark Twain and the Art of Memory," *American Literature*, 53 (May, 1981), 214-231.

"I discount him full ninety percent for embroidery, and what is left is perfect and priceless truth, without a flaw in it anywhere." And in his later years, he told Albert Bigelow Paine, his annointed Boswell, "When I was younger I could remember anything, whether it happened or not; but I am getting old and soon I shall remember only the latter."[36]

He was correct in believing that his memory was most accurate when he was close to events but that even more than most memories, as he aged it tended to become less dependable. Paine quoted the above wry witticism as he told about sitting in on sessions during the author's seventies while Twain dictated reminiscenses to a stenographer—a master fiction writer's and seasoned lecturer's magical performances. Eventually, Paine realized that an artist's soaring imagination . . .

had dominated memory, creating details, even reversing them, yet with a perfect sincerity of purpose on the part of the narrator to set down the literal and unvarnished truth. It was his constant effort to be frank and faithful to facts, to record, to confess, and to condemn without stint . . . the thread of history [,however,] was almost impossible to trace through the marvel of that fabric. . . . Those vividly real personalitities . . . often disagreed in their performance and even in their characters, with the documents in the next room, as I learned by and by when those records, disentangled, began to build the structure of the years.

His gift of dramatization had been exercised too long to

[36] *Mark Twain's Autobiography*, i, 293; *MTB*, iii, 1269.

be discarded now. . . . It was fictional history, with fact as a starting point. . . . Yet there were occasional chapters that were photographically exact, and fitted precisely with the more positive, if less picturesque, materials. It is also true that such chapters were likely to be episodes intrinsically so perfect as to not require the touch of art.[37]

Paine's observations are generally well founded; in this area as in others Twain had a particular way—as many infuriating authors have—of every now and then confounding careful scholars by being inconsistent. Several examples in the first four chapters of the reminiscences that follow illustrate this. Many reminiscences about the author's distant childhood were dictated at the time Paine spoke of, when he was in his seventies, yet many are richly detailed and remarkably accurate.

And some recollections in chapter 4, "Villagers," set down only several years earlier, represent an amazing evocative performance. They take the form of numerous notes, most of them succinct, about the people of Hannibal whom Sam Clemens knew. Sam, remember, was carried to that river town when he wasn't quite four, and he left, never to live there again, when he was seventeen. Anything he learned thereafter about Hannibalites he picked up during five fleeting visits, by means of short conversations, skimpy correspondence, and a few short news stories. He wrote the notes when he was sixty-one and Hannibal was four and a half decades in his past. He

[37] *MTB*, III, 1268–1270.

was living in Weggis, Switzerland, pretty certainly far away from consultants, clippings, or reference books of any kind. But he wrote notes about a hundred and sixty-eight villagers. Independent identifications of fifteen not named and of thirty he named have proved to be impossible. But the accuracy of the biographies of those remaining hundred and twenty-three, so far as it can be checked independently, verifies practically all statements made.

All the same, even in these memoranda that he must have written for his eyes alone, he deviated into fiction every now and then. Indubitably, the village was Hannibal, but the only name he gives it is "St. P.," an abbreviation for St. Petersburg, the name that he had given Hannibal in his books about Tom Sawyer and Huck Finn. Some dates have been changed, and the notes are headed "Villagers of 1840–3," and therefore dated several years too early. The Armstrong family is presented with a melodramatic experience that took place at a different time and in a completely unrelated household. The family of John Marshall Clemens, which figures prominently, is known as the Carpenter family, and though the initials of their first names are kept, the names are changed: Jane Clemens is renamed Joanna Carpenter, and so on. John Marshall Clemens (who becomes Judge Carpenter and who is characterized at greater length and less sympathetically than in the autobiographical dictations) is called the winner of an election that he didn't achieve and a death that differed from his real one.[38]

Unless erosions of memory forced some detours around actuality in these notes and other reminiscent writings, it is hard to say why they were made. After studying a number here and elsewhere, the reader will find that many were functional.

Some changes enabled Twain to develop themes or make interpretative comments. When he had his father win that election "by a great majority" and then catch his death of cold in a winter storm while returning home from the swearing in though he did neither, Twain made an ironic comment or, more accurately, stimulated the reader to think of one. Again, when he had his boyish Marion Rangers during their Civil Wartime service shoot a stranger in the dark of night though, in fact, they did nothing like that, he had them develop an attitude toward the incident preparatory to his eloquent denunciation of war.[39]

---

[38] *Mark Twain's Hannibal, Huck & Tom*, pp. 23–40, 343–369, 370, includes the previously unpublished notes, discusses their composition, and, when it is possible, assesses their accuracy. Three additional identifications have been made and the biographical statements verified.

[39] Twain wrote: "The man was a stranger in the country, that was all we ever found out about him . . . the taking of that unoffensive life seemed such a wanton thing. And it seemed an epitome of war, that all war must be just the killing of strangers . . . whom in other circumstances you would help if you found them in trouble. . . ." The fictitious episode and the comment are not included in chapter 10 hereafter. Another distortion that enhances irony has the author just miss becoming a millionaire in the mines.

Readers of this book may notice some rearrangements of reality that were valuable in other ways. The Sam Clemens of chapters 6–9, as Paine points out, is "a boy of perhaps seventeen" when he signs up to learn the river; but the real-life apprentice was "more than twenty-one years old;" and he had been around, bumming his way across country by working as a tramp printer in St. Louis, New York, Philadelphia, Washington, and Cincinnati. Further, he was "somewhat familiar with steamboats and the general requirements of piloting."[40] The assigned role, that of a young, gullible and naif greenhorn, had proved its great worth for comedy throughout the ages, and like other tried and true jokes was good for laughs here. What is more, the characterization allowed for the development of a narrative thread, one involving a change from ignorance to expertise and from romanticizing to disillusionment. Too, it enables the reader, along with the cub, to become acquainted with a great many facts that are part of the science of piloting. Similar exaggerations of Sam's youth, enthusiasm, and ignorance initiate the chapters about his wartime experiences and his invasion of the Far West.

William Dean Howells, while reviewing the first uniform edition of Twain's works in 1901, saw him

[40] *MTB*, I, 117. See also *Mark Twain & "Huck Finn"*, pp. 40–43. Another instance of a modification that uses a time honored comic device is the highly fictitious account of the author's abortive duel. The comic cowardly reaction of the author is at least as old as Shakespeare's Falstaff.

doing something more novel in his "extended writing" such as his travel books. Many other writers, Howells said, used "some sort of a logical order"—disciplined "impressions and notions . . . into a coherent body" marching "to a conclusion obvious if not inevitable from the start." Twain by contrast "took whatever offered itself to his hand out of that mystical chaos, that divine ragbag, which we call the mind, and left the reader to look after relevancies and sequences for himself. . . . The end you arrive at is the end of the book. . . . You have noticed the author's thoughts, but not necessarily the order of his thinking; he has not made an attempt to trace the threads of association between the things that have followed one another. . . ."

Howells refused to guess whether it was knowingly that Twain used this "fashion we all use in thinking"—one quite familiar to today's readers of *New Yorker* profiles and stream-of-consciousness novels; but he allowed that quite possibly he "pursued it from no wish but to have pleasure in his work, and not fatigue himself or his reader; and his method may be the secret of his vast popularity, but it cannot be the whole secret of it."[41]

On several occasions, Twain supported Howells's guess by indicating that chief aims were to ease the reader's way and to entertain. Not only did he try

[41]Quoted in *My Mark Twain*, pp. 166–169. Howells concludes that Twain "justified" his charm, and that "no writer ever imparted information more inoffensively."

to make his reminiscences and other writings follow the labyrinths of thought, he constantly tried even harder to make them correspond to the patterns of talk. His habit was to read them aloud, modify them, reread them aloud, then amend them again, as often as he had to in order to make them sound right to his mind's ear. Some of his best passages—those about the Quarles farm for instance—he dictated, convinced that by so doing he infused "that subtle something, which makes good talk so much better than the best imitation of it that can be done with a pen."[42]

Almost every page of his that follows will show why very competent critics have admired Twain's style; but of course some pages are particularly outstanding. His preeminence as a pioneer user of literary dialect is demonstrated by the quoted yarns he attributes to Simon Wheeler in chapter 20 and Jim Baker in chapter 22. And passages that show him at his best in straightforward prose are the paragraph picturing antebellum Hannibal before, during, and after the docking of a steamboat there in chapter 6 and the contrast at the end of chapter 7 between the ways a beginner and an experienced pilot viewed a stretch of the great river.[43]

[42]See "Mark Twain and the Mind's Ear" and Marilyn Davis, "Mark Twain's Experiments in Autobiography," *American Literature*, 53 (May, 1981) 202-213.

[43]William M. Gibson, *The Art of Mark Twain* (New York, 1976), pp. 3-32, offers an excellent discussion of Twain's style and cites others in footnotes.

Readers of Twain's reminiscences, therefore, do well to keep constantly in mind their exact nature. They were based upon a memory that sometimes was remarkably retentive and sometimes far from dependable, and they were produced by an imaginative and often playful artist who was more eager to amuse and fascinate readers than he was to be literally accurate. However, because they were based upon extensive and historically important experiences, they have great value not only as entertaining humor and literature but also as chronicles.

## IV

WHEN he pieced together the first-person account that follows, the editor did something that Samuel Clemens, if he were alive, well might like to punish by inflicting painful and lingering torture, and out of sympathy, the editor well might be delighted to join with a helping hand. Inasmuch as Clemens died, however, on April 21, 1910, the editor felt relatively safe as he compiled a superbly written chronological account that Mark Twain wrote but never managed to assemble. And because the editor greatly revered Twain's artistry, he made practically no intentional revisions of the precise wording, and he silently committed only a few revisions and transitional intrusions for the sake of interest and continuity. And although he might have written a few hundred explanatory footnotes pointing out inaccuracies and enlarging upon overly brief passages, he has rigorously—and he believes considerately—held down the number.

As has been indicated, Clemens left the West in 1866. After that year he made his home in the East or in Europe, and there he wrote these memoirs—commotion recollected in relative tranquility.

The following books, listed in the order of their publication, were those drawn upon for *Mark Twain's West*. Those most used are indicated by asterisks: *The Innocents Abroad* (1869), *Roughing It* *(1872), *Sketches New and Old* (1875), *A Tramp Abroad* (1880), *Life on the Mississippi** (1883); *The American Claimant* (1892); *How to Tell a Story and Other Essays* (1897), *Mark Twain's Autobiography*, 2 vols., ed. A. B. Paine* (1924), *Mark Twain in Eruption*, ed. Bernard DeVoto* (1940), *Mark Twain's Hannibal, Huck & Tom*, ed. Walter Blair (1969).

WALTER BLAIR

May 15, 1983

# Mark Twain's West

*The author's memoirs about his boyhood,*
*riverboats and western adventures*

# I

## *Ancestors Stretching Back to Noah's Time*

I WAS BORN the thirtieth of November, 1835, in the almost invisible village of Florida, Monroe County, Missouri. The village contained a hundred people and I increased the population by one per cent. It is more than many of the best men in history could have done for a town. It may not be modest for me to refer to this, but it is true. There is no record of a person doing as much—not even Shakespeare. But I did it for Florida, and it shows that I could have done it for any place—even London.

Recently some one in Missouri has sent me a picture of the house I was born in. Heretofore I have always stated that it was a palace, but I shall be more guarded now.

My parents removed to Missouri about the early 'thirties; I do not remember just when, for I was not born then and cared nothing for such things.

Florida had two streets, each a couple of hundred yards long; the rest of the avenues mere lanes, with rail fences and cornfields on either side. The streets and the lanes were paved with the same material; tough black mud in wet times, deep dust in dry.

Most of the houses were of logs—all of them, indeed, except three or four; these latter were frame

3

ones. There were none of brick, and none of stone.
There was a log church, with a puncheon floor and
slab benches. A puncheon floor is made of logs
whose upper surfaces have been chipped flat with
the adz. The cracks between the logs were not
filled, and there was no carpet; consequently, if you
dropped anything smaller than a peach, it was likely to go on through. The church was perched upon
short sections of logs, which elevated it two or three
feet from the ground. Hogs slept under there, and
whenever the dogs got after them during the service, the minister had to wait till the disturbance
was over. During winter there was always a refreshing breeze up through the puncheon floor; in summer
there were fleas enough for all.

A slab bench is made of the outside cut of a saw-
log, with the bark side down; it is supported on four
sticks driven into auger holes at the ends; it has no
back and no cushions. The church was twilighted
with yellow tallow candles in tin sconces which
hung against the walls. Week days, the church was a
schoolhouse.

There were two stores in the village. My uncle,
John A. Quarles, was proprietor of one of them. It
was a very small establishment, with a few rolls of
"bit"[1] calicoes on half a dozen shelves; a few barrels
of salt mackerel, coffee, and New Orleans sugar behind the counter; stacks of brooms, shovels, axes,
hoes, rakes, and such things here and there; a lot of

[1] a small coin with the nominal value of $12\frac{1}{2}$ cents.

*Birthplace of Sam Clemens, Florida, Missouri.*
Courtesy of the Mark Twain Papers, The Bancroft Library

cheap hats, bonnets, and tinware strung on strings and suspended from the walls; and at the other end of the room was another counter with bags of shot, a cheese or two, and a keg of powder; in front a row of nail kegs and a few pigs of lead, and behind it a barrel or two of New Orleans molasses and native corn whisky on tap. If a boy bought five or ten cents' worth of anything, he was entitled to half a handful of sugar from the barrel; if a woman bought a few yards of calico she was entitled to a spool of thread in addition to the usual gratis "trimmin's"; if a man bought a trifle, he was at liberty to draw and swallow as big a drink of whisky as he wanted.

Everything was cheap: apples, peaches, sweet potatoes, Irish potatoes, and corn, ten cents a bushel; chickens, ten cents apiece; coffee and sugar, five cents a pound; butter, six cents a pound; eggs, three cents a dozen; whisky, ten cents a gallon.

My father was John Marshall Clemens of Virginia; my mother Jane Lampton of Kentucky.

Back of the Virginian Clemenses is a dim procession of ancestors stretching back to Noah's time. According to tradition, some of them were pirates and slavers in Elizabeth's time. But this is no discredit to them, for so were Drake and Hawkins and the others. It was a respectable trade then, and monarchs were partners in it. In my time I have had desires to be a pirate myself. The reader, if he will look deep down in his secret heart will find—but never mind what he will find there. I am not writing

his autobiography, but mine. Later, according to
tradition, one of the procession was ambassador to
Spain in the time of James I, or of Charles I, and
married there and sent down a strain of Spanish
blood to warm us up. Also, according to tradition
this one or another—Geoffrey Clement, by name—
helped to sentence Charles to death. I have not examined into these traditions myself, partly because
I was indolent and partly because I was so busy
polishing up this end of the line and trying to make
it showy; but the other Clemenses claim that they
have made the examination and that it stood the
test. Therefore I have always taken for granted that
I did help Charles out of his troubles, by ancestral
proxy. My instincts have persuaded me, too. Whenever we have a strong and persistent and ineradica-
ble instinct, we may be sure that it is not original
with us, but inherited—inherited from away back
and hardened and perfected by the petrifying influence of time. Now I have been always and unchang-
ingly bitter against Charles, and I am quite certain
that this feeling trickled down to me through the
veins of my forebears from the heart of that judge;
for it is not my disposition to be bitter against people on my own personal account. I am not bitter
against Jeffreys.[2] I ought to be, but I am not. It indicates that my ancestors of James II's time were indifferent to him; I do not know why; I never could

[2]George Jeffreys (1645–1689), as lord chief justice of England, backed James II preceding his abdication in 1688.

make it out; but that is what it indicates. And I have always felt friendly toward Satan. Of course that is ancestral; it must be in the blood, for I could not have originated it.

. . . And so, by the testimony of instinct, backed by the assertions of Clemenses, who said they had examined the records, I have always been obliged to believe that Geoffrey Clement, the martyr maker, was an ancestor of mine, and to regard him with favor, and pride. This has not had a good effect upon me, for it has made me vain, and that is a fault. It has made me set myself above people who were less fortunate in their ancestry, and has moved me to take them down a peg, upon occasion, and say things to them which hurt them before company.

A case of the kind happened in Berlin several years ago. William Walter Phelps was our minister at the Emperor's court then, and one evening he had me to dinner to meet Count S——, a Cabinet Minister. This nobleman was of long and illustrious descent. Of course I wanted to let out the fact that I had some ancestors, too; but I did not want to pull them out of their graves by the ears, and I never could seem to get the chance to work them in in a way that would look sufficiently casual. I suppose Phelps was in the same difficulty. In fact, he looked distraught now and then—just as a person looks who wants to uncover an ancestor purely by accident and cannot think of a way that will seem accidental enough. But at last, after dinner, he made a try. He took us about his drawing-room, showing us the pictures, and finally stopped before a rude and ancient engraving. It was a picture of the court that tried Charles I. There was a pyramid of judges in Puritan slouch hats, and below them three bare-headed secretaries seated at a table. Mr. Phelps put his finger upon one of the three and said, with exulting indifference:

"An ancestor of mine."

I placed my finger on a judge, and retorted with scathing languidness:

"Ancestor of mine. But it is a small matter. I have others."

It was not noble in me to do it. I have always regretted it since. But it landed him. I wonder how he felt! However, it made no difference in our friendship; which shows that he was fine and high, notwithstanding the humbleness of his origin. And it was also creditable in me, too, that I could overlook it. I made no change in my bearing toward him, but always treated him as an equal.

Among the Virginian Clemenses were Jere and Sherrard. Jere Clemens had a wide reputation as a good pistol-shot, and once it enabled him to get on the friendly side of some drummers when they wouldn't have paid any attention to mere smooth words and arguments. He was out stumping the state at the time. The drummers were grouped in front of the stand and had been hired by the opposition to drum while he made his speech. When he was ready to begin he got out his revolver and laid it before him and said, in his soft, silky way:

"I do not wish to hurt anybody and shall try not to, but I have got just a bullet apiece for those six drums, and if you should want to play on them don't stand behind them."

Sherrard Clemens was a Republican Congressman from West Virginia in the war days, and then went out to St. Louis, where the James Clemens branch lived and still lives, and there he became a warm rebel. This was after the war. At the time that he was a Republican I was a rebel; but by the time he had become a rebel I had become (temporarily) a Republican. The Clemenses have always done the best they could to keep the political balances level, no matter how much it might inconvenience them. I did not know what had become of Sherrard Clemens; but once I introduced Senator Hawley to a Republican mass meeting in New England, and then I got a bitter letter from Sherrard from St. Louis. He told me that the Republicans of the North—no, the "mudsills of the North"—had swept away the old aristocracy of the South with fire and sword, and it ill became me, an aristocrat by blood, to train with that kind of swine. Did I forget I was a Lambton?

That was a reference to my mother's side of the house. My mother was a Lambton—Lambton with a p, for some of the American Lamptons could not spell very well in early times, and so the name suffered at their hands. She was a native of Kentucky, and married my father in Lexington in 1823, when she was twenty years old and he was twenty-four. Neither of them had an overplus of property. She brought him two or three Negroes, but nothing else, I think. They removed to the remote and secluded village of Jamestown, in the mountain solitudes of east Tennessee. There their first crop of children was born, but as I was of a later vintage, I do not remember anything about it. I was postponed— postponed to Missouri. Missouri was an unknown new state and needed attractions.

I think that my eldest brother, Orion, my sisters Pamela and Margaret, and my brother Benjamin were born in Jamestown. There may have been others, but as to that I am not sure. It was a great lift for that little village to have my parents come there. It was hoped that they would stay, so that it would become a city. It was supposed that they would stay. And so there was a boom; but by and by they went away, and prices went down, and it was many years before Jamestown got another start. I have written about Jamestown in the *Gilded Age*, a book of mine, but it was from hearsay, not from personal knowledge. My father left a fine estate behind him in the region roundabout Jamestown—more than 100,000 acres. When he died in 1847 he had owned it about twenty years. The taxes were almost nothing (five dollars a year for the whole), and he had always paid them regularly and kept his title perfect. He had always said that the land would not

become valuable in his time, but that it would be a
commodious provision for his children some day. It
contained coal, copper, iron, and timber, and he
said that in the course of time railways would pierce
to that region and then the property would be
property in fact as well as in name. It also produced
a wild grape of a promising sort. He had sent some
samples to Nicholas Longworth of Cincinnati to get
his judgment upon them, and Mr. Longworth had
said that they would make as good wine as his Ca-
tawbas. The land contained all these riches; and
also oil, but my father did not know that, and of
course in those early days he would have cared
nothing about it if he had known it. The oil was not
discovered until about 1895. I wish I owned a couple of acres of the land now, in which case I would
not be writing autobiographies for a living. My father's dying charge was, "Cling to the land and
wait; let nothing beguile it away from you." My
mother's favorite cousin, James Lampton, who figures in my novel *The Gilded Age* and the play dramatizing it as Colonel Sellers, always said of that
land—and said it with blazing enthusiasm, too—
"There's millions in it—millions!" It is true that
James Lampton always said that about everything;
and was always mistaken, too, but this time he was
right; which shows that a man who goes around
with a prophecy-gun ought never to get discouraged. If he will keep up his heart and fire at everything he sees, he is bound to hit something.

Many persons regarded Colonel Sellers as a fiction, an invention, an extravagant impossibility, and did me the honor to call him a "creation"; but they were mistaken. I merely put him on paper as James Lampton was; Lampton was not a person who could be exaggerated. The incidents which looked most extravagant, both in the book and on the stage, were not inventions of mine, but were facts of his life; and I was present when they were developed. Audiences used to come near to dying with laughter over the turnip-eating scene in the play;[3] but, extravagant as the scene was, it was faithful to the facts, in all its absurd details. The thing happened in Lampton's own house, and I was present. In fact, I was myself the guest who ate the turnips. In the hands of a great actor that piteous scene would have dimmed any manly spectator's eyes with tears, and racked his ribs apart with laughter at the same time. But the actor who played the role of Sellers, John T. Raymond, was great in humorous portrayal only. In that he was superb, he was wonderful—in a word, great; in all things else he was a pygmy of pygmies. The real Colonel Sellers, as I knew him in James Lampton, was a pathetic and beautiful spirit, a manly man, a straight and honor-

[3] In a scene dramatizing Chapter XI of *The Gilded Age*, by Mark Twain and Charles Dudley Warner, poverty-stricken Colonel Sellers and his family serve a guest a dinner consisting entirely of water and turnips. Sellers, a genius at becoming ecstatic about anything, delivers a long oration fantastically praising the meal as an ideal one.

able man, a man with a big, foolish, unselfish heart in his bosom, a man born to be loved; and he was loved by all his friends, and by his family worshiped. It is the right word. To them he was but little less than a god. James Lampton, the real Colonel Sellers, was never on the stage. Only half of him was there. Raymond could not play the other half of him; it was above his level.

James Lampton floated, all his days, in a tinted mist of magnificent dreams, and died at last without seeing one of them realized. I saw him last in 1884, when he attended a joint lecture performance that George W. Cable and I gave. He came back stage. It had been twenty-six years since I ate the basin of raw turnips and washed them down with a bucket of water in his house. He had become old and white-headed, but he entered to me in the same old breezy way of his earlier life, and he was all there yet—not a detail wanting; the happy light in his eye, the abounding hope in his heart, the persuasive tongue, the miracle-breeding imagination—they were all there; and before I could turn around he was polishing up his Aladdin's lamp and flashing the secret riches of the world before me. I said to myself: "I did not overdraw him by a shade, I set him down as he was; and he is the same man today. Cable will recognize him." I asked him to excuse me a moment and ran into the next room, which was Cable's. I said:

"I am going to leave your door open so you can

listen. There is a man in there who is interesting."

I went back and asked Lampton what he was doing now. He began to tell me of a "small venture" he had begun in New Mexico through his son; "only a little thing—a mere trifle—partly to amuse my leisure, partly to keep my capital from lying idle, but mainly to develop the boy—develop the boy. Fortune's wheel is ever revolving; he may have to work for his living some day—as strange things have happened in this world. But it's only a little thing—a mere trifle, as I said."

And so it was as he began it. But under his deft hands it grew and blossomed and spread—oh, beyond imagination. At the end of half an hour he finished; finished with the remark, uttered in an adorably languid manner:

"Yes, it is but a trifle, as things go nowadays—a bagatelle—but amusing. It passes the time. The boy thinks great things of it, but he is young, you know, and imaginative; lacks the experience which comes from handling large affairs, and which tempers the fancy and perfects the judgment. I suppose there's a couple of millions in it, possibly three, but not more, I think; still, for a boy, you know, just starting in life, it is not bad. I should not want him to make a fortune—let that come later. It could turn his head, at his time of life, and in many ways be a damage to him."

Then he said something about his having left his pocketbook lying on the table in the main drawing-room at home, and about its being after banking hours, now, and ———.

I stopped him there and begged him to honor Cable and me by being our guest at the lecture—with as many friends as might be willing to do us the like honor. He accepted. And he thanked me as a prince might who had granted us a grace. The reason I stopped his speech about the tickets was because I saw that he was going to ask me to furnish them to him and let him pay next day; and I knew that if he made the debt he would pay it if he had to pawn his clothes. After a little further chat he shook hands heartily and affectionately and took his leave. Cable put his head in at the door and said:

"That was Colonel Sellers."

WHEN I was a boy, everybody was poor, but didn't know it; and everybody was comfortable, and did know it. And there were grades of society—people of good family, people of unclassified family, people of no family. Everybody knew everybody, and was affable to everybody, and nobody put on any visible airs; yet the class lines were quite clearly drawn and the familiar social life of each class was restricted to that class. It was a little democracy which was full of liberty, equality, and Fourth of July, and sincerely so, too; yet you perceived that the aristocratic taint was there. It was there, and nobody found fault with the fact, or ever stopped to reflect that its presence was an inconsistency.

I suppose that this state of things was mainly due to the circumstance that Hannibal's population had come from slave states and still had the institution of slavery with them in their new home. My mother, with her large nature and liberal sympathies, was not intended for an aristocrat, yet through her breeding she was one. Few people knew it, perhaps, for it was an instinct, I think, rather than a principle. So its outward manifestation was likely to be accidental, not intentional, and also not frequent. But I knew of that weak spot. I knew that privately she was proud that the Lambtons, now Earls of Durham, had occupied the family lands for nine hundred years; that they were feudal lords of Lambton Castle and holding the high position of ancestors of hers when the Norman Conqueror came over to divert the Englishry. I argued—cautiously, and with mollifying circumlocutions, for one had to be careful when he was on that holy ground, and mustn't cavort—that there was no particular merit in occupying a piece of land for nine hundred years, with the friendly assistance of an entail; anybody could do it, with intellect or without; therefore the entail was the thing to be proud of, just the entail and nothing else; consequently, she was merely descended from an entail, and she might as well be proud of being descended from a mortgage. Whereas my own ancestry was quite a different and superior thing, because it had the addition of an ancestor—one Clemens—who *did* something; something which was very creditable to him and satisfactory to me, in that he was a member of the court that tried Charles I and delivered him over to the executioner. Ostensibly this was chaff, but at the bottom it was not. I had a very real respect for that ancestor, and this respect has increased with the years, not diminished. He did what he could toward reducing the list of crowned shams of his day. However, I can say this for my mother, that I never heard her refer in any way to her gilded ancestry when any person not a member of the family was present, for she had good American sense. But with other Lamptons whom I have known, it was different. James Lampton "Colonel Sellers" when he was alive, poor old airy soul, one of the earliest things a stranger was likely to hear from his lips was some reference to the "head of our line," flung off with a painful casualness that was wholly beneath criticism as a work of art. It compelled inquiry, of course; it was intended to compel it. Then followed the whole disastrous history of how the Lambton heir came to this country a hundred and fifty years or so ago, disgusted with that foolish fraud, hereditary aristocracy, and married, and shut himself away from the world in the remotenesses of the wilderness, and went to breeding ancestors of future American claimants, while at home in England he was given up as dead and his titles and estates turned over to his younger brother, usurper and personally responsible for the perverse and unseatable usurpers of our day. And the colonel always spoke with studied and courtly deference of the claimant of his day—a second cousin of his—and referred to him with entire seriousness as "the earl." "The earl" was a man of parts, and might have accomplished something for himself but for the calamitous accident of his birth. He was a Kentuckian, and a well-meaning man; but he had no money, and no time to earn any; for all his time was taken up in trying to get me, and others of the tribe, to furnish him capital to fight his claim through the House of Lords with. He had all the documents, all the proofs; he knew he could win. And so he dreamed his life away, always in poverty, sometimes in actual want, and died at last, far from home, and was buried from a hospital by strangers who did not know he was an earl, for he did not look it. That poor fellow used to sign his letters "Durham," and in them he would find fault with me for voting the Republican ticket, for the reason that it was unaristocratic, and by consequence un-Lamptonian. Then along would come a letter from some red-hot Virginian, son of my other branch, and abuse me bitterly for the same vote—on the ground that the Republican was an aristocratic party and it was not becoming in the descendant of a regicide to train with that kind of animal. And so I used to almost wish I hadn't had any ancestors, they were so much trouble to me.

# II

## *A Heavenly Place for a Boy*

M Y FATHER "kept store" in Florida for several years, but had no luck, except that I was born to him. He and the family presently removed to Hannibal, and prospered somewhat.

My uncle, John A. Quarles, was a farmer, and his place was in the country four miles from Florida. He had eight children and about fifteen or twenty Negroes, and was also fortunate in other ways, particularly in his character. I have never met a better man than he was. I was his guest for two or three months every year, from the fourth year after we removed to Hannibal till I was eleven or twelve years old. I have never consciously used him or his wife in a book, but his farm has come very handy to me in literature once or twice. In *Huck Finn* and in *Tom Sawyer, Detective* I moved it down to Arkansas. It was all of six hundred miles, but it was no trouble; it was not a very large farm—five hundred acres perhaps—but I could have done it if it had been twice as large. And as for the morality of it, I cared nothing for that; I would move a state if the exigencies of literature required it.

It was a heavenly place for a boy, that farm of my Uncle John's. The house was a double log one, with a spacious floor (roofed in) connecting it with the kitchen. In the summer the table was set in the middle of that shady and breezy floor, and the sumptuous meals—well, it makes me cry to think of them. Fried chicken, roast pig; ducks and geese, wild and tame turkeys; venison just killed; squirrels, rabbits, pheasants, partridges, prairie-chickens; biscuits, hot batter cakes, hot buckwheat cakes, hot "wheat bread," hot rolls, hot corn pone; fresh corn boiled on the ear, succotash, butter beans, string beans, tomatoes, peas, Irish potatoes, sweet potatoes; buttermilk, sweet milk, "clabber;" watermelons, muskmelons, cantaloupes—all fresh from the garden; apple pie, peach pie, pumpkin pie, peach cobbler, apple dumplings—I can't remember the rest. The way that the things were cooked was perhaps the main splendor—particularly a certain few of the dishes. For instance, the corn bread, the hot biscuits and wheat bread, and the fried chicken. These things have never been properly cooked in the North—in fact, no one there is able to learn the art, so far as my experience goes. The North thinks it knows how to make corn bread, but this is mere superstition. Perhaps no bread in the world is quite so good as Southern corn bread, and perhaps no bread in the world is quite so bad as the Northern imitation of it. The North seldom tries to fry chicken, and this is well; the art cannot be learned north of the line of Mason and Dixon, nor anywhere in Europe. This is not hearsay; it is experience that is

*The Clemens' house on Hill Street, Hannibal, Missouri.*
Courtesy of the Mark Twain Papers, The Bancroft Library

speaking. In Europe it is imagined that the custom of serving different kinds of bread blazing hot is "American," but that is too broad a spread; it is custom in the South, but is much less than that in the North. In the North and in Europe hot bread is considered unhealthy. This is probably just another fussy superstition, like the European superstition that ice-water is unhealthy.

It seems a pity that the world should throw away so many good things merely because they are not wholesome. Yet there are people who strictly deprive themselves of each and every eatable, drinkable, and smokable which has in any way acquired a shady reputation. They pay this price for health. And health is all they get for it. How strange it is! It is like paying out your whole fortune for a cow that has gone dry.

The farmhouse stood in the middle of a very large yard, and the yard was fenced on three sides with rails and on the rear side with high palings; against these stood the smoke-house; beyond the palings was the orchard; beyond the orchard were the Negro quarters and the tobacco fields. The front yard was entered over a stile made of sawed-off logs of graduated heights; I do not remember any gate. In a corner of the front yard were a dozen lofty hickory trees and a dozen black walnuts, and in the nutting season riches were to be gathered there.

Down a piece, abreast the house, stood a little log cabin against the rail fence; and there the woody hill fell sharply away, past the barns, the corn-crib, the stables, and the tobacco-curing house, to a limpid brook which sang along over its gravelly bed and curved and frisked in and out and here and there and yonder in the deep shade of overhanging foliage and vines—a divine place for wading, and it had swimming pools, too, which were forbidden to us and therefore much frequented by us. For we were little Christian children and had early been taught the value of forbidden fruit.

In the little log cabin lived a bedridden white-headed slave woman whom we visited daily and looked upon with awe, for we believed she was upward of a thousand years old and had talked with Moses. The younger Negroes credited these statistics and had furnished them to us in good faith. We accommodated all the details which came to us about her; and so we believed that she had lost her health in the long desert trip coming out of Egypt, and had never been able to get it back again. She had a round bald place on the crown of her head, and we used to creep around and gaze at it in reverent silence, and reflect that it was caused by fright through seeing Pharaoh drowned. We called her "Aunt" Hannah, Southern fashion. She was superstitious, like the other Negroes; also, like them, she was deeply religious. Like them, she had great faith in prayer and employed it in all ordinary exigencies, but not in cases where a dead certainty of result was urgent. Whenever witches were around she tied up the remnant of her wool in little tufts, with white thread, and this promptly made the witches impotent.

All the Negroes were friends of ours, and with those of our own age we were in effect comrades. I say in effect, using the phrase as a modification. We were comrades, and yet not comrades; color and condition interposed a subtle line which both parties were conscious of and which rendered complete fusion impossible. We had a faithful and affectionate good friend, ally, and adviser in "Uncle Dan'l," a middle-aged slave whose head was the best one in the Negro quarter, whose sympathies were wide and warm, and whose heart was honest and simple and knew no guile. He has served me well these many, many years. I have not seen him for more than half a century, and yet spiritually I have had his welcome company a good part of that time, and have staged him in books under his own name and as "Jim," and carted him all around—to Hannibal, down the Mississippi on a raft, and even across the Desert of Sahara in a balloon and he has endured it all with the patience and friendliness and loyalty which were his birthright. It was on the farm that I got my strong liking for his race and my appreciation of certain of its fine qualities. This feeling and this estimate have stood the test of sixty years and more, and have suffered no impairment. The black face is as welcome to me now as it was then.

I can see the farm yet, with perfect clearness. I

can see all its belongings, all its details; the family room of the house, with a "trundle" bed in one corner and a spinning-wheel in another—a wheel whose rising and falling wail, heard from a distance, was the mournfulest of all sounds to me, and made me homesick and low spirited, and filled my atmosphere with the wandering spirits of the dead; the vast fireplace, piled high, on winter nights, with flaming hickory logs from whose ends a sugary sap bubbled out, but did not go to waste, for we scraped it off and ate it; the lazy cat spread out on the rough hearthstones; the drowsy dogs braced against the jambs and blinking; my aunt in one chimney corner, knitting; my uncle in the other, smoking his corn-cob pipe; the slick and carpetless oak floor faintly mirroring the dancing flame tongues and freckled with black indentations where fire coals had popped out and died a leisurely death; half a dozen children romping in the background twilight; "split"-bottomed chairs here and there, some with rockers; a cradle—out of service, but waiting, with confidence; in the early cold mornings a snuggle of children, in shirts and chemises, occupying the hearthstone and procrastinating—they simply could not bear to leave that comfortable place and go out on the wind-swept floor space between the house and kitchen where the general tin basin stood, and wash.

Along outside of the front fence ran the country road, dusty in the summertime, and a good place

for snakes—they liked to lie in it and sun themselves; when they were rattlesnakes or puff adders,
we killed them; when they were black snakes, or
racers, or belonged to the fabled "hoop" breed, we
fled, without shame; but when they were "house
snakes," or "garters," we carried them home and
put them in Aunt Patsy's work basket for a surprise;
for she was prejudiced against snakes, and always
when she took the basket in her lap and they began
to climb out of it, it disordered her mind. She never
could seem to get used to them; her opportunities
went for nothing. And she was always cold toward
bats, too, and could not bear them; and yet I think a
bat is as friendly a bird as there is.

Beyond the road where the snakes sunned themselves was a dense young thicket, and through it a
dim-lighted path led a quarter of a mile; then out of
the dimness one emerged abruptly upon a level
great prairie which was covered with wild strawber-
ry plants, vividly starred with prairie pinks, and
walled in on all sides by forests. The strawberries
were fragrant and fine, and in the season we were
generally there in the crisp freshness of the early
morning, while the dew beads still sparkled upon
the grass and the woods were ringing with the first
songs of the birds.

Down the forest slopes to the left were the
swings. They were made of bark stripped from
hickory saplings. When they became dry they were
dangerous. They usually broke when a child was

forty feet in the air, and this was why so many
bones had to be mended every year. I had no ill
luck myself, but none of my cousins escaped. There
were eight of them, and at one time and another
they broke fourteen arms among them. But it cost
next to nothing because the doctor worked by the
year—twenty-five dollars for the whole family. I remember two of the Florida doctors, Chowning and
Meredith. They not only tended an entire family
for twenty-five dollars a year, but furnished the
medicines themselves. Good measure, too. Only the
largest persons could hold a whole dose. Castor oil
was the principal beverage. The dose was half a
dipperful, with half a dipperful of New Orleans molasses added to help it down and make it taste good,
which it never did. The next standby was calomel;
the next, rhubarb; and the next, jalap. Then they
bled the patient, and put mustard plasters on him.
It was a dreadful system, and yet the death rate was
not heavy. The calomel was nearly sure to salivate
the patient and cost him some of his teeth. There
were no dentists. When teeth became touched with
decay or were otherwise ailing, the doctor knew of
only one thing to do—he fetched his tongs and
dragged them out. If the jaw remained, it was not
his fault. Doctors were not called in cases of ordinary illness; the family grandmother attended to
those. Every old woman was a doctor, and gathered
her own medicines in the woods, and knew how to
compound doses that would stir the vitals of a cast-

iron dog. And then there was the "Indian doctor"; a grave savage, remnant of his tribe, deeply read in the mysteries of nature and the secret properties of herbs; and most backwoodsmen had high faith in his powers and they could tell of wonderful cures achieved by him. In Mauritius, away off yonder in the solitudes of the Indian Ocean, there is a person who answers to our Indian doctor of the old times. He is a Negro, and has had no teaching as a doctor, yet there is one disease which he is master of and can cure and the doctors can't. They send for him when they have a case. It is a child's disease of a strange and deadly sort, and the Negro cures it with a herb medicine which he makes, himself, from a prescription which has come down to him from his father and grandfather. He will not let anyone see it. He keeps the secret of its components to himself, and it is feared that he will die without divulging it; then there will be consternation in Mauritius. I was told these things by the people there, in 1896.

We had the "faith doctor," too, in those early days—a woman. Her specialty was toothache. She was a farmer's old wife and lived five miles from Hannibal. She would lay her hand on the patient's jaw and say, "Believe!" and the cure was prompt. Mrs. Utterback. I remember her very well. Twice I rode out there behind my mother, horseback, and saw the cure performed. My mother was the patient.

Doctor Meredith removed to Hannibal, by and by, and was our family physician there, and saved my life several times. Still, he was a good man and meant well. Let it go.

I was always told that I was a sickly and precarious and tiresome and uncertain child, and lived mainly on allopathic medicines during the first seven years of my life. I asked my mother about this—she was in her eighty-eighth year—and said:

"I suppose that during all that time you were uneasy about me?"

"Yes, the whole time."

"Afraid I wouldn't live?"

After a reflective pause—ostensibly to think out the facts—"No—afraid you would."

The country schoolhouse was three miles from my uncle's farm. It stood in a clearing in the woods and would hold about twenty-five boys and girls. We attended the school with more or less regularity once or twice a week, in summer, walking to it in the cool of the morning by the forest paths, and back in the gloaming at the end of the day. All the pupils brought their dinners in baskets—corn dodger, buttermilk, and other good things—and sat in the shade of the trees at noon and ate them. It is the part of my education which I look back upon with the most satisfaction. My first visit to the school was when I was seven. A strapping girl of fifteen, in the customary sunbonnet and calico dress, asked me if I "used tobacco"—meaning did I chew it. I said no. It roused her scorn. She reported me to all the crowd, and said:

"Here is a boy seven years old who can't chew tobacco."

By the looks and comments which this produced I realized that I was a degraded object, and was cruelly ashamed of myself. I determined to reform. But I only made myself sick; I was not able to learn to chew tobacco. I learned to smoke fairly well, but that did not conciliate anybody and I remained a poor thing, and characterless. I longed to be respected, but I never was able to rise. Children have but little charity for one another's defects.

As I have said, I spent some part of every year at the farm until I was twelve or thirteen years old. The life which I led there with my cousins was full of charm, and so is the memory of it yet. I can call back the solemn twilight and mystery of the deep woods, the earthy smells, the faint odors of the wild flowers, the sheen of rain-washed foliage, the rattling clatter of drops when the wind shook the trees, the far-off hammering of woodpeckers and the muffled drumming of wood pheasants in the remoteness of the forest, the snapshot glimpses of disturbed wild creatures scurrying through the grass—I can call it all back and make it as real as it ever was, and as blessed. I can call back the prairie, and its loneliness and peace, and a vast hawk hanging motionless in the sky, with his wings spread wide and the blue of the vault showing through the fringe of their end feathers. I can see the woods in their autumn dress, the oaks purple, the hickories washed

with gold, the maples and the sumachs luminous
with crimson fires, and I can hear the rustle made
by the fallen leaves as we plowed through them. I
can see the blue clusters of wild grapes hanging
among the foliage of the saplings, and I remember
the taste of them and the smell. I know how the
wild blackberries looked, and how they tasted, and
the same with the pawpaws, the hazelnuts, and the
persimmons; and I can feel the thumping rain, upon
my head, of hickory nuts and walnuts when we
were out in the frosty dawn to scramble for them
with the pigs, and the gusts of wind loosed them
and sent them down. I know the stain of blackberries, and how pretty it is, and I know the stain of
walnut hulls, and how little it minds soap and water, also what grudged experience it had of either of
them. I know the taste of maple sap, and when to
gather it, and how to arrange the troughs and the
delivery tubes, and how to boil down the juice, and
how to hook the sugar after it is made, also how
much better hooked sugar tastes than any that is
honestly come by, let bigots say what they will. I
know how a prize watermelon looks when it is sun-
ning its fat rotundity among pumpkin vines and
"simblins";[1] I know how to tell when it is ripe without "plugging" it; I know how inviting it looks
when it is cooling itself in a tub of water under the
bed, waiting; I know how it looks when it lies on
the table in the sheltered great floor space between

[1]summer squashes.

house and kitchen, and the children gathered for the sacrifice and their mouths watering; I know the crackling sound it makes when the carving knife enters its end, and I can see the split fly along in front of the blade as the knife cleaves its way to the other end; I can see its halves fall apart and display the rich red meat and the black seeds, and the heart standing up, a luxury fit for the elect; I know how a boy looks behind a yard-long slice of that melon, and I know how he feels; for I have been there. I know the taste of the watermelon which has been honestly come by, and I know the taste of the watermelon which has been acquired by art. Both taste good, but the experienced know which tastes best. I know the look of green apples and peaches and pears on the trees, and I know how entertaining they are when they are inside of a person. I know how ripe ones look when they are piled in pyramids under the trees, and how pretty they are and how vivid their colors. I know how a frozen apple looks, in a barrel down cellar in the wintertime, and how hard it is to bite, and how the frost makes the teeth ache, and yet how good it is, notwithstanding. I know the disposition of elderly people to select the specked apples for the children, and I once knew ways to beat the game. I know the look of an apple that is roasting and sizzling on a hearth on a winter's evening, and I know the comfort that comes of eating it hot, along with some sugar and a drench of cream. I know the delicate art and mystery of so

cracking hickory nuts and walnuts on a flatiron with
a hammer that the kernels will be delivered whole,
and I know how the nuts, taken in conjunction with
winter apples, cider, and doughnuts, make old people's old tales and old jokes sound fresh and crisp
and enchanting, and juggle an evening away before
you know what went with the time. I know the look
of Uncle Dan'l's kitchen as it was on the privileged
nights, when I was a child, and I can see the white
and black children grouped on the hearth, with the
firelight playing on their faces and the shadows
flickering upon the walls, clear back toward the cav-
ernous gloom of the rear, and I can hear Uncle
Dan'l telling the immortal tales which Uncle Remus Harris[2] was to gather into his book and charm
the world with, by and by; and I can feel again the
creepy joy which quivered through me when the
time for the ghost story was reached—and the sense
of regret, too, which came over me, for it was always
the last story of the evening and there was nothing
between it and the unwelcome bed.

I can remember the bare wooden stairway in my
uncle's house, and the turn to the left above the
landing, and the rafters and the slanting roof over
my bed, and the squares of moonlight on the floor,
and the white cold world of snow outside, seen
through the curtainless window. I can remember
the howling of the wind and the quaking of the

[2] Joel Chandler Harris (1848–1908) was the creator of a
fictitious Uncle Remus who retold Negro folktales.

house on stormy nights, and how snug and cozy one felt, under the blankets, listening; and how the powdery snow used to sift in, around the sashes, and lie in little ridges on the floor and make the place look chilly in the morning and curb the wild desire to get up—in case there was any. I can remember how very dark that room was, in the dark of the moon, and how packed it was with ghostly stillness when one woke up by accident away in the night, and forgotten sins came flocking out of the secret chambers of the memory and wanted a hearing; and how ill chosen the time seemed for this kind of business; and how dismal was the hoo-hooing of the owl and the wailing of the wolf, sent mourning by on the night wind.

I remember the raging of the rain on that roof, summer nights, and how pleasant it was to lie and listen to it, and enjoy the white splendor of the lightning and the majestic booming and crashing of the thunder. It was a very satisfactory room, and there was a lightning rod which was reachable from the window, an adorable and skittish thing to climb up and down, summer nights, when there were duties on hand of a sort to make privacy desirable.

I remember the 'coon and 'possum hunts, nights with the Negroes, and those long marches through the black gloom of the woods, and the excitement which fired everybody when the distant bay of an experienced dog announced that the hunted was treed; then the wild scramblings and stumblings through briers and bushes and over roots to get to the spot; then the lighting of a fire and the felling of the tree, the joyful frenzy of the dogs and the Negroes, and the weird picture it all made in the red glare—I remember it all well, and the delight that everyone got out of it, except the 'coon.

I remember the pigeon seasons, when the birds would come in millions and cover the trees and by their weight break down the branches. They were clubbed to death with sticks; guns were not necessary and were not used. I remember the squirrel hunts, and prairie-chicken hunts, and wild-turkey hunts, and all that; and how we turned out, mornings, while it was still dark, to go on these expeditions, and how chilly and dismal it was, and how often I regretted that I was well enough to go. A toot on a tin horn brought twice as many dogs as were needed, and in their happiness they raced and scampered about, and knocked small people down, and made no end of unnecessary noise. At the word, they vanished away toward the woods and we drifted silently after them in the melancholy gloom. But presently the gray dawn stole over the world, the birds piped up, then the sun rose and poured light and comfort all around, everything was fresh and dewy and fragrant, and life was a boon again. After three hours of tramping, we arrived back wholesomely tired, overladen with game, very hungry, and just in time for breakfast.

# III

## *The Most Eloquent Person I Have Heard Speak*

M Y SCHOOL DAYS in Hannibal began when I was
four years and a half old. There were no public schools in Missouri in those early days, but there
were two private schools—terms twenty-five cents
per week per pupil and collect it if you can. Mrs.
Horr taught the children in a small log house at the
southern end of Main Street. Mr. Sam Cross taught
the young people of larger growth in a frame
schoolhouse on the hill. I was sent to Mrs. Horr's
school and I remember my first day in that little log
house with perfect clearness; at least I remember an
episode of that first day. I broke one of the rules
and was warned not to do it again, and was told that
the penalty for a second breach was a whipping. I
presently broke the rule again and Mrs. Horr told
me to go out and find a switch and fetch it. I was
glad she appointed me, for I believed I could select
a switch suitable to the occasion with more judiciousness than anybody else.

In the mud I found a cooper's shaving of the old-
time pattern, oak, two inches broad, a quarter of an
inch thick, and rising in a shallow curve at one end.
There were nice new shavings of the same breed
close by but I took this one, although it was rotten.

I carried it to Mrs. Horr, presented it, and stood before her in an attitude of meekness and resignation which seemed to me calculated to win favor and sympathy, but it did not happen. She divided a long look of strong disapprobation equally between me and the shaving; then she called me by my entire name, Samuel Langhorne Clemens—probably the first time I had ever heard it all strung together in one procession—and said she was ashamed of me. I was to learn later that when a teacher calls a boy by his entire name it means trouble. She said she would try and appoint a boy with a better judgment than mine in the matter of switches, and it saddens me yet when I remember how many faces lighted up with the hope of getting that appointment. Jim Dunlap got it, and when he returned with the switch of his choice I recognized he was an expert.

Mrs. Horr was a New England lady of middle age with New England ways and principles, and she always opened school with prayer and a chapter from the New Testament; also she explained the chapter with a brief talk. In one of these talks she dwelt upon the text, "Ask and ye shall receive," and said that whosoever prayed for a thing with earnestness and strong desire need not doubt that his prayer would be answered.

I was so forcibly struck by this information and so gratified by the opportunities which it offered that this was probably the first time I had heard of it. I thought I would give it a trial. I believed in

Mrs. Horr thoroughly and I had no doubts as to the result. I prayed for gingerbread. Margaret Kooneman, who was the baker's daughter, brought a slab of gingerbread to school every morning; she had always kept it out of sight before but when I finished my prayer and glanced up, there it was in easy reach and she was looking the other way. In all my life I believe I never enjoyed an answer to prayer more than I enjoyed that one; and I was a convert, too. I had no end of wants and they had always remained unsatisfied up to that time, but I meant to supply them and extend them now that I had found out how to do it.

But this dream was like almost all the other dreams we indulge in in life, there was nothing in it. I did as much praying during the next two or three days as any one in that town, I suppose, and I was very sincere and earnest about it too, but nothing came of it. I found that not even the most powerful prayer was competent to lift that gingerbread again, and I came to the conclusion that if a person remains faithful to his gingerbread and keeps his eye on it, he need not trouble himself about your prayers.

Something about my conduct and bearing troubled my mother, and she took me aside and questioned me concerning it with much solicitude. I was reluctant to reveal to her the change that had come over me, for it would grieve me to distress her kind heart, but at last I confessed, with many tears, that I had ceased to be a Christian. She was heartbroken, and asked me why.

I said it was because I had found out that I was a Christian for revenue only and I could not bear the thought of that, it was so ignoble.

She gathered me to her breast and comforted me and I gathered from what she said that if I would continue in that condition I would never be lonesome.

WHEN my mother died, in October, 1890, she was well along in her eighty-eighth year, a mighty age, a well-contested fight for life for one who at forty was so delicate of body as to be accounted a confirmed invalid and destined to pass soon away. I knew her well during the first twenty-five years of my life; but after that I saw her only at wide intervals, for we lived many days' journey apart. I am not proposing to write about her, but merely to talk about her; not give her formal history, but merely to make illustrative extracts from it, so to speak; furnish flashlight glimpses of her character, not a processional view of her career. Technically speaking, she had no career; but she had a character, and it was of a fine and striking and lovable sort.

What becomes of the multitudinous photographs which one's mind takes of people? Out of the million which my mental camera must have taken of this first and closest friend, only one clear and strongly defined one of early date remains. She was forty years old then, and I was eight. She held me

*Sam's mother, Jane Clemens,*
*from a portrait by Brady in 1859.*
Courtesy of the Mark Twain Papers, The Bancroft Library

by the hand, and we were kneeling by the bedside of my brother, two years older than I, who lay dead, and the tears were flowing down her cheeks unchecked. And she was moaning. That dumb sign of anguish was perhaps new to me, since it made upon me a very strong impression—an impression which holds its place still with the picture which it helped to intensify and make memorable.

She had a small and slender body, but a large heart; a heart so large that everybody's grief and everybody's joys found welcome in it, and hospitable accommodation. The greatest difference which I find between her and the rest of the people whom I have known, is this, and it is a remarkable one: those others felt a strong interest in a few things, whereas to the very day of her death she felt a strong interest in the whole world and everything and everybody in it. In all her life she never knew such a thing as a half-hearted interest in affairs and people, or an interest which drew a line and left out certain affairs and was indifferent to certain people. The invalid who takes a strenuous and indestructible interest in everything and everybody but himself, and to whom a dull moment is an unknown thing and an impossibility, is a formidable adversary for disease and a hard invalid to vanquish. I am certain that it was this feature of my mother's makeup that carried her so far toward ninety.

Her interest in people and in all other animals was warm, personal and friendly. She always found something to excuse, and as a rule to love, in the toughest of them; even if she had to put it there herself. She was the natural ally and friend of the friendless. It was believed that, Presbyterian as she was, she could be beguiled into saying a soft word for the devil himself, and so the experiment was tried. The abuse of Satan began; one conspirator after another added his bitter word, his malign reproach, his pitiless censure, till at last, sure enough, the unsuspecting subject of the trick walked into the trap. She admitted that the indictment was sound, that Satan was utterly wicked and abandoned, just as these people had said; *but* would any claim that he had been treated fairly? A sinner was but a sinner; Satan was just that, like the rest. What saves the rest?—their own efforts alone? No—or none might ever be saved. To their feeble efforts is added the mighty help of pathetic, appealing, imploring prayers that go up daily out of all the churches in Christendom and out of myriads upon myriads of pitying hearts. But who prays for Satan? Who, in eighteen centuries, has had the common humanity to pray for the one sinner that needed it most, our one fellow and brother who most needed a friend yet had not a single one, the one sinner among us all who had the highest and clearest *right* to every Christian's daily and nightly prayers, for the plain and unassailable reason that his was the first and greatest need, he being among sinners the supremest?

This friend of Satan was a most gentle spirit, and

an unstudied and unconscious pathos was her native speech. When her pity or her indignation was stirred by hurt or shame inflicted upon some defenseless person or creature, she was the most eloquent person I have heard speak. It was seldom eloquence of a fiery or violent sort, but gentle, pitying, persuasive, appealing; and so genuine and so nobly and simply worded and so touchingly uttered, that many times I have seen it win the reluctant and splendid applause of tears. Whenever anybody or any creature was being oppressed, the fears that belonged to her sex and her small stature retired to the rear and her soldierly qualities came promptly to the front. One day in our village I saw a vicious devil of a Corsican, a common terror in the town, chasing his grown daughter past cautious male citizens with a heavy rope in his hand, and declaring he would wear it out on her. My mother spread her door wide to the refugee, and then, instead of closing and locking it after her, stood in it and stretched her arms across it, barring the way. The man swore, cursed, threatened her with his rope; but she did not flinch or show any sign of fear; she only stood straight and fine, and lashed him, shamed him, derided him, defied him in tones not audible to the middle of the street, but audible to the man's conscience and dormant manhood; and he asked her pardon and gave her his rope and said with a most great and blasphemous oath that she was the bravest woman he ever saw; and so went his way without another word and troubled her no more. He and she were always good friends after that, for in her he had found a long-felt want—somebody who was not afraid of him.

One day in St. Louis she walked out into the street and greatly surprised a burly cartman who was beating his horse over the head with the butt of his heavy whip; for she took the whip away from him and then made such a persuasive appeal in behalf of the ignorantly offending horse that he was tripped into saying he was to blame; and also into volunteering a promise which of course he couldn't keep, for he was not built in that way—a promise that he wouldn't ever abuse a horse again.

That sort of interference in behalf of abused animals was a common thing with her all her life; and her manner must have been without offense and her good intent transparent, for she always carried her point, and also won the courtesy, and often the friendly applause, of the adversary. All the race of dumb animals had a friend in her. By some subtle sign the homeless, hunted, bedraggled, and disreputable cat recognized her at a glance as the born refuge and champion of his sort—and followed her home. His instinct was right, he was as welcome as the prodigal son. We had nineteen cats at one time, in 1845. And there wasn't one in the lot that had any character, not one that had any merit, except the cheap and tawdry merit of being unfortunate. They were a vast burden to us all—including my

mother—but they were out of luck, and that was
enough; they had to stay. However, better these
than no pets at all; children must have pets, and we
were not allowed to have caged ones. An imprisoned creature was out of the question—my mother
would not have allowed a rat to be restrained of its
liberty.

We lived in a slaveholding community; indeed,
when slavery perished my mother had been in daily
touch with it for sixty years. Yet, kind-hearted and
compassionate as she was, I think she was not conscious that slavery was a bald, grotesque, and un-
warrantable usurpation. She had never heard it assailed in any pulpit, but had heard it defended and
sanctified in a thousand; her ears were familiar with
Bible texts that approved it, but if there were any
that disapproved it they had not been quoted by
her pastors; as far as her experience went, the wise
and the good and the holy were unanimous in the
conviction that slavery was right, righteous, sacred,
the peculiar pet of the Deity, and a condition which
the slave himself ought to be daily and nightly
thankful for. Manifestly, training and association
can accomplish strange miracles. As a rule our
slaves were convinced and content. So, doubtless,
are the far more intelligent slaves of a monarchy;
they revere and approve their masters, the monarch
and the noble, and recognize no degradation in the
fact that they are slaves.

However, there was nothing about the slavery of

the Hannibal region to rouse one's dozing humane instincts to activity. It was the mild domestic slavery, not the brutal plantation article. Cruelties were very rare, and exceedingly and wholesomely unpopular. To separate and sell the members of a slave family to different masters was a thing not well liked by the people, and so it was not often done, except in the settling of estates. I have no recollection of ever seeing a slave auction in that town; but I am suspicious that that is because the thing was a common and commonplace spectacle, not an uncommon and impressive one. I vividly remember seeing a dozen black men and women chained to one another, once, and lying in a group on the pavement, awaiting shipment to the Southern slave market. Those were the saddest faces I have ever seen. Chained slaves could not have been a common sight, or this picture would not have made so strong and lasting an impression upon me.

The "nigger trader" was loathed by everybody. He was regarded as a sort of human devil who bought and conveyed poor helpless creatures to hell—for to our whites and blacks alike the Southern plantation was simply hell; no milder name could describe it. If the threat to sell an incorrigible slave "down the river" would not reform him, nothing would—his case was past cure.

It is commonly believed that an infallible effect of slavery was to make such as lived in its midst hard hearted. I think it had no such effect—speaking in general terms. I think it stupefied everybody's humanity, as regarded the slave, but stopped there. There were no hard-hearted people in our town—I mean there were no more than would be found in any other town of the same size in any other country; and in my experience hard-hearted people are very rare everywhere.

In my schoolboy days I had no aversion to slavery. I was not aware that there was anything wrong about it. No one arraigned it in my hearing; the local papers said nothing against it; the local pulpit taught us that God approved it, that it was a holy thing, and that the doubter need only look in the Bible if he wished to settle his mind—and then the texts were read aloud to us to make the matter sure; if the slaves themselves had an aversion to slavery, they were wise and said nothing. In Hannibal we seldom saw a slave misused; on the farm, never.

There was, however, one small incident of my boyhood days which touched this matter, and it must have meant a good deal to me or it would not have stayed in my memory, clear and sharp, vivid and shadowless, all these slow-drifting years. We had a little slave boy whom we had hired from some one, there in Hannibal. He was from the eastern shore of Maryland, and had been brought away from his family and his friends, halfway across the American continent to be sold. He was a cheery spirit, innocent and gentle, and the noisiest creature that ever was, perhaps. All day long he was singing, whistling, yelling, whooping, laughing—it was maddening, devastating, unendurable. At last, one day, I lost all my temper, and went raging to my mother and said Sandy had been singing for an hour without a single break, and I couldn't stand it, and *wouldn't* she please shut him up. The tears came into her eyes and her lip trembled, and she said something like this:

"Poor thing, when he sings it shows that he is not remembering, and that comforts me; but when he is still I am afraid he is thinking, and I cannot bear it. He will never see his mother again; if he can sing, I must not hinder it, but be thankful for it. If you were older, you would understand me; then that friendless child's noise would make you glad."

It was a simple speech and made up of small words, but it went home, and Sandy's noise was not a trouble to me any more. She never used large words, but she had a natural gift for making small ones do effective work. She was capable with her tongue to the last—especially when a meanness or an injustice roused her spirit. She has come handy to me several times in my books, where she figures as Tom Sawyer's Aunt Polly. I fitted her out with a dialect and tried to think up other improvements for her, but did not find any. I used Sandy once, also; it was in *Tom Sawyer*. I tried to get him to whitewash the fence, but it did not work. I do not remember what name I called him by in the book.

MY MOTHER had a good deal of trouble with me, but I think she enjoyed it. She had none at all with my brother Henry, who was two years younger than I, and I think that the unbroken monotony of his goodness and truthfulness and obedience would have been a burden to her but for the relief and variety which I furnished in the other direction. I was a tonic. I was valuable to her. I never thought of it before, but now I see it. I never knew Henry to do a vicious thing toward me, or toward anyone else— but he frequently did righteous ones that cost me as heavily. It was his duty to report me, when I needed reporting and neglected to do it myself, and he was very faithful in discharging that duty. He is Sid in *Tom Sawyer*. But Sid was not Henry. Henry was a very much finer and better boy than ever Sid was.

It was Henry who called my mother's attention to the fact that the thread with which she had sewed my collar together to keep me from going in swimming had changed color. My mother would not have discovered it but for that, and she was manifestly piqued when she recognized that that prominent bit of circumstantial evidence had escaped her sharp eye. That detail probably added a detail to my punishment. It is human. We generally visit our shortcomings on somebody else when there is a possible excuse for it—but no matter. I took it out of Henry. There is always compensation for such as are unjustly used. I often took it out of him—sometimes as an advance payment for something which

I hadn't yet done. These were occasions when the opportunity was too strong a temptation, and I had to draw on the future. I did not need to copy this idea from my mother, and probably didn't. It is most likely that I invented it for myself. Still, she wrought upon that principle upon occasion.

If the incident of the broken sugar bowl is in *Tom Sawyer*—I don't remember whether it is or not— that is an example of it.[1] Henry never stole sugar. He took it openly from the bowl. His mother knew he wouldn't take sugar when she wasn't looking, but she had some doubts about me. Not exactly doubts, either. She knew very well I *would*. One day when she was not present Henry took sugar from her prized and precious old-English sugar bowl, which was an heirloom in the family—and he managed to break the bowl. It was the first time I had ever had a chance to tell anything on him, and I was inexpressibly glad. I told him I was going to tell on him, but he was not disturbed. When my mother came in and saw the bowl lying on the floor in fragments, she was speechless for a minute. I allowed that silence to work; I judged it would increase the effect. I was waiting for her to ask, "Who did that?"—so that I could fetch out my news. But it was an error of calculation. When she got through with her silence she didn't ask anything about it— she merely gave me a crack on the skull with her thimble that I felt all the way down to my heels.

[1] The incident is in *Tom Sawyer*.

Then I broke out with my injured innocence, expecting to make her very sorry that she had punished the wrong one. I expected her to do something remorseful and pathetic. I told her that I was not the one—it was Henry. But there was no upheaval. She said, without emotion: "It's all right. It isn't any matter. You deserve it for something you've done that I didn't know about; and if you haven't done it, why then you deserve it for something that you are going to do that I shan't hear about."

There was a stairway outside the house, which led up to the rear part of the second story. One day Henry was sent on an errand, and he took a tin bucket along. I knew he would have to ascend those stairs, so I went up and locked the door on the inside, and came down into the garden, which had been newly plowed and was rich in choice, firm clods of black mold. I gathered a generous equipment of these and ambushed him. I waited till he had climbed the stairs and was near the landing and couldn't escape. Then I bombarded him with clods, which he warded off with his tin bucket the best he could, but without much success, for I was a good marksman. The clods smashing against the weatherboarding fetched my mother out to see what was the matter, and I tried to explain that I was amusing Henry. Both of them were after me in a minute, but I knew the way over that high board fence and escaped for that time. After an hour or two, when I ventured back, there was no one around and I thought the incident was closed. But it was not so. Henry was ambushing me. With an unusually competent aim for him, he landed a stone on the side of my head which raised a bump there which felt like the Matterhorn. I carried it to my mother straightway for sympathy, but she was not strongly moved. It seemed to be her idea that incidents like this would eventually reform me if I harvested enough of them. So the matter was only educational. I had had a sterner view of it than that before.

# IV

## *Villagers*

Tom Nash was a boy of my own age—the post-master's son. About 1849, the Mississippi was frozen across, and he and I went skating one night, probably without permission. I cannot see why we should go skating in the night unless without permission, for there could be no considerable amusement to be gotten out of skating late at night if nobody was going to object to it. About midnight, when we were more than half a mile out toward the Illinois shore, we heard some ominous rumbling and grinding and crashing going on between us and the home side of the river, and we knew what it meant—the river was breaking up. We started for home, pretty badly scared. We flew along at full speed whenever the moonlight sifting down between the clouds enabled us to tell which was ice and which was water. In the pauses we waited, started again whenever there was a good bridge of ice, paused again when we came to naked water, and waited in distress until a floating vast cake should bridge that place. It took us an hour to make the trip—a trip which we made in a misery of apprehension all the time. But at last we arrived within a very brief distance of the shore. We waited again. There

was another place that needed bridging. All about
us the ice was plunging and grinding along and pil-
ing itself up in mountains on the shore, and the
dangers were increasing, not diminishing. We grew
very impatient to get to solid ground, so we started
too early and went springing from cake to cake.
Tom made a miscalculation and fell short. He got a
bitter bath, but he was so close to shore that he only
had to swim a stroke or two—then his feet struck
hard bottom and he crawled out. I arrived a little
later, without accident. We had been in a drenching
perspiration and Tom's bath was a disaster for him.
He took to his bed, sick, and had a procession of
diseases. The closing one was scarlet fever, and he
came out of it stone deaf. Within a year or two
speech departed, of course. But some years later he
was taught to talk, after a fashion—one couldn't always make out what it was he was trying to say. Of
course he could not modulate his voice, since he
couldn't hear himself talk. When he supposed he
was talking low and confidentially, you could hear
him in Illinois.

In 1902, I was invited by the University of Missouri to come out there and receive the honorary
degree of LL.D. I took that opportunity to spend a
week in Hannibal—a city now, a village in my day.
It had been fifty-five years since Tom Nash and I
had had that adventure. When I was at the railway
station ready to leave Hannibal, there was a great
crowd of citizens there. I saw Tom Nash approach-

*Hannibal, Missouri about 1850*
*from a painting by Henry Lewis.*
Courtesy of the Missouri Historical Society

ing me across a vacant space, and I walked toward him, for I recognized him at once. He was old and white-headed, but the boy of fifteen was still visible in him. He came up to me, made a trumpet of his hands at my ear, nodded his head toward the citizens, and said, confidentially—in a yell like a fog horn—"Same damned fools, Sam."

## SCHOOLMATES

IF I wanted to describe Dawson's, the last school that I attended in Hannibal, I could save myself the trouble by conveying the description of it to these pages from *Tom Sawyer*. I can remember the drowsy and inviting summer sounds that used to float in through the open windows from that distant boy-Paradise, Cardiff Hill, and intermingle with the murmurs of the studying pupils and make them the more dreary by the contrast. I remember Andy Fuqua, the oldest pupil—a man of twenty-five. I remember the youngest pupil, Nannie Owsley, a child of seven. I remember George RoBards, about eighteen or twenty years old, the only pupil who studied Latin. I remember Mr. Dawson very well. I remember his boy, Theodore, who was as good as he could be. In fact he was inordinately good, extravagantly good, offensively good, detestably good, and he had pop-eyes, and I would have drowned him if I had had a chance.

In that school we were all about on an equality and so far as I remember, the passion of envy had no place in our hearts, except in the case of Arch Fuqua—the other one's brother. Of course we all went barefoot in the summertime. Arch Fuqua was about my own age—ten or eleven. In the winter we could stand him, because he wore shoes then, and his great gift was hidden from our sight and we were enabled to forget it. But in the summertime he was a bitterness to us. He was our envy, for he could double back his big toe and let it fly and you could hear it snap thirty yards. There was not another boy in the school that could approach this feat. He had not a rival as regards a physical distinction—except in Theodore Eddy, who could wiggle his ears like a horse. But he was no real rival, because you couldn't hear him work his ears; so all the advantage lay with Arch Fuqua.

I remember the names of some of these schoolmates, and by fitful glimpses, even their faces rise before me for a moment—only just long enough to be recognized; then they vanish. I catch glimpses of George RoBards—slender, pale, studious, bending over his book and absorbed in it, his long straight black hair hanging down below his jaws like a pair of curtains on the sides of his face. I can see him give his head a toss and flirt one of the curtains back around his head—to get it out of his way, apparently; really to show off. In that day it was a great thing among the boys to have hair of so flexible a sort that it could be flung back in that way, with a flirt of the head. George RoBards was the envy of us all. For there was no hair among us that was so competent for this exhibition as his.

George was a fine young fellow in all ways. He and Mary Moss were sweethearts and pledged to eternal constancy, from the time when they were merely children. But Mr. Lakenan arrived now and became a resident. He took an important position in the little town at once, and maintained it. He brought with him a distinguished reputation as a lawyer. He was educated, cultured; he was grave even to austerity; he was dignified in his conversation and deportment. He was a rather oldish bachelor—as bachelor oldishness was estimated in that day. He was a rising man. He was contemplated with considerable awe by the community, and as a catch he stood at the top of the market. That blooming and beautiful thing, Mary Moss, attracted his favor. He laid siege to her and won. Everybody said she accepted him to please her parents, not herself. They were married. And everybody again, testifying, said he continued her schooling all by himself, proposing to educate her up to standard and make her a meet companion for him. These things may have been true. They may not have been true. But they were interesting. George went away, presently, to some far-off region and there he died—of a broken heart, everybody said. That could be true, for he had good cause. He would go far before he would find another Mary Moss.

John RoBards was the little brother of George, a

small chap with silky golden curtains to his face
which dangled to his shoulders and below, and
could be flung back ravishingly. When he was
twelve years old he crossed the plains with his father amid the rush of the gold seekers of '49; and I
remember the departure of the cavalcade when it
spurred westward. We were all there to see and to
envy. And I can still see that proud little chap sailing by on a great horse, with his long locks streaming out behind. We were all on hand to gaze and
envy when he returned, two years later, in unimag-
inable glory—for he had traveled. None of us had
ever been forty miles from home. But he had
crossed the continent. He had been in the gold
mines, that fairyland of our imagination. And he
had done a still more wonderful thing. He had been
in ships—in ships on the actual ocean; in ships on
three actual oceans. For he had sailed down the
Pacific and round the Horn among icebergs and
through snowstorms and wild wintry gales, and had
sailed on and turned the corner and flown northward in the trades and up through the blistering
equatorial waters—and there in his brown face were
the proofs of what he had been through. We would
have sold our souls to Satan for the privilege of
trading places with him.

Another schoolmate was John Meredith, a boy of
a quite uncommonly sweet and gentle disposition.
He grew up, and when the Civil War broke out he
became a sort of guerrilla chief on the Confederate

side, and I was told that in his raids upon Union families in the country parts of Monroe County— in earlier times the friends and familiars of his father—he was remorseless in his devastations and sheddings of blood. It seems almost incredible that this could have been that gentle comrade of my school days; yet it can be true, for Robespierre when he was young was like that.

Will Bowen was another schoolmate, and so was his brother, Sam, who was his junior by a couple of years. Before the Civil War broke out both became St. Louis and New Orleans pilots. While Sam was still very young he had a curious adventure. He fell in love with a girl of sixteen, only child of a very wealthy German brewer. He wanted to marry her, but he and she both thought that the papa would not only not consent, but would shut his door against Sam. The old man was not so disposed, but they were not aware of that. He had his eye upon them, and it was not a hostile eye. That indiscreet young couple got to living together surreptitiously. Before long the old man died. When the will was examined it was found that he had left the whole of his wealth to Mrs. Samuel A. Bowen. Then the poor things made another mistake. They rushed down to the French suburb, Carondelet, and got a magistrate to marry them and date the marriage back a few months. The old brewer had some nieces and nephews and cousins, and different kinds of assets of that sort, and they traced out the fraud and proved it

and got the property. This left Sam with a girl wife
on his hands and the necessity of earning a living
for her at the pilot wheel. After a few years Sam and
another pilot were bringing a boat up from New
Orleans when the yellow fever broke out among the
few passengers and the crew. Both pilots became
stricken with it and there was nobody to take their
place at the wheel. The boat was landed at the head
of Island 82 to wait for succor. Death came swiftly
to both pilots—and there they lie buried, unless the
river has cut the graves away and washed the bones
into the stream, a thing which has probably happened long ago.

## NOTES ON OTHER VILLAGERS

*Mrs. Holiday.* Was a Mac Donald, born Scotch.
Wore her father's ivory miniature—a British General in the Revolution. Lived on Holiday's Hill. Well
off. Hospitable. Fond of having parties of young
people. Widow. Old but anxious to marry. Always
consulting fortune-tellers; always managed to make
them understand that she had been promised three
by the first fraud. They always confirmed the
prophecy. She finally died before the prophecies
had a full chance.

*Ed. Hyde, Dick Hyde.* Tough and dissipated. Ed
held his uncle down while Dick tried to kill him
with a pistol which refused to fire.

*Blankenships.* Both parents were paupers and
drunkards; the girls were charged with prostitution;

not proven. Tom, a kindly young heathen. Bence, a fisherman. These children were never sent to school or church. In *Huckleberry Finn* I have drawn Tom exactly as he was.[1] He was ignorant, unwashed, insufficiently fed; but he had as good a heart as any boy had. His liberties were totally unrestricted. He was the only really independent person—boy or man—in the community, and by consequence he was tranquilly and continuously happy, and was envied by all the rest of us.

*Woodson Blankenship*, Tom's father, was at one time Town Drunkard, an exceedingly well-defined and unofficial office in those days. He succeeded General Gaines, and for a time he was sole and only incumbent in the office; but afterward Jimmy Finn proved competency and disputed the place with him, so we had two town drunkards at one time. During Jimmy Finn's term he was not finical; he was not hypercritical; he was largely and handsomely democratic—and slept in the deserted tanyard with the hogs. My father tried to reform him once, but did not succeed.

*Injun Joe.* My father once tried to reform Injun Joe, the halfbreed. That also was a failure, and we boys were glad. For Injun Joe, drunk, was interesting and a benefaction to us, but Injun Joe, sober, was a dreary spectacle.

Injun Joe got lost in the great cave three miles

[1]Tom Blankenship was the prototype of the character, Huckleberry Finn.

below Hannibal, a tangled wilderness of narrow and lofty clefts and passages. It was an easy place to get lost in; anybody could do it—including the bats. Injun Joe would have starved to death if the bats had run short. But there was no chance of that; there were myriads of them. In the book *Tom Sawyer* I starved him entirely to death in the cave, but that was in the interest of art; it never happened.

The cave was an uncanny place, for it contained a corpse—the corpse of a young girl of fourteen. It was in a glass cylinder inclosed in a copper one which was suspended from a rail which bridged a narrow passage. The body was preserved in alcohol, and it was said that loafers and rowdies used to drag it up by the hair and look at the dead face. The girl was the daughter of a St. Louis surgeon of extraordinary ability and wide celebrity. He was an eccentric man and did many strange things. He put the poor thing in that forlorn place himself.

*Letitia Honeyman.* Married a showy stranger. Turned out to be a thief and swindler. She and her baby waited while he served a long term. At the end of it her youth was gone, and her cheery ways.

*Ratcliffes.* One son lived in a bark hut up at the still house branch and at intervals came home at night and emptied the larder. Back door left open purposely; and if notice was taken of him he would not come.

*Another son* had to be locked into a small house in a corner of the yard—and chained. Fed through a

*Tom Blankenship's (Huck Finn) house
in Hannibal, Missouri.*
Courtesy of the Frazer Studio

hole. Would not wear clothes, winter or summer. Could not have fire. Religious mania. Believed his left hand had committed a mortal sin and must be sacrificed. Got hold of a hatchet, and chopped it off. He died in that small house.

*One son* became a fine physician and in California ventured to marry; but went mad and finished his days in an asylum.

*Ousley.* A prosperous merchant. Smoked fragrant cigars—regalias—5¢ apiece. Killed old Smar; then acquitted. His party brought him huzzaing in from Palmyra at midnight after the trial. But there was a cloud upon him—a social chill—and he presently moved away.

*Mrs. Sexton* (she pronounced it *Saxton* to make it finer, the nice, kind-hearted, smirky, smily dear Christian creature—Methodist.)

*Margaret.* Pretty child of 14. Boarders in 1844 house. Simon and Hartley were rivals. Mrs. S. talked much of N-Yorliuns; and hints and sighs of better days there, departed never to return.

*Cloak of the time*, flung back, lined with bright plaid. Worn with a swagger. Most rational garment that ever was.

*Slouch hat*, worn gallusly.

*Hoop-skirts coming in.*

*Literature.* Byron, Scott, Cooper, Marryatt, Boz. Pirates and Knights preferred to other society. Songs tended to regrets for bygone days and vanished joys: Oft in the Stilly Night; Last Rose of

Summer; The Last Link; Bonny Doon; Old Dog Tray; for the lady I love will soon be a bride; Gaily the Troubadour; Bright Alforata.

*Negro Melodies* the same trend: Old Kentucky Home; (de day goes by like a shadow on de wall, wid sorrow where all was delight;) Massa's in de Cold Ground; Swanee River.

Any young person would have been proud of a "strain" of Indian blood. Bright Alforata of the blue Juniata got her strain from "a far distant fount."

All that sentimentality and romance among young folk seem puerile, now, but when one examines it and compares it with the ideals of today, it was the preferable thing. It was soft, sappy, melancholy; but money had no place in it. To get rich was no one's ambition—it was not in any young person's thoughts. The heroes of these young people—even the pirates—were moved by lofty impulses: they waded in blood, in the distant fields of war and adventure and upon the pirate deck, to rescue the helpless, not to make money; they spent their blood and made their self-sacrifices for "honor's" sake, not to capture a giant fortune; they married for love, not for money and position. It was an intensely sentimental age, but it took no sordid form. The Californian rush for wealth in '49 introduced the change and begot the lust for money which is the rule of life today, and the hardness and cynicism which is the spirit of today.

The three "rich" men were not worshiped, and

not envied. They were not arrogant, nor assertive, nor tyrannical, nor exigent. It was California that changed the spirit of the people and lowered their ideals to the plane of today.

*Unbeliever.* There was but one—Blennerhasset, the young Kentucky lawyer, a fascinating cuss—and they shuddered to hear him talk. They expected a judgment to fall upon him at any moment. They believed the devil would come for him in person some stormy night.

He was very profane, and blasphemous. He was vain of being prayed for in the revivals; vain of being singled out for this honor always by every new revivalist; vain of the competition between these people for his capture; vain that it was the ambition of each to hang this notable scalp at his belt. The young ladies were ambitious to convert him.

*Chastity.* There was the utmost liberty among young people—but no young girl was ever insulted or seduced, or even scandalously gossiped about. Such things were not even dreamed of in that society, much less spoken of and referred to.

Two or three times, in the lapse of years, married women were whispered about, but never an unmarried one.

*Daily Packet Service* to Keokuk. The merchants—envied by all the untraveled town—made trips to the great city (of 30,000 souls). St. L papers had pictures of Planters House, and sometimes an engraved letter-head had a picture of the city front,

with the boats sardined at the wharf and the modest
spire of the little Cath Cathedral showing prominently; and at last when a minor citizen realized the
dream of his life and traveled to St. Louis, he was
thrilled to the marrow when he recognized the rank
of boats and the spire and the Planters, and was
amazed at the accuracy of the pictures and at the
fact that the things were realities and not inventions
of the imagination. He talked St. Louis, and nothing
but S. L. and its wonders for months and months
afterward. "Call *that* a fire-uniform! you ought to
see a turn-out in St L.—blocks and blocks and
blocks of red shirts and helmets, and more engines
and hosecarts and hook and ladder Co's—my!"

*4th July.* Banners. Declaration and Spreadeagle
speech in the public square. Procession—Sunday
schools, Masons, Odd Fellows, Temperance Society, Cadets of Temperance, the Co of St P Greys, the
Fantastics (oh, so funny!) and of course the Fire Co
and Sam R. Maybe in the woods. Collation in the
cool shade of a tent. Gingerbread in slabs; lemon-
ade; ice cream. Opened with prayer—closed with a
blessing.

*The House Beautiful.* Mr. Dickens declined to
agree that the Mississippi steamboats were "magnificent," or that they should be referred to as "floating palaces"—terms which had always been applied
to them; terms which did not over-express the admiration with which the people viewed them.

Mr. Dickens's position was unassailable, possibly;

*The famous Planters House on Fourth Street, St. Louis.*
Courtesy of the Missouri Historical Society

the people's position was certainly unassailable. If
Mr. Dickens was comparing these boats with the
crown jewels; or with the Taj, or with the Matterhorn; or with some other priceless or wonderful
thing which he had seen, they were not magnificent—he was right. The people compared them
with what *they* had seen; and, thus measured, thus
judged, the boats were magnificent—the term was
the correct one, it was not at all too strong. The
people were as right as was Mr. Dickens. The
steamboats were finer than anything on shore. Compared with superior dwelling-houses and first-class
hotels in the valley, they were indubitably magnificent, they were "palaces." To a few people living in
New Orleans and St. Louis they were not magnificent, perhaps; not palaces; but to the great majority
of those populations, and to the entire populations
spread over both banks between Baton Rouge and
St. Louis, they were palaces; they were the citizen's
dream of what magnificence was, and satisfied it.

Every town and village along that vast stretch of
double river-frontage had a best dwelling, finest
dwelling, mansion—the home of its wealthiest and
most conspicuous citizen. It is easy to describe it:
large grassy yard with paling fence painted white and
in fair repair; brick walk from gate to door; big,
square, two-story "frame" house, painted white and
porticoed like a Grecian temple—with this difference, that the imposing fluted columns and Corin-
thian capitals were a pathetic sham, being made of

white pine, and painted; iron knocker; brass door-knob—discolored, for lack of polishing. Within, an uncarpeted hall, of planed boards; opening out of it, a parlor, fifteen feet by fifteen—in some instances five or ten feet larger; ingrain carpet; mahogany center-table; lamp on it, with green-paper shade—standing on a gridiron, so to speak, made of high-colored yarns, by the young ladies of the house, and called a lamp-mat; several books, piled and disposed, with cast-iron exactness, according to an inherited and unchangeable plan; among them, Tupper, much penciled; also, *Friendship's Offering*, and *Affection's Wreath*, with their sappy inanities illustrated in die-away mezzotints; also, Ossian; *Alonzo and Melissa*, maybe *Ivanhoe*; also "Album," full of original "poetry" of the Thou-hast-wounded-the-spirit-that-loved-thee breed; two or three goody-goody works—*Shepherd of Salisbury Plain*, etc.; current number of the chaste and innocuous *Godey's Lady's Book*, with painted fashion-plate of wax-figure women with mouths all alike—lips and eyelids the same size—each five-foot woman with a two-inch wedge sticking from under her dress and letting on to be half of her foot. Polished air-tight stove (new and deadly invention), with pipe passing through a board which closes up the discarded good old fireplace. On each end of the wooden mantel, over the fireplace, a large basket of peaches and other fruits, natural size, all done in plaster, rudely, or in wax, and painted to resemble the originals—

*The grandeur of the Mississippi River steamboats.*
*Top: Main cabin of* The Grand Republic.
*Bottom: Dining salon of* The City of Monroe.
Courtesy of the Missouri Historical Society

which they don't. Over middle of mantel, engraving—"Washington Crossing the Delaware"; on the wall by the door, copy of it done in thunder-and-lightning crewels by one of the young ladies—work of art which would have made Washington hesitate about crossing, if he could have foreseen what advantage was going to be taken of it. Piano—kettle in disguise—with music, bound and unbound, piled on it, and on a stand near by: "Battle of Prague"; "Bird Waltz"; "Arkansas Traveler"; "Rosin the Bow"; "Marseillaise Hymn"; "On a Lone Barren Isle" (St. Helena); "The Last Link Is Broken"; "She Wore a Wreath of Roses the Night When Last We Met"; "Go, Forget Me, Why Should Sorrow o'er That Brow a Shadow Fling"; "Hours That Were to Memory Dearer"; "Long, Long Ago"; "Days of Absence"; "A Life on the Ocean Wave, a Home on the Rolling Deep"; "Bird at Sea"; and spread open on the rack where the plaintive singer has left it, "*Ro*-holl on, silver *moo*-hoon, guide the *trav*-el-err on his *way*," etc. Tilted pensively against the piano, a guitar—guitar capable of playing the Spanish fandango by itself, if you give it a start. Frantic work of art on the wall—pious motto, done on the premises, sometimes in colored yarns, sometimes in faded grasses: progenitor of the "God Bless Our Home" of modern commerce. Framed in black moldings on the wall, other works of art, conceived and committed on the premises, by the young ladies; being grim black-and-white crayons; landscapes, mostly:

lake, solitary sailboat, petrified clouds, pregeological trees on shore, anthracite precipice; name of the criminal conspicuous in the corner. Lithograph, "Napoleon Crossing the Alps." Lithograph, "The Grave at St. Helena." Steel plates, Trumbull's "Battle of Bunker Hill," and the "Sally from Gibraltar." Copper plates, "Moses Smiting the Rock," and "Return of the Prodigal Son." In big gilt frame, slander of the family in oil: papa holding a book ("Constitution of the United States"); a guitar leaning against mamma, blue ribbons fluttering from its neck; the young ladies, as children, in slippers and scalloped pantalettes, one embracing toy horse, the other beguiling kitten with ball of yarn, and both simpering up at mamma, who simpers back. These persons all fresh, raw, and red—apparently skinned. Opposite, in gilt frame, grandpa and grandma, at thirty and twenty-two, stiff, old-fashioned, high-collared, puff-sleeved, glaring pallidly out from a background of solid Egyptian night. Under a glass French clock dome, large bouquet of stiff flowers done in corpsy-white wax. Pyramidal what-not in the corner, the shelves occupied chiefly with bric-à-brac of the period, disposed with an eye to best effect: shell, with the Lord's Prayer carved on it; and another shell—of the long-oval sort, narrow, straight orifice, three inches long, running from end to end—portrait of Washington carved on it; not well done; the shell had Washington's mouth, originally—artist should have built to that. These two

are memorials of the long-ago bridal trip to New
Orleans and the French Market. Other bric-à-brac:
Californian "specimens"—quartz, with gold wart
adhering; old Guinea-gold locket, with circlet of ancestral hair in it; Indian arrow-heads, of flint; pair of
bead moccasins, from uncle who crossed the Plains;
three "alum" baskets of various colors—being skele-
ton-frame of wire, clothed on with cubes of crystal-
lized alum in the rock-candy style—works of art
which were achieved by the young ladies; their dou-
bles and duplicates to be found upon all what-nots
in the land; convention of desiccated bugs and butterflies pinned to a card; painted toy dog, seated
upon bellows attachment—drops its under-jaw and
squeaks when pressed upon; sugar-candy rabbit—
limbs and features merged together, not strongly
defined; pewter presidential-campaign medal; miniature cardboard wood-sawyer, to be attached to the
stovepipe and operated by the heat; small Napoleon, done in wax; spread-open daguerreotypes of
dim children, parents, cousins, aunts, and friends,
in all attitudes but customary ones; no templed por-
tico at back, and manufactured landscape stretching
away in the distance—that came in later, with the
photograph; all these vague figures lavishly chained
and ringed—metal indicated and secured from
doubt by stripes and splashes of vivid gold bronze;
all of them too much combed, too much fixed up;
and all of them uncomfortable in inflexible Sunday
clothes of a kind which the spectator cannot realize

could ever have been in fashion; husband and wife
generally grouped together—husband sitting, wife
standing, with hand on his shoulder—and both preserving, all these fading years, some traceable effect
of the daguerreotypist's brisk "Now smile, if you
please!" Bracketed over what-not—place of special
sacredness—an outrage in watercolor, done by the
young niece that came on a visit long ago, and died.
Pity, too; for she might have repented of this in
time. Horsehair chairs, horsehair sofa which keeps
sliding from under you. Window-shades, of oil stuff,
with milkmaids and ruined castles stenciled onto
them in fierce-looking colors. Lambrequins dependent from gaudy boxings of beaten tin, gilded.
Bedrooms with rag carpets and bedsteads of the
"corded" sort, with a sag in the middle, the cords
needing tightening; snuffy feather-bed—not aired
often enough; cane-seat chairs, splint-bottomed rock-
er; looking-glass on wall, school-slate size, veneer-
ed frame; inherited bureau; wash-bowl and pitcher,
possibly—but not certainly; brass candlestick, tallow candle, snuffers. Nothing else in the room. Not
a bathroom in the house; and no visitor likely to
come along who has ever seen one.

That was the residence of the principal citizen,
all the way from the suburbs of New Orleans to the
edge of St. Louis. When he stepped aboard a big
fine steamboat, he entered a new and marvelous
world: chimney-tops cut to counterfeit a spraying
crown of plumes—and maybe painted red; pilot-

house, hurricane-deck, boiler-deck guards, all gar-
nished with white wooden filigree-work of fanciful
patterns; gilt acorns topping the derricks; gilt deer-
horns over the big bell; gaudy symbolical picture
on the paddle-box, possibly; big roomy boiler-deck
painted blue, and furnished with Windsor arm-
chairs; inside, a far-receding snow-white "cabin";
porcelain knob and oil-picture on every stateroom
door; curving patterns of filigree-work touched up
with gilding, stretching overhead all down the con-
verging vista; big chandeliers every little way, each
an April shower of glittering glass-drops; lovely
rainbow-light falling everywhere from the colored
glazing of the skylights; the whole a long-drawn,
resplendent tunnel, a bewildering and soul-satisfy-
ing spectacle! in the ladies' cabin a pink and white
Wilton carpet, as soft as mush, and glorified with a
ravishing pattern of gigantic flowers. Then the Bridal Chamber—the animal that invented that idea was
still alive and unhanged, at that day—Bridal Chamber whose pretentious flummery was necessarily
overawing to the now tottering intellect of that ho-
sannahing citizen. Every stateroom had its couple of
cozy clean bunks, and perhaps a looking-glass and a
snug closet; and sometimes there was even a wash-
bowl and pitcher, and part of a towel which could
only be told from mosquito-netting by an expert—
though generally these things were absent, and the
shirt-sleeved passengers cleansed themselves at a
long row of stationary bowls in the barber shop,

where were also public towels, public combs, and public soap.

Take the steamboat which I have just described, and you have her in her highest and finest, and most pleasing, and comfortable, and satisfactory estate.

*The Minstrel Show.* I remember the first Negro musical show I ever saw. It must have been in the early forties. It was a new institution. In our village of Hannibal we had not heard of it before, and it burst upon us as a glad and stunning surprise.

The show remained a week and gave a performance every night. Church members did not attend these performances, but all the worldlings flocked to them and were enchanted. Church members did not attend shows out there in those days. The minstrels appeared with coal-black hands and faces and their clothing was a loud and extravagant burlesque of the clothing worn by the plantation slave of the time; not that the rags of the poor slave were burlesqued, for that would not have been possible; burlesque could have added nothing in the way of extravagance to the sorrowful accumulation of rags and patches which constituted his costume; it was the form and color of his dress that was burlesqued. Standing collars were in fashion in that day, and the minstrel appeared in a collar which engulfed and hid the half of his head and projected so far forward that he could hardly see sideways over its points. His coat was sometimes made of curtain calico with a swallowtail that hung nearly to his heels and had buttons as big as a blacking box. His shoes were rusty and clumsy and cumbersome, and five or six sizes too large for him. There were many variations upon this costume and they were all extravagant, and were by many believed to be funny.

The minstrel used a very broad Negro dialect; he used it competently and with easy facility, and it was so funny—delightfully and satisfyingly funny. However, there was one member of the minstrel troupe of those early days who was not extravagantly dressed and did not use the Negro dialect. He was clothed in the faultless evening costume of the white society gentleman and used a stilted, courtly, artificial, and painfully grammatical form of speech, which the innocent villagers took for the real thing as exhibited in high and citified society, and they vastly admired it and envied the man who could frame it on the spot without reflection and deliver it in this easy and fluent and artistic fashion. "Bones" sat at one end of the row of minstrels, "Banjo" sat at the other end, and the dainty gentleman just described sat in the middle. This middleman was the spokesman of the show. The neatness and elegance of his dress, the studied courtliness of his manners and speech, and the shapeliness of his undoctored features made him a contrast to the rest of the troupe and particularly to "Bones" and "Banjo." "Bones" and "Banjo" were the prime jokers and whatever funniness was to be gotten out of paint and exaggerated clothing they utilized to the limit.

Their lips were thickened and lengthened using bright red paint to such a degree that their mouths resembled slices cut in a ripe watermelon.

The original ground plan of the minstrel show was maintained without change for a good many years. There was no curtain to the stage in the beginning; while the audience waited they had nothing to look at except the row of empty chairs back of the footlights; presently the minstrels filed in and were received with a wholehearted welcome; they took their seats, each with his musical instrument in his hand; then the aristocrat in the middle began with a remark like this:

"I hope, gentlemen, I have the pleasure of seeing you in your accustomed excellent health, and that everything has proceeded prosperously with you since last we had the good fortune to meet."

"Bones" would reply for himself and go on and tell about something in the nature of peculiarly good fortune that had lately fallen to his share; but in the midst of it he would be interrupted by "Banjo," who would throw doubt upon his statement of the matter; then a delightful jangle of assertion and contradiction would break out between the two; the quarrel would gather emphasis, the voices would grow louder and louder and more and more energetic and vindictive, and the two would rise and approach each other, shaking fists and instruments and threatening bloodshed, the courtly middleman meantime imploring them to preserve the peace

and observe the proprieties—but all in vain, of
course. Sometimes the quarrel would last five minutes, the two contestants shouting deadly threats in
each other's faces with their noses not six inches
apart, the house shrieking with laughter all the
while at this happy and accurate imitation of the
usual and familiar Negro quarrel, then finally both
of the malignants would gradually back away from
each other, each making impressive threats as to
what was going to happen the "next time" each
should have the misfortune to cross the other's
path; then they would sink into their chairs and
growl back and forth at each other across the front
of the line until the house had had time to recover
from its convulsions and hysterics and quiet down
to a semblance of order.

The aristocrat in the middle of the row would
now make a remark which was surreptitiously intended to remind one of the end men of an experience of his of a humorous nature and fetch it out of
him—which it always did. It was usually an experience of a stale and moldy sort and as old as America. One of these things, which always delighted the
audience of those past days until the minstrels wore
it threadbare, was "Bones's" account of the perils
which he had once endured during a storm at sea.
The storm lasted so long that in the course of time
all the provisions were consumed. Then the middleman would inquire anxiously how the people
managed to survive.

"Bones" would reply, "We lived on eggs."

"You lived on eggs! Where did you get eggs?"

"Every day, when the storm was so very bad, the Captain laid *to*."

During the first five years that joke convulsed the house, but after that the population of the United States had heard it so many times that they respected it no longer and always received it in a deep and reproachful and indignant silence, along with others of its caliber which had achieved disfavor by long service.

The minstrel troupes had good voices and both their solos and their choruses were a delight to me as long as the Negro show continued in existence. In the beginning the songs were rudely comic, but a little later sentimental songs were introduced.

The minstrel show was born in the early forties and it had a prosperous career for about thirty-five years; then it degenerated into a variety show and was nearly all variety show with a Negro act or two thrown in incidentally. The real Negro show has been stone dead for thirty years. To my mind it was a thoroughly delightful thing, and a most competent laughter-compeller and I am sorry it is gone.

# V

# Orion and Sam Clemens, Printers

M^Y BROTHER, Orion Clemens, was born in Jamestown, Tennessee, in 1825. He was the family's
first-born and antedated me ten years.

Orion's boyhood was spent in that wee little log
hamlet of Jamestown up there among the knobs—so
called—of East Tennessee, among a very sparse
population of primitives who were as ignorant of
the outside world and as unconscious of it as the
other wild animals were that inhabited the forest
around. The family migrated to Florida, Missouri,
then moved to Hannibal, Missouri, when Orion was
ten years old. When he was fifteen or sixteen he was
sent to St. Louis and there he learned the printer's
trade. One of his characteristics was eagerness. He
woke with an eagerness about some matter or other
every morning; it consumed him all day; it perished
in the night and he was on fire with a fresh new
interest the next morning before he could get his
clothes on. He exploited in this way three hundred
and sixty-five red-hot new eagernesses every year of
his life—until he died sitting at a table with a pen in
his hand, in the early morning, jotting down the
conflagration for that day and preparing to enjoy
the fire of it until night should extinguish it. He

was then seventy-two years old. But I am forgetting another characteristic, a very pronounced one. That was his deep glooms, his despondencies, his despairs; these had their place in each and every day along with the eagernesses. Thus his day was divided—no, not divided, mottled—from sunrise to midnight with alternating brilliant sunshine and black cloud. Every day he was the most joyous and hopeful man that ever was, I think, and also every day he was the most miserable man that ever was.

While he was in his apprenticeship in St. Louis he got well acquainted with Edward Bates, a very fine man, an honorable and upright man, and a distinguished lawyer. He patiently allowed Orion to bring to him each new project; he discussed it with him and extinguished it by argument and irresistible logic—at first. But after a few weeks he found that this labor was not necessary; that he could leave the new project alone and it would extinguish itself the same night. Orion thought he would like to become a lawyer. Mr. Bates encouraged him, and he studied law nearly a week, then of course laid it aside to try something new. He wanted to become an orator. Mr. Bates gave him lessons. Mr. Bates walked the floor reading from an English book aloud and rapidly turning the English into French, and he recommended this exercise to Orion. But as Orion knew no French, he took up that study and wrought at it with enthusiasm two or three days; then gave it up. During his apprenticeship in St.

Louis he joined a number of churches, one after another, and taught in the Sunday schools—changing his Sunday school every time he changed his religion. He was correspondingly erratic in his politics — Whig today, Democrat next week, and anything fresh that he could find in the political market the week after. I may remark here that throughout his long life he was always trading religions and enjoying the change of scenery. I will also remark that his sincerity was never doubted; his truthfulness was never doubted; and in matters of business and money his honesty was never questioned. Notwithstanding his forever-recurring changes and caprices, his principles were always kept high, and absolutely unshakable.

He was the strangest compound that ever got mixed in a human mold. Such a person as that is given to acting upon impulse and without reflection; that was Orion's way. Everything he did he did with conviction and enthusiasm and with a vainglorious pride in the thing he was doing—and no matter what that thing was, whether good, bad or indifferent, he repented of it every time in sackcloth and ashes before twenty-four hours had sped. Except in the matter of grounded principle, he was as unstable as water. You could dash his spirits with a single word; you could raise them into the sky again with another one. You could break his heart with a word of disapproval; you could make him as happy as an angel with a word of approval. And there was no occasion to put any sense or any vestige of mentality of any kind into these miracles; anything you might say would answer.

He had another conspicuous characteristic, and it was the father of those which I have just spoken of. This was an intense lust for approval. He was so eager to be approved, so girlishly anxious to be approved by anybody and everybody, without discrimination, that he was commonly ready to forsake his notions, opinions, and convictions at a moment's notice in order to get the approval of any person who disagreed with them. I wish to be understood as reserving his fundamental principles all the time. He never forsook those to please anybody. Born and reared among slaves and slaveholders, he was yet an abolitionist from his boyhood to his death. He was always truthful; he was always sincere; he was always honest and honorable. But in light matters—matters of small consequence, like religion and politics and such things—he never acquired a conviction that could survive a disapproving remark from a cat.

He was always dreaming; he was a dreamer from birth, and this characteristic got him into trouble now and then. Once when he was twenty-three or twenty-four years old, and was become a journeyman, he conceived the romantic idea of coming to Hannibal without giving us notice, in order that he might furnish to the family a pleasant surprise. If he had given notice, he would have been informed that we had changed our residence, and that that gruff, old bass-voiced sailorman, Doctor Meredith, our family physician, was living in the house which we had formerly occupied, and that Orion's former room in that house was now occupied by Doctor Meredith's two ripe old-maid sisters. Orion arrived at Hannibal per steamboat in the middle of the night, and started with his customary eagerness on his excursion, his mind all on fire with his romantic project and building and enjoying his surprise in advance. He was always enjoying things in advance; it was the make of him. He never could wait for the event, but he must build it out of dream-stuff and enjoy it beforehand—consequently sometimes when the event happened he saw that it was not as good as the one he had invented in his imagination, and so he had lost profit by not keeping the imaginary one and letting the reality go.

When he arrived at the house he went around to the back door and slipped off his boots and crept upstairs and arrived at the room of those old maids without having wakened any sleepers. He undressed in the dark and got into bed and snuggled up against somebody. He was a little surprised, but not much, for he thought it was our brother Ben. It was winter, and the bed was comfortable, and the supposed Ben added to the comfort—and so he was dropping off to sleep very well satisfied with his progress so far and full of happy dreams of what was going to happen in the morning. But something else was going to happen sooner than that, and it happened now. The old maid that was being crowded squirmed and struggled, and presently came to a half waking condition and protested against the crowding. That voice paralyzed Orion. He couldn't move a limb; he couldn't get his breath; and the crowded one began to paw around, found Orion's new whiskers, and screamed, "Why, it's a man!" This removed the paralysis, and Orion was out of the bed and clawing around in the dark for his clothes in a fraction of a second. Both maids began to scream, so Orion did not wait to get his whole outfit. He started with such parts of it as he could grab. He flew to the head of the stairs and started down, and he was paralyzed again at that point, because he saw the faint yellow flame of a candle soaring up the stairs from below and he judged that Doctor Meredith was behind it, and he was. He had no clothes on to speak of, but no matter, he was well enough fixed for an occasion like this, because he had a butcher knife in his hand. Orion shouted to him, and this saved his life, for the doctor recognized his voice. Then, in those deep sea-going bass tones of his that I used to admire so much when I was a little boy, he explained to Orion the change that had been made, told him where to find the Clemens family, and closed with some quite unnecessary advice about posting himself before he undertook another adventure like that—advice which Orion probably never needed again.

When my father died, in 1847, the disaster happened—as is the customary way with such things—just at the very moment when our fortunes had changed and we were about to be comfortable once more, after several years of grinding poverty and privation which had been inflicted upon us by the dishonest act of one Ira Stout, to whom my father had lent several thousand dollars—a fortune in those days and in that region. My father had just been elected clerk of the Surrogate Court.[1] This modest prosperity was not only quite sufficient for us and for our ambitions, but he was so esteemed—held in such high regard and honor throughout the county—that his occupancy of that dignified office would, in the opinion of everybody, be his possession as long as he might live. He went to Palmyra, the county-seat, to be sworn in, about the end of February. In returning home, horseback, twelve miles, a storm of sleet and rain assailed him and he arrived at the house in a half-frozen condition. Pleurisy followed and he died on the 24th of March.

Thus our splendid new fortune was snatched from us and we were in the depths of poverty again. It is the way such things are accustomed to happen.

The Clemens family was penniless again.

Orion did not come to Hannibal until two or three years after my father's death. He remained in

[1] Here as elsewhere, Mark Twain improved upon actuality: John Marshall Clemens had not been elected to the office of clerk of the court.

St. Louis. He was a journeyman printer and earning wages. Out of his wage he supported my mother and my brother Henry, who was two years younger than I. My sister Pamela helped in this support by taking piano pupils. Thus we got along, but it was pretty hard sledding. I was not one of the burdens, because I was taken from school at once[2] upon my father's death and placed in the office of the Hannibal *Courier*, as printer's apprentice, and Mr. Ament, the editor and proprietor of the paper, allowed me the usual emolument of the office of apprentice—that is to say, board and clothes, but no money. The clothes consisted of two suits a year, but one of the suits always failed to materialize and the other suit was not purchased so long as Mr. Ament's old clothes held out. I was only about half as big as Ament, consequently his shirts gave me the uncomfortable sense of living in a circus tent, and I had to turn up his pants to my ears to make them short enough.

There were two other apprentices. One was Wales McCormick, seventeen or eighteen years old, and a giant. When he was in Ament's clothes they fitted him as the candle mold fits the candle—thus he was generally in a suffocated condition, particularly in the summertime. He was a reckless, hilarious, admirable creature; he had no principles and was delightful company. At first, the apprentices

[2]In fact, the boy attended Dawson's school—perhaps part-time—for some months after his father's death.

*Sam Clemens as a printer's apprentice in 1850.*
Courtesy of the Mark Twain Papers, The Bancroft Library

had to feed in the kitchen with the old slave cook
and her very handsome and bright and well-behaved
young mulatto daughter. For his own amusement—
for he was not generally laboring for other people's
amusement—Wales was constantly and persistently,
loudly and elaborately making love to that mulatto girl and distressing the life out of her and worrying
the old mother to death. She would say, "Now
Marse Wales, Marse Wales, can't you behave yourself?" With encouragement like that, Wales would
naturally renew his attentions and emphasize them.
It was killingly funny to Ralph and me. And, to
speak truly, the old mother's distress about it was
merely a pretense. She quite well understood that
by the customs of slaveholding communities it was
Wales's right to make love to that girl if he wanted
to. But the girl's distress was very real. She had a
refined nature, and she took all Wales's extravagant
lovemaking in earnest.

We got but little variety in the way of food at
that kitchen table, and there wasn't enough of it,
anyway. So we apprentices used to keep alive by
arts of our own—that is to say, we crept into the
cellar nearly every night, by a private entrance
which we had discovered, and we robbed the cellar
of potatoes and onions and such things, and carried
them downtown to the printing office, where we
slept on pallets on the floor, and cooked them at
the stove and had very good times.

As I have indicated, Mr. Ament's economies were

of a pretty close and rigid kind. By and by, when
we apprentices were promoted from the basement
to the ground floor and allowed to sit at the family
table, along with the one journeyman, Pet MacMur-
ray, the economies carried on. Mrs. Ament was
a bride. She had attained to that distinction very
recently, after waiting a good part of a lifetime for
it, and she was the right woman in the right place,
according to the Amentian idea, for she did not
trust the sugar bowl to us, but sweetened our coffee
herself. That is, she went through the motions. She
didn't really sweeten it. She seemed to put one
heaping teaspoonful of brown sugar into each cup,
but, according to Wales, that was a deceit. He said
she dipped the spoon in the coffee first to make the
sugar stick, and then scooped the sugar out of the
bowl with the spoon upside down, so that the effect
to the eye was a heaped-up spoon, whereas the sugar on it was nothing but a layer. This all seems
perfectly true to me, and yet that thing would be so
difficult to perform that I suppose it really didn't
happen, but was one of Wales's lies.

I have said that Wales was reckless, and he was. It
was the ever-bubbling and indestructible good spirits
flowing from the joy of youth. I think there wasn't
anything that that vast boy wouldn't do to procure
five minutes' entertainment for himself. One never
knew where he would break out next. Among his
shining characteristics was the most limitless and
adorable irreverence. There didn't seem to be any-

thing serious in life for him; there didn't seem to be anything that he revered.

Once the celebrated founder of the, at that time, new and widespread sect called Campbellites arrived in our village from Kentucky, and it made a prodigious excitement. The farmers and their families drove or tramped into the village from miles around to get a sight of the illustrious Alexander Campbell and to have a chance to hear him preach. When he preached in a church many had to be disappointed, for there was no church that would begin to hold all the applicants; so in order to accommodate all, he preached in the open air in the public square, and that was the first time in my life that I had realized what a mighty population this planet contains when you get them all together.

He preached a sermon on one of these occasions which he had written especially for that occasion. All the Campbellites wanted it printed, so that they could save it and read it over and over again, and get it by heart. So they drummed up sixteen dollars, which was a large sum then, and for this great sum Mr. Ament contracted to print five hundred copies of that sermon and put them in yellow paper covers. It was a sixteen-page duodecimo pamphlet, and it was a great event in our office. As we regarded it, it was a book, and it promoted us to the dignity of book printers. Moreover, no such mass of actual money as sixteen dollars, in one bunch, had ever entered that office on any previous occasion. People didn't pay for their paper and for their advertising in money; they paid in dry goods, sugar, coffee, hickory or oak wood, turnips, pumpkins, onions, watermelons—and it was very seldom indeed that a man paid in money, and when that happened we thought there was something the matter with him.

We set up the great book in pages—eight pages to a form—and by help of a printer's manual we managed to get the pages in their apparently crazy but really sane places on the imposing-stone. We printed that form on a Thursday. Then we set up the remaining eight pages, locked them into a form, and struck a proof. Wales read the proof, and presently was aghast, for he had struck a snag. And it was a bad time to strike a snag, because it was Saturday; it was approaching noon; Saturday afternoon was our holiday, and we wanted to get away and go fishing. At such a time as this Wales struck that snag and showed us what had happened. He had left out a couple of words in a thin-spaced page of solid matter and there wasn't another break-line for two or three pages ahead. What in the world was to be done? Overrun all those pages in order to get in the two missing words? Apparently there was no other way. It would take an hour to do it. Then a revise must be sent to the great minister; we must wait for him to read the revise; if he encountered any errors we must correct them. It looked as if we might lose half the afternoon before we could get away. Then Wales had one of his brilliant ideas. In the line in

which the "out" had been made occurred the name
Jesus Christ. Wales reduced it in the French way to
J. C. It made room for the missing words, but it took
99 per cent of the solemnity out of a particularly
solemn sentence. We sent off the revise and waited.
We were not intending to wait long. In the circumstances we meant to get out and go fishing before
that revise should get back, but we were not speedy
enough. Presently that great Alexander Campbell
appeared at the far end of that sixty-foot room, and
his countenance cast a gloom over the whole place.
He strode down to our end and what he said was
brief, but it was very stern, and it was to the point.
He read Wales a lecture. He said, "So long as you
live, don't you ever diminish the Saviour's name
again. Put it *all* in." He repeated this admonition a
couple of times to emphasize it, then he went away.

In that day the common swearers of the region
had a way of their own of *emphasizing* the Saviour's
name when they were using it profanely, and this
fact intruded itself into Wales's incorrigible mind.
It offered to him an opportunity for a momentary
entertainment which seemed to him to be more
precious and more valuable than even fishing and
swimming could afford. So he imposed upon himself the long and weary and dreary task of overrun-
ning all those three pages in order to improve upon
his former work and incidentally and thoughtfully
improve upon the great preacher's admonition. He
enlarged the offending J. C. into Jesus H. Christ.

Wales knew that would make prodigious trouble, and it did. But it was not in him to resist. I don't remember what his punishment was, but he was not the person to care for that. He had already collected his dividend.

It was during my first year's apprenticeship in the *Courier* office that I did a thing which I have been trying to regret for fifty-five years. It was a summer afternoon and just the kind of weather that a boy prizes for river excursions and other frolics, but I was a prisoner. The others were all gone holidaying. I was alone and sad. I had committed a crime of some sort and this was the punishment. I must lose my holiday, and spend the afternoon in solitude besides. I had the printing-office all to myself, there in the third story. I had one comfort, and it was a generous one while it lasted. It was the half of a long and broad watermelon, fresh and red and ripe. I gouged it out with a knife, and I found accommodation for the whole of it in my person—though it did crowd me until the juice ran out of my ears. There remained then the shell, the hollow shell. It was big enough to do duty as a cradle. I didn't want to waste it, and I couldn't think of anything to do with it which could afford entertainment. I was sitting at the open window which looked out upon the sidewalk of the main street three stories below, when it occurred to me to drop it on somebody's head. I doubted the judiciousness of this, and I had some compunctions about it, too, because so much

of the resulting entertainment would fall to my
share and so little to the other person. But I thought
I would chance it. I watched out of the window for
the right person to come along—the safe person—
but he didn't come. Every time there was a candidate he or she turned out to be an unsafe one, and I
had to restrain myself. But at last I saw the right one
coming. It was my brother Henry. He was the best
boy in the whole region. He never did harm to anybody, he never offended anybody. He was exasper-
atingly good. He had an overflowing abundance of
goodness—but not enough to save him this time. I
watched his approach with eager interest. He came
strolling along, dreaming his pleasant summer
dream and not doubting but that Providence had
him in His care. If he had known where I was he
would have had less confidence in that superstition.
As he approached his form became more and more
foreshortened. When he was almost under me he
was so foreshortened that nothing of him was visible
from my high place except the end of his nose and
his alternately approaching feet. Then I poised the
watermelon, calculated my distance, and let it go,
hollow side down. The accuracy of that gunnery
was beyond admiration. He had about six steps to
make when I let that canoe go, and it was lovely to
see those two bodies gradually closing in on each
other. If he had had seven steps to make, or five
steps to make, my gunnery would have been a failure. But he had exactly the right number to make,

and that shell smashed down right on the top of his head and drove him into the earth up to the chin, the chunks of that broken melon flying in every direction like a spray. I wanted to go down there and condole with him, but it would not have been safe. He would have suspected me at once. I expected him to suspect me, anyway, but as he said nothing about this adventure for two or three days—I was watching him in the meantime in order to keep out of danger—I was deceived into believing that this time he didn't suspect me. It was a mistake. He was only waiting for a sure opportunity. Then he landed a cobblestone on the side of my head which raised a bump there so large that I had to wear two hats for a time. I carried this crime to my mother, for I was always anxious to get Henry into trouble with her and could never succeed. I thought that I had a sure case this time when she should come to see that murderous bump. I showed it to her, but she said it was no matter. She didn't need to inquire into the circumstances. She knew I had deserved it, and the best way would be for me to accept it as a valuable lesson, and thereby get profit out of it.

About 1849 or 1850 Orion severed his connection with the printing-house in St. Louis and came up to Hannibal and bought a weekly paper called the Hannibal *Journal*, together with its plant and its good-will, for the sum of five hundred dollars cash. He borrowed the cash, at ten per cent interest, from an old farmer named Johnson who lived five miles out of town. Then he reduced the subscription price of the paper from two dollars to one dollar. He reduced the rates for advertising in about the same proportion, and thus he created one absolute and unassailable certainty—to wit: that the business would never pay him a single cent of profit. He took me out of the *Courier* office and engaged my services in his own at three dollars and a half a week, which was an extravagant wage, but Orion was always generous, always liberal with everybody except himself. It cost him nothing in my case, for he never was able to pay me a single penny as long as I was with him. By the end of the first year he found he must make some economies. The office rent was cheap, but it was not cheap enough. He could not afford to pay rent of any kind, so he moved the whole plant into the house we lived in, and it cramped the dwelling-place cruelly. He kept that paper alive during four years, but I have at this time no idea how he accomplished it. Toward the end of each year he had to turn out and scrape and scratch for the fifty dollars of interest due Mr. Johnson, and that fifty dollars was about the only cash he ever received or paid out, I suppose, while he was proprietor of that newspaper, except for ink and printing-paper. The paper was a dead failure. It had to be that from the start. Finally he handed it over to Mr. Johnson, and went up to Muscatine, Iowa, and acquired a small interest in a weekly newspaper there. It was not a sort of property to marry on—but no matter. He came across a winning and pretty girl who lived in Quincy, Illinois, a few miles below Keokuk, and they became engaged. He was always falling in love with girls, but by some accident or other he had never gone so far as engagement before. And now he achieved nothing but misfortune by it, because he straightway fell in love with a Keokuk girl—at least he imagined that he was in love with her, whereas I think she did the imagining for him. The first thing he knew he was engaged to her; and he was in a great quandary. He didn't know whether to marry the Keokuk one or the Quincy one, or whether to try to marry both of them and suit everyone concerned. But the Keokuk girl soon settled that for him. She was a master spirit and she ordered him to write the Quincy girl and break off that match, which he did. Then he married the Keokuk girl and they began a struggle for life which turned out to be a difficult enterprise, and very unpromising.

To gain a living in Muscatine was plainly impossible, so Orion and his new wife went to Keokuk to live, for she wanted to be near her relatives. He bought a little bit of a job-printing plant—on credit, of course—and at once put prices down to where not even the apprentices could get a living out of it.

I had not joined the Muscatine migration. Just before that happened (which I think was in 1853) I disappeared one night and fled to St. Louis. There I worked in the composing-room of the *Evening*

*Sam Clemens at age 18, shortly before he set out*
*to become a riverboat pilot.*
Courtesy of the Mark Twain Papers, The Bancroft Library

*News* for a time, and then started on my travels to see the world. The world was New York City, Philadelphia, and Washington, D.C. After being away for several months, I rejoined the family and again worked for Orion.

I worked in that little job office in Keokuk as much as two years, I should say, without ever collecting a cent of wages, for Orion was never able to pay anything—but Dick Higham and I had good times. I don't know what Dick got, but it was probably only uncashable promises.

One day in the mid-winter of 1856 or 1857—I think it was 1856—I was walking along the main street of Keokuk in the middle of the forenoon. It was bitter weather—so bitter that that street was deserted, almost. A light dry snow was blowing here and there on the ground and on the pavement, swirling this way and that way and making all sorts of beautiful figures, but very chilly to look at. The wind blew a piece of paper past me and it lodged against a wall of a house. Something about the look of it attracted my attention and I gathered it in. It was a fifty-dollar bill, the only one I had ever seen, and the largest assemblage of money I had ever seen in one spot. I advertised it in the papers and suffered more than a thousand dollars' worth of solicitude and fear and distress during the next few days lest the owner should see the advertisement and come and take my fortune away. As many as four days went by without an applicant; then I could endure this kind of misery no longer. I felt sure that another four could not go by in this safe and secure way. I felt that I must take that money out of danger. So I bought a ticket for Cincinnati and went to that city. I worked there several months in the printing-office of Wrightson & Company.

Meantime, Orion sweat along with his little job office in Keokuk, and he and his wife were living with his wife's family—ostensibly as boarders, but it is not likely that Orion was ever able to pay the board. On account of charging nothing for the work done in his job office, he had almost nothing to do there. He was never able to get it through his head that work done on a profitless basis deteriorates and is presently not worth anything, and that customers are obliged to go where they can get better work, even if they must pay better prices for it. He had plenty of time, and he took up Blackstone again. He also put up a sign which offered his services to the public as a lawyer. He never got a case, in those days, nor even an applicant, although he was quite willing to transact law business for nothing and furnish the stationery himself.

Presently he moved to a wee little hamlet called Alexandria, two or three miles down the river, and he put up that sign there. He got no bites. He was by this time very hard aground. But by this time I was beginning to earn a wage of two hundred and fifty dollars a month as pilot, and so I supported him thenceforth until 1861.

# VI

## *To Be a Steamboatman*

WHEN I was a boy, there was but one permanent ambition among my comrades in our village. That was, to be a steamboatman. We had transient ambitions of other sorts, but they were only transient. When a circus came and went, it left us all burning to become clowns; the first Negro minstrel show that ever came to our section left us all suffering to try that kind of life; now and then we had a hope that, if we lived and were good, God would permit us to be pirates. These ambitions faded out, each in its turn; but the ambition to be a steamboatman always remained.

Once a day a cheap, gaudy packet arrived upward from St. Louis, and another downward from Keokuk. Before these events, the day was glorious with expectancy; after them, the day was a dead and empty thing. Not only the boys, but the whole village, felt this. After all these years I can picture that old time to myself now, just as it was then: the white town drowsing in the sunshine of a summer's morning; the streets empty, or pretty nearly so; one or two clerks sitting in front of the Water Street stores, with their splint-bottomed chairs tilted back against the wall, chins on breasts, hats slouched over their faces, fast asleep—with shingle-shavings enough around to show what broke them down; a sow and a litter of pigs loafing along the sidewalk, doing a good business in watermelon rinds and seeds; two or three lonely little freight piles scattered about the "levee;" a pile of "skids" on the slope of the stone-paved wharf, and the fragrant town drunkard asleep in the shadow of them; two or three wood flats at the head of the wharf, but nobody to listen to the peaceful lapping of the wavelets against them; the great Mississippi, the majestic, the magnificent Mississippi, rolling its mile-wide tide along, shining in the sun; the dense forest away on the other side; the "point" above the town, and the "point" below, bounding the river-glimpse and turning it into a sort of sea, and withal a very still and brilliant and lonely one. Presently a film of dark smoke appears above one of those remote "points;" instantly a Negro drayman, famous for his quick eye and prodigious voice, lifts up the cry, "S-t-e-a-m-boat a-comin'!" and the scene changes! The town drunkard stirs, the clerks wake up, a furious clatter of drays follows, every house and store pours out a human contribution, and all in a twinkling the dead town is alive and moving. Drays, carts, men, boys, all go hurrying from many quarters to a common center, the wharf. Assembled there, the people fasten their eyes upon the coming boat as upon a wonder they are seeing for the first time. And the boat *is* rather a handsome sight, too.

She is long and sharp and trim and pretty; she has two tall, fancy-topped chimneys, with a gilded device of some kind swung between them; a fanciful pilot-house, all glass and "gingerbread," perched on top of the "texas" deck behind them; the paddle-boxes are gorgeous with a picture or with gilded rays above the boat's name; the boiler deck, the hurricane deck, and the texas deck are fenced and ornamented with clean white railings; there is a flag gallantly flying from the jack-staff; the furnace doors are open and the fires glaring bravely; the upper decks are black with passengers; the captain stands by the big bell, calm, imposing, the envy of all; great volumes of the blackest smoke are rolling and tumbling out of the chimneys—a husbanded grandeur created with a bit of pitch pine just before arriving at a town; the crew are grouped on the forecastle; the broad stage is run far out over the port bow, and an envied deck-hand stands picturesquely on the end of it with a coil of rope in his hand; the pent steam is screaming through the gauge-cocks; the captain lifts his hand, a bell rings, the wheels stop; then they turn back, churning the water to foam, and the steamer is at rest. Then such a scramble as there is to get aboard, and to get ashore, and to bring on freight and to discharge freight, all at one and the same time; and such a yelling and cursing as the mates facilitate it all with! Ten minutes later the steamer is under way again, with no flag on the jack-staff and no black smoke issuing from the chimneys. After ten more minutes the town is dead again, and the town drunkard asleep by the skids once more.

My father was a justice of the peace, and I supposed he possessed the power of life and death over all men and could hang anybody that offended him. This was distinction enough for me as a general thing; but the desire to be a steamboatman kept intruding, nevertheless. I first wanted to be a cabin-boy, so that I could come out with a white apron on and shake a tablecloth over the side, where all my old comrades could see me; later I thought I would rather be the deckhand who stood on the end of the stage-plank with the coil of rope in his hand, because he was particularly conspicuous. But these were only day-dreams—they were too heavenly to be contemplated as real possibilities. By and by one of our boys went away. He was not heard of for a long time. At last he turned up as apprentice engineer or "striker" on a steamboat. This thing shook the bottom out of all my Sunday school teachings. That boy had been notoriously worldly, and I just the reverse; yet he was exalted to this eminence, and I left in obscurity and misery. There was nothing generous about this fellow in his greatness. He would always manage to have a rusty bolt to scrub while his boat tarried at our town, and he would sit on the inside guard and scrub it, where we all could see him and envy him and loathe him. And whenever his boat was laid up he would come home and swell around the town in his blackest and greasiest clothes, so that nobody could help remembering that he was a steamboatman; and he used all sorts of steamboat technicalities in his talk, as if he were so used to them that he forgot common people could not understand them.

This creature's career could produce but one result, and it speedily followed. Boy after boy managed to get on the river. The minister's son became an engineer. The doctor's and the postmaster's sons became "mud clerks;" the wholesale liquor dealer's son became a barkeeper on a boat; four sons of the chief merchant, and two sons of the county judge, became pilots. Pilot was the grandest position of all. The pilot, even in those days of trivial wages, had a princely salary—from a hundred and fifty to two hundred and fifty dollars a month, and no board to pay. Two months of his wages would pay a preacher's salary for a year. Now some of us were left disconsolate. We could not get on the river—at least our parents would not let us.

So by and by I ran away. I said I would never come home again till I was a pilot and could come in glory. But somehow I could not manage it. I went meekly aboard a few of the boats that lay packed together like sardines at the long St. Louis wharf, and very humbly inquired for the pilots, but got only a cold shoulder and short words from mates and clerks. I had to make the best of this sort of treatment for the time being, but I had comforting daydreams of a future when I should be a great and honored pilot, with plenty of money, and could kill some of these mates and clerks and pay for them.

Months afterward the hope within me struggled to a reluctant death, and I found myself without an ambition. But I was ashamed to go home. I was in Cincinnati, and I set to work to map out a new career. I had been reading about the recent exploration of the river Amazon by an expedition sent out by our government. It was said that the expedition, owing to difficulties, had not thoroughly explored a part of the country lying about the head-waters, some four thousand miles from the mouth of the river. It was only about fifteen hundred miles from Cincinnati to New Orleans, where I could doubtless get a ship. I had thirty dollars left; I would go and complete the exploration of the Amazon.[1] This was all the thought I gave to the subject. I never was great in matters of detail. I packed my valise, and took passage on an ancient tub called the *Paul Jones*, for New Orleans. For the sum of sixteen dollars I had the scarred and tarnished splendors of her main saloon principally to myself, for she was not a creature to attract the eye of wiser travelers.

[1]Typically, Mark Twain makes his narrator much more naive than the actual Sam Clemens had been. In 1856, Sam, who was in his twenty-second year, had recently been reading William Lewis Herndon's *Exploration of the Valley of the Amazon* (1853), a two-volume official report which gave far more plausible reasons for migrating to South America than the one that the humorist mentioned here.

*The busy riverfront at St. Louis.*
Courtesy of the Missouri Historical Society

When we presently got under way and went poking down the broad Ohio, I became a new being and the subject of my own admiration. I was a traveler! A word never had tasted so good in my mouth before. I had an exultant sense of being bound for mysterious lands and distant climes which I never have felt in so uplifting a degree since.

What with lying on the rocks four days at Louisville, and some other delays, the poor old *Paul Jones* fooled away about two weeks in making the voyage from Cincinnati to New Orleans. This gave me a chance to get acquainted with one of the pilots, and he taught me how to steer the boat, and thus made the fascination of river life more potent than ever for me.

In New Orleans, I soon discovered two things.[2] One was that a vessel would not be likely to sail for the mouth of the Amazon under ten or twelve years; and the other was that the nine or ten dollars still left in my pocket would not suffice for so impossible an exploration as I had planned, even if I could afford to wait for a ship. Therefore it followed that I must contrive a new career. The *Paul Jones* was now bound for St. Louis. I planned a siege against my pilot, and at the end of three hard days he surrendered. He agreed to teach me the Mississippi

[2]Another inventive enhancement of Sam Clemens' naivete. Actually, he gave up the Amazonian project and arranged for his apprenticeship when the boat was 900 miles north of New Orleans.

River from New Orleans to St. Louis for five hundred dollars, payable out of the first wages I should receive after graduating. I entered upon the small enterprise of "learning" twelve or thirteen hundred miles of the great Mississippi River with the easy confidence of my time of life. If I had really known what I was about to require of my faculties, I should not have had the courage to begin. I supposed that all a pilot had to do was to keep his boat in the river, and I did not consider that that could be much of a trick, since it was so wide.

The boat backed out from New Orleans at four in the afternoon, and it was "our watch" until eight. Mr. Bixby, my chief, "straightened her up," plowed her along past the sterns of the other boats that lay at the Levee, and then said, "Here, take her; shave those steamships as close as you'd peel an apple." I took the wheel, and my heartbeat fluttered up into the hundreds; for it seemed to me that we were about to scrape the side off every ship in the line, we were so close. I held my breath and began to claw the boat away from the danger; and I had my own opinion of the pilot who had known no better than to get us into such peril, but I was too wise to express it. In half a minute I had a wide margin of safety intervening between the *Paul Jones* and the ships; and within ten seconds more I was set aside in disgrace, and Mr. Bixby was going into danger again and flaying me alive with abuse of my cowardice. I was stung, but I was obliged to admire the easy confidence with which my chief loafed from side to side of his wheel, and trimmed the ships so closely that disaster seemed ceaselessly imminent. When he had cooled a little he told me that the easy water was close ashore and the current outside, and therefore we must hug the bank, up-stream, to get the benefit of the former, and stay well out, down-stream, to take advantage of the latter. In my own mind I resolved to be a down-stream pilot and leave the up-streaming to people dead to prudence.

Now and then Mr. Bixby called my attention to certain things. Said he, "This is Six-Mile Point." I assented. It was pleasant enough information, but I could not see the bearing of it. I was not conscious that it was a matter of any interest to me. Another time he said, "This is Nine-Mile Point." Later he said, "This is Twelve-Mile Point." They were all about level with the water's edge; they all looked about alike to me; they were monotonously unpicturesque. I hoped Mr. Bixby would change the subject. But no; he would crowd up around a point, hugging the shore with affection, and then say: "The slack water ends here, abreast this bunch of China trees; now we cross over." So he crossed over. He gave me the wheel once or twice, but I had no luck. I either came near chipping off the edge of a sugar-plantation, or I yawed too far from shore, and so dropped back into disgrace again and got abused.

The watch was ended at last, and we took supper and went to bed. At midnight the glare of a lantern shone into my eyes, and the night watchman said:

"Come, turn out!"

And then he left. I could not understand this extraordinary procedure; so I presently gave up trying and dozed off to sleep. A short while later the watchman was back again, and this time he was gruff. I was annoyed. I said:

"What do you want to come bothering around here in the middle of the night for? Now, as like as not, I'll not get to sleep again tonight."

The watchman said:

"Well, if this ain't good, I'm blessed."

The "off-watch" was just turning in, and I heard some brutal laughter from them, and such remarks as "Hello, watchman! ain't the new cub turned out yet? He's delicate, likely. Give him some sugar in a rag, and then send for the chambermaid to sing 'Rock-a-bye Baby,' to him."

About this time Mr. Bixby appeared on the scene. Something like a minute later I was climbing the pilot-house steps with some of my clothes on and the rest in my arms. Mr. Bixby was close behind, commenting. Here was something fresh—this thing of getting up in the middle of the night to go to work. It was a detail in piloting that had never occurred to me at all. I knew that boats ran all night, but somehow I had never happened to reflect that somebody had to get up out of a warm bed to run them. I began to fear that piloting was not quite so romantic as I had imagined it was.

It was a rather dingy night, although a fair number of stars could be seen. The big mate was at the wheel, and he had the old tub pointed at a star and was holding her straight up the middle of the river. The shores on either hand were not much more than half a mile apart, but they seemed wonderfully far away and ever so vague and indistinct. The mate said:

"We've got to land at Jones's plantation, sir."

The vengeful spirit in me exulted. I said to myself, "I wish you joy of your job, Mr. Bixby; you'll have a good time finding Mr. Jones's plantation such a night as this; and I hope you never *will* find it as long as you live."

Mr. Bixby said to the mate:

"Upper end of the plantation, or the lower?"

"Upper."

"I can't do it. The stumps there are out of water at this stage. It's no great distance to the lower, and you'll have to get along with that."

"All right, sir. If Jones don't like it, he'll have to lump it, I reckon."

And then the mate left. My exultation began to cool and my wonder to come up. Here was a man who not only proposed to find this plantation on such a night, but to find either end of it you preferred. I dreadfully wanted to ask a question, but I was carrying about as many short answers as my cargo-room would admit of, so I held my peace. All I desired to ask Mr. Bixby was the simple question whether he was ass enough to really imagine he was going to find that plantation on a night when all plantations were exactly alike and all of the same color. But I held in. I used to have fine inspirations of prudence in those days.

Mr. Bixby made for the shore and soon was scraping it, just the same as if it had been daylight. And not only that, but singing:

"Father in heaven, the day is declining," etc.

It seemed to me that I had put my life in the keeping of a peculiarly reckless outcast. Presently he turned on me and said:

"What's the name of the first point above New Orleans?"

I was gratified to be able to answer promptly, and I did. I said I didn't know.

"Don't *know*?"

This manner jolted me. I was down at the foot again, in a moment. But I had to say just what I had said before.

"Well, you're a smart one!" said Mr. Bixby. "What's the name of the *next* point?"

Once more I didn't know.

"Well, this beats anything. Tell me the name of *any* point or place I told you." I studied awhile and decided that I couldn't.

"Look here! What do you start out from, above Twelve-Mile Point, to cross over?"

"I—I—don't know."

"You—you—don't know?" mimicking my drawling manner of speech. "What *do* you know?"

"I—I—nothing, for certain."

"By the great Cæsar's ghost, I believe you! You're the stupidest dunderhead I ever saw or ever heard of, so help me Moses! The idea of *you* being a pilot—*you*! Why, you don't know enough to pilot a cow down a lane."

Oh, but his wrath was up! He was a nervous man, and he shuffled from one side of his wheel to the other as if the floor was hot. He would boil awhile to himself, and then overflow and scald me again.

"Look here! What do you suppose I told you the names of those points for?"

I tremblingly considered a moment, and then the devil of temptation provoked me to say:

"Well to—to—be entertaining, I thought."

This was a red rag to the bull. He raged and stormed so (he was crossing the river at the time) that I judged it made him blind, because he ran over the steering-oar of a trading-scow. Of course the traders sent up a volley of red-hot profanity. Never was a man so grateful as Mr. Bixby was; because he was brimful, and here were subjects who could *talk back*. He threw open a window, thrust his head out, and such an irruption followed as I never had heard before. The fainter and farther away the scowmen's curses drifted, the higher Mr. Bixby lifted his voice and the weightier his adjectives grew. When he closed the window he was empty. You could have drawn a seine through his system and not caught curses enough to disturb your mother with. Presently he said to me in the gentlest way:

"My boy, you must get a little memorandum-book; and every time I tell you a thing, put it down right away. There's only one way to be a pilot, and that is to get this entire river by heart. You have to know it just like A B C."

That was a dismal revelation to me; for my memory was never loaded with anything but blank cartridges. However, I judged that it was best to make some allowances, for doubtlessly Mr. Bixby was "stretching." Presently he pulled a rope and struck a few strokes on the big bell. The stars were all gone now, and the night was as black as ink. I could hear the wheels churn along the bank, but I was not entirely certain that I could see the shore. Then the voice of the invisible watchman called up from the hurricane deck:—

"What's this, sir?"

"Jones's plantation."

I said to myself, I wish I might venture to offer a small bet that it wasn't. Mr. Bixby handled the engine bells, and in due time the boat's nose came to the land, a man skipped ashore, a darky's voice on the bank said, "Gimme de k'yarpet-bag, Mars' Jones," and the next moment we were standing up the river again, all serene. I reflected deeply awhile.

# VII

## *The Shape of the River*

BY THE TIME we had gone seven or eight hundred miles up the river, I had learned to be a tolerably plucky up-stream steersman, in daylight; and before we reached St. Louis I had made a trifle of progress in night work, but only a trifle. I had a note-book that fairly bristled with the names of towns, "points," bars, islands, bends, reaches, etc.; but the information was to be found only in the note-book—none of it was in my head. It made my heart ache to think I had only got half of the river set down; for as our watch was four hours off and four hours on, day and night, there was a long four-hour gap in my book for every time I had slept since the voyage began.

My chief was presently hired to go on a big New Orleans boat, and I packed my satchel and went with him. She was a grand affair. When I stood in her pilot-house I was so far above the water that I seemed perched upon a mountain; and her decks stretched so far away, fore and aft, below me, that I wondered how I could ever have considered the little *Paul Jones* a large craft. There were other differences, too. The *Paul Jones's* pilot-house was a cheap, dingy, battered rattletrap, and cramped for room; but here was a sumptuous glass temple; room enough to have a dance in; showy red and gold window-curtains; an imposing sofa; leather cushions and a back to the high bench where visiting pilots sit, to spin yarns and "look at the river"; bright, fanciful "cuspidores," instead of a broad wooden box filled with sawdust; nice new oilcloth on the floor! a hospitable big stove for winter; a wheel as high as my head, costly with inlaid work; a wire tiller-rope; bright brass knobs for the bells; and a tidy, white-aproned, black "texas-tender," to bring up tarts and ices and coffee during mid-watch, day and night. Now this was "something like"; and so I began to take heart once more to believe that piloting was a romantic sort of occupation after all. The moment we were under way I began to prowl about the great steamer and fill myself with joy.

When I returned to the pilot-house St. Louis was gone, and I was lost. Here was a piece of river which was all down in my book, but I could make neither head nor tail of it: you understand, it was turned around. I had seen it when coming up-stream, but I had never faced about to see how it looked when it was behind me. My heart broke again, for it was plain that I had got to learn this troublesome river *both ways*.

However, at the end of what seemed a tedious while, I had managed to pack my head full of bars, islands, towns, "points," and bends; and a curiously inanimate mass of lumber it was, too. Inasmuch as I could shut my eyes and reel off a good long string of these names without leaving out more than ten miles of river in every fifty, I began to feel that I could take a boat down to New Orleans if I could make her skip those little gaps. But of course my complacency could hardly get start enough to lift my nose a trifle into the air, before Mr. Bixby would think of something to fetch it down again. One day he turned on me with this settler:

"What is the shape of Walnut Bend?"

He might as well have asked me my grandmother's opinion of protoplasm. I reflected respectfully, and then said I didn't know it had any particular shape. My gun-powdery chief went off with a bang, of course, and then went on loading and firing until he was out of adjectives.

I had learned long ago that he only carried just so many rounds of ammunition, and was sure to subside into a very placable and even remorseful old smoothbore as soon as they were all gone. That word "old" is merely affectionate; he was not more than thirty-four. I waited. By and by he said:

"My boy, you've got to know the *shape* of the river perfectly. It is all there is left to steer by on a very dark night. Everything else is blotted out and gone. But mind you, it hasn't the same shape in the night that it has in the daytime."

"How on earth am I ever going to learn it, then?"

"How do you follow a hall at home in the dark? Because you know the shape of it. You can't see it."

"Do you mean to say that I've got to know all the million trifling variations of shape in the banks of this interminable river as well as I know the shape of the front hall at home?"

"On my honor, you've got to know them *better* than any man ever did know the shapes of the halls in his own house."

"I wish I was dead!"

"Now I don't want to discourage you, but—"

"Well, pile it on me; I might as well have it now as another time."

"You see, this has got to be learned; there isn't any getting around it. A clear starlight night throws such heavy shadows that, if you didn't know the shape of a shore perfectly, you would claw away from every bunch of timber, because you would take the black shadow of it for a solid cape; and you see you would be getting scared to death every fifteen minutes by the watch. You would be fifty yards from shore all the time when you ought to be within fifty feet of it. You can't see a snag in one of those shadows, but you know exactly where it is, and the shape of the river tells you when you are coming to it. Then there's your pitch-dark night; the river is a very different shape on a pitch-dark night from what it is on a star-light night. All shores seem to be straight lines, then, and mighty dim ones, too; and you'd *run* them for straight lines, only you know better. You boldly drive your boat right into what seems to be a solid, straight wall (you knowing

*Captain Horace Bixby who taught Sam Clemens
how to pilot.*
Courtesy of the Walter Blair Collection

very well that in reality there is a curve there), and that wall falls back and makes way for you. Then here's your gray mist. You take a night when there's a grisly, drizzly, gray mist, and then there isn't *any* particular shape to a shore. A gray mist would tangle the head of the oldest man that ever lived. Well, then, different kinds of *moonlight* change the shape of the river in different ways. You see—"

"Oh, don't say any more, please! Have I got to learn the shape of the river according to all these five hundred thousand different ways? If I tried to carry all that cargo in my head it would make me stoop-shouldered."

"*No!* you only learn *the* shape of the river; and you learn it with such absolute certainty that you can always steer by the shape that's *in your head.*"

"Very well, I'll try it; but, after I have learned it, can I depend on it? Will it keep the same form and not go fooling around?"

Before Mr. Bixby could answer, Mr. W. came in to take the watch, and he said:

"Bixby, you'll have to look out for President's Island, and all that country clear away up above the Old Hen and Chickens. The banks are caving and the shape of the shores changing like everything. Why, you wouldn't know the point above 40. You can go up inside the old sycamore snag, now."[1]

[1] It may not be necessary, but still it will be no harm to explain that "inside" means between the snag and the shore.—Mark Twain's footnote.

So that question was answered. Here were leagues of shore changing shape. My spirits were down in the mud again. Two things seemed pretty apparent to me. One was, that in order to be a pilot a man had got to learn more than any one man ought to be allowed to know; and the other was, that he must learn it over again in a different way every twenty-four hours.

I went to work now to learn the shape of the river; and of all the eluding and ungraspable objects that ever I tried to get mind or hands on, that was the chief. I would fasten my eyes upon a sharp, wooded point that projected far into the river some miles ahead of me, and go to laboriously photographing its shape upon my brain; and just as I was beginning to succeed to my satisfaction, we would draw up toward it and the exasperating thing would begin to melt away and fold back into the bank! If there had been a conspicuous dead tree standing upon the very point of the cape, I would find that tree inconspicuously merged into the general forest, and occupying the middle of a straight shore, when I got abreast of it! No prominent hill would stick to its shape long enough for me to make up my mind what its form really was, but it was as dissolving and changeful as if it had been a mountain of butter in the hottest corner of the tropics. Nothing ever had the same shape when I was coming down-stream that it had borne when I went up. I mentioned these little difficulties to Mr. Bixby. He said:

"That's the very main virtue of the thing. If the shapes didn't change every three seconds they wouldn't be of any use. Take this place where we are now, for instance. As long as that hill over yonder is only one hill, I can boom right along the way I'm going; but the moment it splits at the top and forms a V, I know I've got to scratch to starboard in a hurry, or I'll bang this boat's brains out against a rock; and then the moment one of the prongs of the V swings behind the other, I've got to waltz to larboard again, or I'll have a misunderstanding with a snag that would snatch the keelson right out of this steamboat as neatly as if it were a sliver in your hand. If that hill didn't change its shape on bad nights there would be an awful steamboat graveyard around here inside of a year."

It was plain that I had got to learn the shape of the river in all the different ways that could be thought of—upside down, wrong end first, inside out, fore-and-aft, and "thort-ships"—and then also know what to do on gray nights when it hadn't any shape at all. So I set about it. In the course of time I began to get the best of this knotty lesson, and my self-complacency moved to the front once more. Mr. Bixby was all fixed, and ready to start it to the rear again. He opened on me after this fashion:

"How much water did we have in the middle crossing at Hole-in-the-Wall, trip before last?"

I considered this an outrage. I said:

"On every trip the leadsmen are singing through

that tangled place for three-quarters of an hour on a stretch. How do you reckon I can remember such a mess as that?"

"My boy, you've got to remember it. You've got to remember the exact spot and the exact marks the boat lay in when we had the shoalest water, in every one of the five hundred shoal places between St. Louis and New Orleans; and you mustn't get the shoal soundings and marks of one trip mixed up with the shoal soundings and marks of another, either, for they're not often twice alike. You must keep them separate."

When I came to myself again, I said:

"When I get so that I can do that, I'll be able to raise up the dead, and then I won't have to pilot a steamboat to make a living. I want to retire from this business. I want a slush-bucket and a brush; I'm only fit to be a roustabout. I haven't got brains enough to be a pilot; and if I had I wouldn't have the strength enough to carry them around, unless I went on crutches."

"Now drop that! When I say I'll learn[2] a man the river, I mean it. And you can depend on it, I'll learn him or kill him."

There was no use in arguing with a person like this. I promptly put such a strain on my memory that by and by even the shoal water and the countless crossing-marks began to stay with me. But the

[2] "Teach" is not in the river vocabulary.—Mark Twain's footnote.

result was just the same. I never could more than
get one knotty thing learned before another presented itself. Now I had often seen pilots gazing at
the water and pretending to read it as if it were a
book; but it was a book that told me nothing. A
time came at last, however, when Mr. Bixby seemed
to think me far enough advanced to bear a lesson on
water-reading. So he began:

"Do you see that long, slanting line on the face of
the water? Now, that's a reef. Moreover, it's a bluff
reef. There is a solid sand bar under it that is nearly
as straight as the side of a house. There's plenty
of water close up to it, but mighty little on top of
it. If you were to hit it you would knock the boat's
brains out. Do you see where the line fringes out at
the upper end and begins to fade away?"

"Yes, sir."

"Well, that is a low place; that is the head of the
reef. You can climb over there, and not hurt anything. Cross over, now, and follow along close under the reef—easy water there—not much current."

I followed the reef along till I approached the
fringed end. Then Mr. Bixby said:

"Now get ready. Wait till I give the word. She
won't want to mount the reef; a boat hates shoal
water. Stand by—wait—*wait*—and keep her in hand.
*Now* cramp her down! Snatch her! snatch her!"

He seized the other side of the wheel and helped
to spin it around until it was hard down, and then
we held. The boat resisted, and refused to answer for

a while, and next she came surging to starboard, mounted the reef, and sent a long, angry ridge of water foaming away from her bows.

"Now watch her; watch her like a cat, or she'll get away from you. When she fights strong and the tiller slips a little, in a jerky, greasy sort of way, let up on her a trifle; it is the way she tells you at night that the water is too shoal; but keep edging her up, little by little, toward the point. You are well up on the bar now; there is a bar under every point, because the water that comes down around it forms an eddy and allows the sediment to sink. Do you see those fine lines on the face of the water that branch out like the ribs of a fan? Well, those are little reefs; you want to just miss the ends of them, but run them pretty close. Now look out—look out! Don't you crowd that slick, greasy-looking place; there ain't nine feet there; she won't stand it. She begins to smell it; look sharp, I tell you! Oh, blazes, there you go! Stop the starboard wheel! Quick! Ship up to back! Set her back!"

The engine bells jingled and the engines answered promptly, shooting white columns of steam far aloft out of the 'scape-pipes, but it was too late. The boat had "smelt" the bar in good earnest; the foamy ridges that radiated from her bows suddenly disappeared, a great dead swell came rolling forward, and swept ahead of her, she careened far over to larboard, and went tearing away toward the shore as if she were about scared to death. We were a good mile from where we ought to have been when we finally got the upper hand of her again.

THE FACE of the water, in time, became a wonderful book—a book that was a dead language to the uneducated passenger, but which told its mind to me without reserve, delivering its most cherished secrets as clearly as if it uttered them with a voice. And it was not a book to be read once and thrown aside, for there was a new story to tell everyday. Throughout the long twelve hundred miles there was never a page that was void of interest, never one that you could leave unread without loss, never one that you would want to skip, thinking you could find higher enjoyment in some other thing. There never was so wonderful a book written by man; never one whose interest was so absorbing, so unflagging, so sparklingly renewed with every reperusal. The passenger who could not read it was charmed with a peculiar sort of faint dimple on its surface (on the rare occasions when he did not overlook it altogether); but to the pilot that was an *italicized* passage; indeed, it was more than that, it was a legend of the largest capitals, with a string of shouting exclamation-points at the end of it, for it meant that a wreck or a rock was buried there that could tear the life out of the strongest vessel that ever floated. It is the faintest and simplest expression the water ever makes, and the most hideous to a pilot's eye. In truth, the passenger who could not read this book saw nothing but all manner of pretty pictures in it, painted by the sun and shaded by the clouds, whereas to the trained eye these were not pictures at all, but the grimmest and most dead-earnest of reading matter.

Now when I had mastered the language of this water, and had come to know every trifling feature that bordered the great river as familiarly as I knew the letters of the alphabet, I had made a valuable acquisition. But I had lost something, too. I had lost something which could never be restored to me while I lived. All the grace, the beauty, the poetry, had gone out of the majestic river! I still kept in mind a certain wonderful sunset which I witnessed when steamboating was new to me. A broad expanse of the river was turned to blood; in the middle distance the red hue brightened into gold, through which a solitary log came floating, black and conspicuous; in one place a long, slanting mark lay sparkling upon the water; in another the surface was broken by boiling, tumbling rings, that were as many-tinted as an opal; where the ruddy flush was faintest, was a smooth spot that was covered with graceful circles and radiating lines, ever so delicately traced; the shore on our left was densely wooded, and the somber shadow that fell from this forest was broken in one place by a long, ruffled trail that shone like silver; and high above the forest wall a clean-stemmed dead tree waved its single leafy bough that glowed like a flame in the unobstructed splendor that was flowing from the sun. There were graceful curves, reflected images, soft distances, woody heights; and over the whole scene, the dissolving lights drifted steadily, enriching it every passing moment with new marvels of coloring.

I stood like one bewitched. I drank it in, in a speechless rapture. The world was new to me, and I had never seen anything like this at home. But as I have said, a day came when I began to cease from noting the glories and the charms which the moon and the sun and the twilight wrought upon the river's face; another day came when I ceased altogether to note them. Then, if that sunset scene had been repeated, I should have looked upon it without rapture, and should have commented upon it inwardly after this fashion: "This sun means that we are going to have wind tomorrow; that floating log means that the river is rising, small thanks to it; that slanting mark on the water refers to a bluff reef which is going to kill somebody's steamboat one of these nights, if it keeps on stretching out like that; those tumbling 'boils' show a dissolving bar and a changing channel there; the lines and circles in the slick water over yonder are a warning that that troublesome place is shoaling up dangerously; that silver streak in the shadow of the forest is the 'break' from a new snag, and he has located himself in the very best place he could have found to fish for steamboats; that tall dead tree, with only a single living branch, is not going to last long, and then how is a body ever going to get through this blind place at night without the friendly old landmark?"

No, the romance and beauty were all gone from the river. All the value any feature of it had for me now was the amount of usefulness it could furnish toward compassing the safe piloting of a steamboat. Since those days, I have pitied doctors from my heart. What does the lovely flush in a beauty's cheek mean to a doctor but a "break" that ripples above some deadly disease? Are not all her visible charms sown thick with what are to him the signs and symbols of hidden decay? Does he ever see her beauty at all, or doesn't he simply view her professionally, and comment upon her unwholesome condition all to himself? And doesn't he sometimes wonder whether he has gained most or lost most by learning his trade?

# VIII

## *A Curious and Wonderful Science*

Bᴜᴛ I am wandering from what I was intending to
do; that is, make plainer than perhaps appears
in the previous chapters some of the peculiar requirements of the science of piloting. First of all,
there is one faculty which a pilot must incessantly
cultivate until he has brought it to absolute perfection. Nothing short of perfection will do. That faculty is memory. He cannot stop with merely thinking a thing is so and so; he must *know* it; for this is
eminently one of the "exact" sciences. With what
scorn a pilot was looked upon, in the old times, if
he ever ventured to deal in that feeble phrase "I
think," instead of the vigorous one, "I know!" One
cannot easily realize what a tremendous thing it is
to know every trivial detail of twelve hundred miles
of river and know it with absolute exactness. If you
will take the longest street in New York, and travel
up and down it, conning its features patiently until
you know every house and window and lamppost
and big and little sign by heart, and know them so
accurately that you can instantly name the one you
are abreast of when you are set down at random in
that street in the middle of an inky black night, you
will then have a tolerable notion of the amount and

the exactness of a pilot's knowledge who carries the Mississippi River in his head. And then, if you will go on until you know every street-crossing, the character, size, and position of the crossing-stones, and the varying depth of mud in each of these numberless places, you will have some idea of what the pilot must know in order to keep a Mississippi steamer out of trouble. Next, if you will take half of the signs in that long street, and *change their places* once a month, and still manage to know their new positions accurately on dark nights, and keep up with these repeated changes without making any mistakes, you will understand what is required of a pilot's peerless memory by the fickle Mississippi.

I think a pilot's memory is about the most wonderful thing in the world. To know the Old and New Testaments by heart, and be able to recite them glibly, forward or backward, or begin at random anywhere in the book and recite both ways and never trip or make a mistake, is no extravagant mass of knowledge, and no marvelous facility, compared to a pilot's massed knowledge of the Mississippi and his marvelous facility in the handling of it. I make this comparison deliberately, and believe I am not expanding the truth when I do it. Many will think my figure too strong, but pilots will not.

And how easily and comfortably the pilot's memory does its work; how placidly effortless is its way; how *unconsciously* it lays up its vast stores, hour by hour, day by day, and never loses or mislays a single valuable package of them all! Take an instance. Let a leadsman cry, "Half twain![1] half twain! half twain! half twain! half twain!" until it becomes as monotonous as the ticking of a clock; let conversation be going on all the time, and the pilot be doing his share of the talking, and no longer consciously listening to the leadsman; and in the midst of this endless string of half twains let a single "quarter twain!" be interjected, without emphasis, and then the half-twain cry go on again, just as before: two or three weeks later that pilot can describe with precision the boat's position in the river when that quarter twain was uttered, and give you such a lot of head-marks, stern-marks, and side-marks to guide you, that you ought to be able to take the boat there and put her in that same spot again yourself! The cry of "quarter twain" did not really take his mind from his talk, but his trained faculties instantly photographed the bearings, noted the change of depth, and laid up the important details for future reference without requiring any assistance from *him* in the matter. If you were walking and talking with a friend, and another friend at your side kept up a monotonous repetition of the vowel sound A, for several blocks, and then in the midst interjected an R, thus, A, A, A, A, A, R, A, A, A, etc., and gave

[1] As the humorist would explain to his Nevada newspaper editor when he adopted his pseudonym in 1863, *twain* "is an old river term, a leadsman's call, signifying two fathoms— twelve feet." *Mark Twain*, therefore, meant "safe water."

the R no emphasis, you would not be able to state, two or three weeks afterward, that the R had been put in, nor be able to tell what objects you were passing at the moment it was done. But you could if your memory had been patiently and laboriously trained to do that sort of thing mechanically.

Give a man a tolerably fair memory to start with, and piloting will develop it into a very colossus of capability. But *only in the matters it is daily drilled in.* A time would come when the man's faculties could not help noticing landmarks and soundings, and his memory could not help holding on to them with the grip of a vise; but if you asked that same man at noon what he had had for breakfast, it would be ten chances to one that he could not tell you. Astonishing things can be done with the human memory if you will devote it faithfully to one particular line of business.

At the time that wages soared so high on the Missouri River, my chief, Mr. Bixby, went up there and learned more than a thousand miles of that stream with an ease and rapidity that were astonishing. When he had seen each division *once* in the daytime and *once* at night, his education was so nearly complete that he took out a "daylight" license; a few trips later he took out a full license, and went to piloting day and night—and he ranked A 1, too.

Mr. Bixby placed me as steersman for a while under a pilot whose feats of memory were a constant marvel to me. However, his memory was born in him, I think, not built. For instance, somebody would mention a name. Instantly Mr. Brown would break in:

"Oh, I knew *him*. Sallow-faced, red-headed fellow, with a little scar on the side of his throat, like a splinter under the flesh. He was only in the Southern trade six months. That was about thirteen years ago. I made a trip with him. There was five feet in the upper river then; the *Henry Blake* grounded at the foot of Tower Island drawing four and a half; the *George Elliott* unshipped her rudder on the wreck of the *Sunflower*___"

"Why, the *Sunflower* didn't sink until___"

"*I* know when she sunk; it was three years before that, on the 2d of December; Asa Hardy was captain of her, and his brother John was first clerk; and it was his first trip in her, too; Tom Jones told me these things a week afterward in New Orleans; he was first mate of the *Sunflower*. Captain Hardy stuck a nail in his foot the 6th of July of the next year, and died of the lockjaw on the 15th. His brother John died two years after—3d of March—erysipelas. I never saw either of the Hardys—they were Alleghany River men—but people who knew them told me all these things. And they said Captain Hardy wore yarn socks winter and summer, and his first wife's name was Jane Shook; she was from New England—and his second one died in a lunatic asylum. It was in the blood. She was from Lexington, Kentucky. Name was Horton before she was married."

And so on, by the hour, the man's tongue would go. He could *not* forget anything. It was simply impossible. The most trivial details remained as distinct and luminous in his head, after they had lain there for years, as the most memorable events. His was not simply a pilot's memory; its grasp was universal. If he were talking about a trifling letter he had received seven years before, he was pretty sure to deliver you the entire screed from memory. And then, without observing that he was departing from the true line of his talk, he was more than likely to hurl in a long-drawn parenthetical biography of the writer of that letter; and you were lucky indeed if he did not take up that writer's relatives, one by one, and give you their biographies, too.

Such a memory as that is a great misfortune. To it, all occurrences are of the same size. Its possessor cannot distinguish an interesting circumstance from an uninteresting one. As a talker, he is bound to clog his narrative with tiresome details and make himself an insufferable bore. Moreover, he cannot stick to his subject. He picks up every little grain of memory he discerns in his way, and so is led aside. Mr. Brown would start out with the honest intention of telling you a vastly funny anecdote about a dog. He would be "so full of laugh" that he could hardly begin; then his memory would start with the dog's breed and personal appearance; drift into a history of his owner; of his owner's family, with descriptions of weddings and burials that had occurred in it, together with recitals of congratulatory verses and obituary poetry provoked by the same; then this memory would recollect that one these events occurred during the celebrated "hard winter" of such-and-such a year, and a minute description of that winter would follow, along with the names of people who were frozen to death, and statistics showing the high figures which pork and hay went up to. Pork and hay would suggest corn and fodder; corn and fodder would suggest cows and horses; cows and horses would suggest the circus and certain celebrated bare-back riders; the transition from the circus to the menagerie was easy and natural; from the elephant to equatorial Africa was but a step; then of course the heathen savages would suggest religion; and at the end of three or four hours' tedious jaw, the watch would change, and Brown would go out of the pilot-house muttering extracts from sermons he had heard years before about the efficacy of prayer as a means of grace. And the original first mention would be all you had learned about that dog, after all this waiting and hungering.

A pilot must have a memory; but there are two higher qualities which he must also have. He must have good and quick judgment and decision, and a cool, calm courage that no peril can shake. Give a man the merest trifle of pluck to start with, and by the time he has become a pilot he cannot be unmanned by any danger a steamboat can get into; but one cannot quite say the same for judgment. Judgment is a matter of brains, and a man must *start* with a good stock of that article or he will never succeed as a pilot.

The growth of courage in the pilot house is steady all the time, but it does not reach a high and satisfactory condition until some time after the young pilot has been "standing his own watch" alone and under the staggering weight of all the responsibilities connected with the position. When the apprentice has become pretty thoroughly acquainted with the river, he goes clattering along so fearlessly with his steamboat, night or day, that he presently begins to imagine that it is *his* courage that animates him; but the first time the pilot steps out and leaves him to his own devices he finds out it was the other man's. He discovers that the article has been left out of his own cargo altogether. The whole river is bristling with exigencies in a moment; he is not prepared for them; he does not know how to meet them; all his knowledge forsakes him; and within fifteen minutes he is as white as a sheet and scared almost to death. Therefore pilots wisely train these cubs by various strategic tricks to look danger in the face a little more calmly. A favorite way of theirs is to play a friendly swindle upon the candidate.

Mr. Bixby served me in this fashion once, and for years afterward I used to blush, even in my sleep, when I thought of it. I had become a good steersman; so good, indeed, that I had all the work to do on our watch, night and day. Mr. Bixby seldom made a suggestion to me; all he ever did was to take the wheel on particularly bad nights or in particularly bad crossings, land the boat when she needed to be landed, play gentleman of leisure nine-tenths of the watch, and collect the wages. The lower river was about bank-full, and if anybody had questioned my ability to run any crossing between Cairo and New Orleans without help or instruction, I should have felt irreparably hurt. The idea of being afraid of any crossing in the lot, in the *daytime*, was a thing too preposterous for contemplation. Well, one matchless summer's day I was bowling down the bend above Island 66, brimful of self-conceit and carrying my nose as high as a giraffe's, when Mr. Bixby said:

"I am going below awhile. I suppose you know the next crossing?"

This was almost an affront. It was about the plainest and simplest crossing in the whole river. One couldn't come to any harm, whether he ran it right or not; and as for depth, there never had been any bottom there. I knew all this, perfectly well.

"Know how to *run* it? Why, I can run it with my eyes shut."

"How much water is there in it?"

"Well, that is an odd question. I couldn't get bottom there with a church steeple."

"You think so, do you?"

The very tone of the question shook my confidence. That was what Mr. Bixby was expecting. He left, without saying anything more. I began to imagine all sorts of things. Mr. Bixby, unknown to me, of course, sent somebody down to the forecastle with some mysterious instructions to the leadsmen, another messenger was sent to whisper among the officers, and then Mr. Bixby went into hiding behind a smoke-stack where he could observe results. Presently the captain stepped out on the hurricane-deck; next the chief mate appeared; then a clerk. Every moment or two a straggler was added to my audience; and before I got to the head of the island I had fifteen or twenty people assembled down there under my nose. I began to wonder what the trouble was. As I started across, the captain glanced aloft at me and said, with a sham uneasiness in his deep voice:

"Where is Mr. Bixby?"

"Gone below, sir."

But that did the business for me. My imagination began to construct dangers out of nothing, and they multiplied faster than I could keep the run of them. All at once I imagined I saw shoal water ahead! The wave of coward agony that surged through me then came near dislocating every joint in me. All my confidence in that crossing vanished. I seized the bell-rope; then dropped it, ashamed; seized it again; dropped it once more; clutched it tremblingly once again, and pulled it so feebly that I could hardly hear the stroke myself. Captain and mate sang out instantly, and both together:

"Starboard lead there! and quick about it!"

This was another shock. I began to climb the wheel like a squirrel; but I would hardly get the boat started to port before I would see new dangers on that side, and away I would spin to the other; only to find perils accumulating to starboard, and be crazy to get to port again. Then came the leadsman's sepulchral cry:

"D-e-e-p four!"

Deep four in a bottomless crossing! The terror of it took my breath away.

"M-a-r-k three! M-a-r-k three! Quarter-less-three! Half twain!"

This was frightful! I seized the bell-ropes and stopped the engines.

"Quarter twain! Quarter twain! *Mark* twain!"

I was helpless. I did not know what in the world to do. I was quaking from head to foot, and I could have hung my hat on my eyes, they stuck out so far.

"Quarter-*less*-twain! Nine-and-a-*half*!"

We were *drawing* nine! My hands were a nerveless flutter. I could not ring a bell intelligibly with them. I flew to the speaking-tube and shouted to the engineer:

"Oh, Ben, if you love me, *back* her! Quick, Ben! Oh, back the immortal *soul* out of her!"

I heard the door close gently. I looked around, and there stood Mr. Bixby, smiling a bland, sweet smile. Then the audience on the hurricane-deck sent up a thundergust of humiliating laughter. I saw it all, now, and I felt meaner than the meanest man in human history. I laid in the lead, set the boat in her marks, came ahead on the engines, and said:

"It was a fine trick to play on an orphan, *wasn't* it? I suppose I'll never hear the last of how I was ass enough to heave the lead at the head of 66."

"Well, no, you won't, maybe. In fact I hope you won't; for I want you to learn something by that experience. Didn't you *know* there was no bottom in that crossing?"

"Yes, sir, I did."

"Very well, then. You shouldn't have allowed me or anybody else to shake your confidence in that knowledge. Try to remember that. And another thing: when you get into a dangerous place, don't turn coward. That isn't going to help matters any."

It was a good enough lesson, but pretty hardly learned. Yet about the hardest part of it was that for months I so often had to hear a phrase which I had conceived a particular distaste for. It was, "Oh, Ben, if you love me, back her!"

IN MY preceding chapters I have tried, by going into the minutiæ of the science of piloting, to carry the reader step by step to a comprehension of what the science consists of; and at the same time I have tried to show him that it is a very curious and wonderful science, too, and very worthy of his attention. If I have seemed to love my subject, it is no surprising thing, for I loved the profession far better than any I have followed since, and I took a measureless pride in it. The reason is plain: a pilot, in those days, was the only unfettered and entirely independent human being that lived on the earth. Kings are but the hampered servants of parliament and the people; parliaments sit in chains forged by their constituency; the editor of a newspaper cannot be independent, but must work with one hand tied behind him by party and patrons, and be content to utter only half or two-thirds of his mind; no clergyman is a free man and may speak the whole truth, regardless of his parish's opinions; writers of all kinds are manacled servants of the public. We write frankly and fearlessly, but then we "modify" before we print. In truth, every man and woman and child has a master, and worries and frets in servitude; but, in the day I write of, the Mississippi pilot had *none*. The captain could stand upon the hurricane-deck, in the pomp of a very brief authority, and give him five or six orders while the vessel backed into the stream, and then that skipper's reign was over. The moment that the boat was under way in the river, she was under the sole and unquestioned control of the pilot. He could do with her exactly as he pleased, run her when and whither he chose, and tie her up to the bank whenever his judgment said that that course was best. His movements were entirely free; he consulted no one, he received commands from nobody, he promptly resented even the merest suggestions. Indeed, the law of the United States forbade him to listen to commands or suggestions, rightly considering that the pilot necessarily knew better how to handle the boat than anybody could tell him. So here was the novelty of a king without a keeper, an absolute monarch who was absolute in sober truth and not by a fiction of words.

# IX

## *Extra Lessons and a Catastrophe*

DURING the two or two and a half years of my apprenticeship I served under many pilots, and had experience of many kinds of steamboatmen and many varieties of steamboats; for it was not always convenient for Mr. Bixby to have me with him, and in such cases he sent me with somebody else. I am to this day profiting somewhat by that experience; for in that brief, sharp schooling, I got personally and familiarly acquainted with about all the different types of human nature that are to be found in fiction, biography, or history. The fact is daily borne in upon me that the average shore-employment requires as much as forty years to equip a man with this sort of an education. When I say I am still profiting by this thing, I do not mean that it has constituted me a judge of men—no, it has not done that, for judges of men are born, not made. My profit is various in kind and degree, but the feature of it which I value most is the zest which that early experience has given to my later reading. When I find a well-drawn character in fiction or biography I generally take a warm personal interest in him, for the reason that I have known him before—met him on the river.

The figure that comes before me oftenest, out of the shadows of that vanished time, is that of Brown, of the steamer *Pennsylvania*—the man referred to in a former chapter, whose memory was so good and tiresome. He was a middle-aged, long, slim, bony, smooth-shaven, horse-faced, ignorant, stingy, malicious, snarling, fault-hunting, mote-magnifying tyrant. I early got the habit of coming on watch with dread at my heart. No matter how good a time I might have been having with the off-watch below, and no matter how high my spirits might be when I started aloft, my soul became lead in my body the moment I approached the pilot-house.

I often wanted to kill Brown, but this would not answer. A cub had to take everything his boss gave, in the way of vigorous comment and criticism; and we all believed that there was a United States law making it a penitentiary offense to strike or threaten a pilot who was on duty. However, I could *imagine* myself killing Brown; there was no law against that; and that was the thing I used always to do the moment I was abed. Instead of going over my river in my mind, as was my duty, I threw business aside for pleasure, and killed Brown. I killed Brown every night for months; not in old, stale, commonplace ways, but in new and picturesque ones—ways that were sometimes surprising for freshness of design and ghastliness of situation and environment.

Brown was *always* watching for a pretext to find fault; and if he could find no plausible pretext, he would invent one. He would scold you for shaving a shore, and for not shaving it; for hugging a bar, and for not hugging it; for "pulling down" when not invited, and for *not* pulling down when not invited, for firing up without orders, and for waiting *for* orders. In a word, it was his invariable rule to find fault with *everything* you did; and another invariable rule of his was to throw all his remarks (to you) into the form of an insult.

Finally, I got into serious trouble. Brown was steering; I was "pulling down." It was shortly after I had helped my younger brother come aboard the *Pennsylvania* as an assistant "mud-clerk." Henry appeared on the hurricane-deck, and shouted to Brown to stop at some landing or other, a mile or so below. Brown gave no intimation that he had heard anything. But that was his way: he never condescended to take notice of an under-clerk. The wind was blowing; Brown was deaf (although he always pretended he wasn't), and I very much doubted if he had heard the order. If I had had two heads, I would have spoken; but as I had only one, it seemed judicious to take care of it; so I kept still.

Presently, sure enough, we went sailing by that plantation. Captain Klinefelter appeared on deck, and said:

"Let her come around, sir, let her come around. Didn't Henry tell you to land here?"

"*No*, sir!"

"I sent him up to do it."

"He *did* come up; and that's all the good it done, the dod-derned fool. He never said anything."

"Didn't *you* hear him?" asked the captain of me.

Of course I didn't want to be mixed up in this business, but there was no way to avoid it; so I said:

"Yes, sir."

I knew what Brown's next remark would be, before he uttered it. It was:

"Shut your mouth! You never heard anything of the kind."

I closed my mouth, according to instructions. An hour later Henry entered the pilot-house, unaware of what had been going on. He was a thoroughly inoffensive boy, and I was sorry to see him come, for I knew that Brown would have no pity on him. Brown began, straightway:

"Here! Why didn't you tell me we'd got to land at that plantation?"

"I did tell you, Mr. Brown."

"It's a lie!"

I said:

"You lie, yourself. He did tell you."

Brown glared at me in unaffected surprise; and for as much as a moment he was entirely speechless; then he shouted to me:

"I'll attend to your case in a half a minute!" then to Henry, "And you leave the pilot-house!"

It was pilot law, and must be obeyed. The boy started out, and even had his foot on the upper step outside the door, when Brown, with a sudden access of fury, picked up a ten-pound lump of coal and sprang after him; but I was between, with a heavy stool, and I hit Brown a good honest blow which stretched him out.

I had committed the crime of crimes—I had lifted my hand against a pilot on duty! I supposed I was booked for the penitentiary sure, and couldn't be booked any surer if I went on and squared my long account with this person while I had the chance; consequently I stuck to him and pounded him with my fists a considerable time. I do not know how long, the pleasure of it probably made it seem longer than it really was; but in the end he struggled free and jumped up and sprang to the wheel: a very natural solicitude, for, all this time, here was this steamboat tearing down the river at the rate of fifteen miles an hour and nobody at the helm! Yet, Eagle Bend was two miles wide at this bank-full stage, and correspondingly long and deep: and the boat was steering herself straight down the middle and taking no chances. Still, that was only luck, a body *might* have found her charging into the woods.

Perceiving at a glance that the *Pennsylvania* was in no danger, Brown gathered up the big spy-glass, war-club fashion, and ordered me out of the pilot-house with more than Comanche bluster. But I was not afraid of him now; so, instead of going, I tarried, and criticized his grammar. I reformed his ferocious speeches for him, and put them into good English, calling his attention to the advantage of pure English over the bastard dialect of the Pennsylvania collieries whence he was extracted. He could have done his part to admiration in a cross-fire of mere vituperation, of course; but he was not equipped for this species of controversy; so he presently laid aside his glass and took the wheel, muttering and shaking his head; and I retired to the bench. The racket had brought everybody to the hurricane-deck, and I trembled when I saw the old captain looking up from amid the crowd. I said to myself, "Now I *am* done for!" for although, as a rule, he was so fatherly and indulgent toward the boat's family, and so patient of minor shortcomings, he could be stern enough when the fault was worth it.

I tried to imagine what he *would* do to a cub pilot who had been guilty of such a crime as mine, committed on a boat guard-deep with costly freight and alive with passengers. Our watch was nearly ended. I thought I would go and hide somewhere till I got a chance to slide ashore. So I slipped out of the pilot-house, and down the steps, and around to the texas-door, and was in the act of gliding within, when the captain confronted me! I dropped my head, and he stood over me in silence a moment or two, then said impressively:

"Follow me."

I dropped into his wake; he led the way to his parlor in the forward end of the texas. We were alone, now. He closed the after door; then moved

slowly to the forward one and closed that. He sat
down; I stood before him. He looked at me some
little time, then said:

"So you have been fighting Mr. Brown?"

I answered meekly:

"Yes, sir."

"Do you know that is a very serious matter?"

"Yes, sir."

"Are you aware that this boat was plowing down
the river for fully five minutes with no one at the
wheel?"

"Yes, sir."

"Did you strike him first?"

"Yes, sir."

"What with?"

"A stool, sir."

"Hard?"

"Middling, sir."

"Did it knock him down?"

"He—he fell, sir."

"Did you follow up? Did you do anything more?"

"Yes, sir."

"What did you do?"

"Pounded him, sir."

"Pounded him?"

"Yes, sir."

"Did you pound him much? that is, severely?"

"One might call it that, sir, maybe."

"I'm deucèd glad of it! Hark ye, never mention
that I said that. You have been guilty of a great

crime; and don't you ever be guilty of it again, on this boat. *But*—lay for him ashore! Give him a good sound thrashing, do you hear? I'll pay the expenses. Now go—and mind you, not a word of this to anybody. Clear out with you! You've been guilty of a great crime, you whelp!"

I slid out, happy with the sense of a close shave and a mighty deliverance; and I heard him laughing to himself and slapping his fat thighs after I had closed his door.

When Brown came off watch he went straight to the captain, who was talking with some passengers on the boiler-deck, and demanded that I be put ashore in New Orleans—and added:

"I'll never turn a wheel on this boat again while that cub stays."

The captain said:

"But he needn't come round when you are on watch, Mr. Brown."

"I won't even stay on the same boat with him. *One* of us has got to go ashore."

"Very well," answered the captain, "let it be yourself," and resumed his talk with the passengers.

During the brief remainder of the trip I knew how an emancipated slave feels, for I was an emancipated slave myself.

WE LAY three days in New Orleans, but the captain did not succeed in finding another pilot, so he proposed that I should stand a daylight watch and leave the night watches to George Ealer. But I was afraid; I had never stood a watch of any sort by myself, and I believed I should be sure to get into trouble in the head of some chute, or ground the boat in a near cut through some bar or other. Brown remained in his place, but he would not travel with me. So the captain gave me an order on the captain of the *A. T. Lacey* for a passage to St. Louis, and said he would find a new pilot there and my steersman's berth could then be resumed. The *Lacey* was to leave a couple of days after the *Pennsylvania*.

The night before the *Pennsylvania* left, Henry and I sat chatting on a freight pile on the levee till midnight. The subject of the chat, mainly, was one which I think we had not exploited before—steamboat disasters. One was then on its way to us, little as we suspected it; the water which was to make the steam which should cause it was washing on past a point fifteen hundred miles up the river while we talked—but it would arrive at the right time and the right place. We doubted if persons not clothed with authority were of much use in cases of disaster, still they might be of *some* use; and if a disaster ever fell within our experience we would stick to the boat, and give such minor service as chance might throw to us. Henry remembered this when the disaster came, and acted accordingly.

The *Lacey* started up the river two days behind the *Pennsylvania*. We touched at Greenville, Mississippi, a couple of days out, and somebody shouted:

"The *Pennsylvania* is blown up at Ship Island, and a hundred and fifty lives lost!"

At Napoleon, Arkansas, the same evening, we got an extra, issued by a Memphis paper, which gave some particulars. It mentioned my brother, and said he was not hurt.

Further up the river we got a later extra. My brother was again mentioned, but this time as being hurt beyond help. We did not get full details of the catastrophe until we reached Memphis. This is the sorrowful story:

It was six o'clock on a hot summer morning. The *Pennsylvania* was creeping along, north of Ship Island, about sixty miles below Memphis, on a half-head of steam, towing a wood-flat which was fast being emptied. George Ealer was in the pilot-house—alone, I think; the second engineer and a striker had the watch in the engine-room; the second mate had the watch on deck; George Black, Mr. Wood, and my brother, clerks, were asleep, as were also Brown and the head engineer, the carpenter, the chief mate, and one striker; Captain Klinefelter was in the barber's chair, and the barber was preparing to shave him. There were a good many cabin passengers aboard, and three or four hundred deck passengers—so it was said at the time—and not very many of them were astir. The wood being nearly all out of the flat now, Ealer rang to "come ahead" full of steam, and the next moment four of the eight boilers exploded with a thunderous crash, and the whole forward third of the boat was hoisted toward the sky! The main part of the mass, with the chimneys, dropped upon the boat again, a mountain of riddled and chaotic rubbish—and then, after a little, fire broke out.

Many people were flung to considerable distances and fell in the river; among these were Mr. Wood and my brother and the carpenter. The carpenter was still stretched upon his mattress when he struck the water seventy-five feet from the boat. Brown, the pilot, and George Black, chief clerk, were never seen or heard of after the explosion. The barber's chair, with Captain Klinefelter in it and unhurt, was left with its back overhanging vacancy—everything forward of it, floor and all, had disappeared; and the stupefied barber, who was also unhurt, stood with one toe projecting over space, still stirring his lather unconsciously and saying not a word.

When George Ealer saw the chimneys plunging aloft in front of him, he knew what the matter was; so he muffled his face in the lapels of his coat, and pressed both hands there tightly to keep this protection in its place so that no steam could get to his nose or mouth. He had ample time to attend to these details while he was going up and returning. He presently landed on top of the unexploded boilers, forty feet below the former pilot-house, accompanied by his wheel and a rain of other stuff, and enveloped in a cloud of scalding steam. All of the many who breathed that steam died; none escaped.

But Ealer breathed none of it. He made his way to the free air as quickly as he could; and when the steam cleared away he returned and climbed up on the boilers again, and patiently hunted out each and every one of his chessmen and the several joints of his flute.

By this time the fire was beginning to threaten. Shrieks and groans filled the air. A great many persons had been scalded, a great many crippled; the explosion had driven an iron crowbar through one man's body—I think they said he was a priest. He did not die at once, and his sufferings were very dreadful. A young French naval cadet of fifteen, son of a French admiral, was fearfully scalded, but bore his tortures manfully. Both mates were badly scalded, but they stood to their posts, nevertheless. They drew the wood-boat aft, and they and the captain fought back the frantic herd of frightened immigrants till the wounded could be brought there and placed in safety first.

When Mr. Wood and Henry fell in the water they struck out for shore, which was only a few hundred yards away; but Henry presently said he believed he was not hurt (what an unaccountable error!) and therefore would swim back to the boat and help save the wounded. So they parted and Henry returned.

By this time the fire was making fierce headway, and several persons who were imprisoned under the ruins were begging piteously for help. All efforts to conquer the fire proved fruitless, so the buckets were presently thrown aside and the officers fell to with axes and tried to cut the prisoners out. A striker was one of the captives; he said he was not injured, but could not free himself, and when he saw that the fire was likely to drive away the workers he begged that some one would shoot him, and thus save him from the more dreadful death. The fire did drive the axmen away, and they had to listen, helpless, to this poor fellow's supplications till the flames ended his miseries.

The fire drove all into the wood-flat that could be accommodated there; it was cut adrift then, and it and the burning steamer floated down the river toward Ship Island. They moored the flat at the head of the island, and there, unsheltered from the blazing sun, the half-naked occupants had to remain, without food or stimulants, or help for their hurts, during the rest of the day. A steamer came along, finally, and carried the unfortunates to Memphis, and there the most lavish assistance was at once forthcoming. By this time Henry was insensible. The physicians examined his injuries and saw that they were fatal, and naturally turned their main attention to patients who could be saved.

Forty of the wounded were placed upon pallets on the floor of a great public hall, and among these was Henry. There the ladies of Memphis came every day, with flowers, fruits, and dainties and delicacies of many kinds, and there they remained and nursed the wounded. All the physicians stood watches there, and all the medical students; and the rest of the town furnished money, or whatever else was wanted. And Memphis knew how to do all these things well; for many a disaster like the *Pennsylvania's* had happened near her doors, and she was experienced, above all other cities on the river, in the gracious office of the Good Samaritan.

The sight I saw when I entered that large hall was new and strange to me. Two long rows of prostrate forms—more than forty in all—and every face and head a shapeless wad of loose raw cotton. It was a gruesome spectacle. I watched there six days and nights, and a very melancholy experience it was. There was one daily incident which was peculiarly depressing: this was the removal of the doomed to a chamber apart. It was done in order that the *morale* of the other patients might not be injuriously affected by seeing one of their number in the death agony. The fated one was always carried out with as little stir as possible, and the stretcher was always hidden from sight by a wall of assistants; but no matter: everybody knew what that cluster of bent forms, with its muffled step and its slow movement, meant; and all eyes watched it wistfully, and a shudder went abreast of it like a wave.

I saw many poor fellows removed to the "death-room," and saw them no more afterward. But I saw our chief mate carried thither more than once. His hurts were frightful, especially his scalds. He was clothed in linseed oil and raw cotton to his waist, and resembled nothing human. He was often out of his mind; and then his pains would make him rave and shout and sometimes shriek. Then, after a period of dumb exhaustion, his disordered imagination would suddenly transform the great apartment into a fore-castle, and the hurrying throng of nurses into the crew; and he would come to a sitting posture and shout, "Hump yourselves, *hump* yourselves, you petrifactions, snail-bellies, pall-bearers! going to be all *day* getting that hatful of freight out?" and supplement this explosion with a firmament obliterating irruption of profanity which nothing could stay or stop till his crater was empty. And now and then while these frenzies possessed him, he would tear off handfuls of the cotton and expose his cooked flesh to view. It was horrible. It was bad for the others, of course—this noise and these exhibitions; so the doctors tried to give him morphine to quiet him. But, in his mind or out of it, he would not take it. He said his wife had been killed by that treacherous drug, and he would die before he would take it. He suspected that the doctors were concealing it in his ordinary medicines and in his water, so he ceased from putting either to his lips. Once, when he had been without water during two sweltering days, he took the dipper in his hand, and the sight of the limpid fluid, and the misery of his thirst, tempted him almost beyond his strength; but he mastered himself and threw it away, and after that he allowed no more to be brought near him. Three times I saw him carried to the death-room, insensible and supposed to be dying; but each time he revived, cursed his attendants, and demanded to be taken back among his comrades. He lived to be mate of a steamboat again.

But he was the only one who went to the death-room and returned alive. Dr. Peyton, a principal physician, and rich in all the attributes that go to constitute high and flawless character, did all that educated judgment and trained skill could do for Henry; but, as the newspapers had said in the beginning, his hurts were past help. On the evening of the sixth day his wandering mind busied itself with matters far away, and his nerveless fingers "picked at his coverlet." His hour had struck; we bore him to the death-room, poor boy.

IN DUE course I got my license. I was a pilot, full-fledged from April 1859 until the Spring of 1861. I dropped into casual employments; no misfortunes resulting, intermittent work gave place to steady and protracted engagements. Time drifted smoothly and prosperously on, and I supposed—and hoped—that I was going to follow the river the rest of my days, and die at the wheel when my mission was ended. But by and by the war came, commerce was suspended, my occupation was gone.

# X

## *A Campaign That Failed*

YOU HAVE heard from a great many people who
did something in the war; is it not fair and right
that you listen a little moment to one who started
out to do something in it, but didn't? Thousands
entered the war, got just a taste of it, and then
stepped out again permanently. These, by their
very numbers, are respectable, and are therefore entitled to a sort of voice—not a loud one, but a modest one; not a boastful one, but an apologetic one.
They ought not to be allowed much space among
better people—people who did something. I grant
that; but they ought at least to be allowed to state
why they didn't do anything, and also to explain
the process by which they didn't do anything. Surely this kind of light must have a sort of value.

Out West there was a good deal of confusion in
men's minds during the first months of the great
trouble—a good deal of unsettledness, of leaning
first this way, then that, then the other way. It was
hard for us to get our bearings.

I was piloting on the Mississippi when the news
came that South Carolina had gone out of the Union on the 20th of December, 1860. In the summer
of 1861, the first wash of the wave of war broke

upon the shores of Missouri. Our state was invaded by the Union forces. They took possession of St. Louis, Jefferson Barracks, and some other points. The Governor, who was Claib Jackson, issued his proclamation calling out fifty thousand militia to repel the invader.

I was visiting in Hannibal. Several of us got together in a secret place by night and formed ourselves into a military company. One Tom Lyman, a young fellow of a good deal of spirit but of no military experience, was made captain; I was made second lieutenant. We had no first lieutenant; I do not know why; it was long ago. There were fifteen of us. By the advice of an innocent connected with the organization we called ourselves the Marion Rangers. I do not remember that any one found fault with the name. I did not; I thought it sounded quite well. The young fellow who proposed this title was perhaps a fair sample of the kind of stuff we were made of. He was young, ignorant, good-natured, well-meaning, trivial, full of romance, and given to reading chivalric novels and singing forlorn love-ditties. He had some pathetic little nickel-plated aristocratic instincts, and detested his name, which was Dunlap; detested it, partly because it was nearly as common in that region as Smith, but mainly because it had a plebeian sound to his ear. So he tried to ennoble it by writing it in this way: *d'Unlap.* That contented his eye, but left his ear unsatisfied, for people gave the new name the same old pronunciation—emphasis on the front end of it. He then did the bravest thing that can be imagined—a thing to make one shiver when one remembers how the world is given to resenting shams and affectations; he began to write his name so: *d'Un Lap.*

That is one sample of us. Another was Ed Stevens, son of the town jeweler—trim-built, handsome, graceful, neat as a cat; bright, educated, but given over entirely to fun. There was nothing serious in life to him. As far as he was concerned, this military expedition of ours was simply a holiday. I should say that about half of us looked upon it in the same way; not consciously, perhaps, but unconsciously. We did not think; we were not capable of it. As for myself, I was full of unreasoning joy to be done with turning out of bed at midnight and then four in the morning for a while; grateful to have a change, new scenes, new occupations, a new interest. In my thoughts that was as far as I went; I did not go into the details; as a rule, one doesn't at twenty-four.

Another sample was Smith, the blacksmith's apprentice. This vast donkey had some pluck, of a slow and sluggish nature, but a soft heart; at one time he would knock a horse down for some impropriety, and at another he would get homesick and cry. However, he had one ultimate credit to his count which some of us hadn't; he stuck to the w‍ and was killed in battle at last.

Jo Bowers, another sample, was a good-nature‍

huge, flax-headed lubber; lazy, sentimental, full of harmless brag, a grumbler by nature; an experienced, industrious, ambitious, and often quite picturesque liar, and yet not a successful one, for he had had no intelligent training, but was allowed to come up just any way. This life was serious enough to him, and seldom satisfactory. But he was a good fellow, anyway, and the boys all liked him. He was made orderly sergeant; Stevens was made corporal.

These samples will answer—and they are quite fair ones. Well, this herd of cattle started for the war. What could you expect of them? They did as well as they knew how; but, really, what was justly to be expected of them? Nothing, I should say. That is what they did.

We waited for a dark night, for caution and secrecy were necessary; then, toward midnight, we stole in couples and from various directions to the Griffith place, beyond the town; from that point we set out together on foot. Hannibal lies at the extreme southeastern corner of Marion County, on the Mississippi River; our objective point was the hamlet of New London, ten miles away, in Ralls County.

The first hour was all fun, all idle nonsense and laughter. But that could not be kept up. The steady trudging came to be like work; the play had somehow oozed out of it; the stillness of the woods and the somberness of the night began to throw a depressing influence over the spirits of the boys, and presently the talking died out and each person shut himself up in his own thoughts. During the last half of the second hour nobody said a word.

Now we approached a log farm-house where, according to report, there was a guard of five Union soldiers. Lyman called a halt; and there, in the deep gloom of the overhanging branches, he began to whisper a plan of assault upon that house, which made the gloom more depressing than it was before. It was a crucial moment; we realized, with a cold suddenness, that here was no jest—we were standing face to face with actual war. We were equal to the occasion. In our response there was no hesitation, no indecision: we said that if Lyman wanted to meddle with those soldiers, he could go ahead and do it; but if he waited for us to follow him, he would wait a long time.

Lyman urged, pleaded, tried to shame us, but it had no effect. Our course was plain, our minds were made up: we would flank the farm-house—go out around. And that was what we did.

We struck into the woods and entered upon a rough time, stumbling over roots, getting tangled in vines, and torn by briers. At last we reached an open place in a safe region, and sat down, blown and hot, to cool off and nurse our scratches and bruises. Lyman was annoyed, but the rest of us were cheerful; we had flanked the farm-house, we had made our first military movement, and it was a success; we had nothing to fret about, we were feeling just the other way. Horse-play and laughing began again; the expedition was become a holiday frolic once more.

Then we had two more hours of dull trudging and ultimate silence and depression; then, about dawn, we straggled into New London, soiled, heel-blistered, fagged with our little march, and all of us except Stevens in a sour and raspy humor and privately down on the war. We stacked our shabby old shotguns in Colonel Ralls's barn, and then went in a body and breakfasted with that veteran of the Mexican War. Afterward he took us to a distant meadow, and there in the shade of a tree we listened to an old-fashioned speech from him, full of gunpowder and glory, full of that adjective-piling, mixed metaphor and windy declamation which were regarded as eloquence in that ancient time and that remote region; and then he swore us upon the Bible to be faithful to the State of Missouri and to drive all invaders from her soil, no matter whence they might come or under what flag they might march.

Then we formed in line of battle and marched four miles to a shady and pleasant piece of woods on the border of the far-reaching expanses of a flowery prairie. It was an enchanting region for war—our kind of war.

We pierced the forest about half a mile, and took up a strong position, with some low, wooded, and rocky hills behind us, and a purling, limpid creek in front. Straightway, half the command were in swimming and the other half fishing. The ass with the French name gave this position a romantic title, but it was too long, so the boys shortened and simplified it to Camp Ralls.

We occupied an old maple-sugar camp, whose half-rotted troughs were still propped against the trees. A long corn-crib served for sleeping-quarters for the battalion. On our left, half a mile away, were Mason's farm and house; and he was a friend to the cause. Shortly after noon the farmers began to arrive from several directions, with mules and horses for our use, and these they lent us for as long as the war might last, which they judged would be about three months. The animals were of all sizes, all colors, and all breeds. They were mainly young and frisky, and nobody in the command could stay on them long at a time; for we were town boys, and ignorant of horsemanship.

I will anticipate here sufficiently to say that we did learn to ride, after some day's practice, but never well. We could not learn to like our animals; they were not choice ones, and most of them had annoying peculiarities of one kind or another.

However, I will get back to where I was—our first afternoon in the sugar-camp. The sugar-troughs came very handy as horse-troughs, and we had plenty of corn to fill them with. I ordered Sergeant Bowers to feed my mule; but he said that if I reckoned he went to war to be a dry-nurse to a mule, it wouldn't take me very long to find out my mistake.

I believed that this was insubordination, but I was full of uncertainties about everything military, and so I let the thing pass, and went and ordered Smith, the blacksmith's apprentice, to feed the mule; but he merely gave me a large, cold, sarcastic grin, such as an ostensibly seven-year-old horse gives you when you lift his lip and find he is fourteen, and turned his back on me. I then went to the captain, and asked if it were not right and proper and military for me to have an orderly. He said it was, but as there was only one orderly in the corps, it was but right that he, himself, should have Bowers on his staff. Bowers said he wouldn't serve on anybody's staff; and if anybody thought he could make him, let him try it. So, of course, the thing had to be dropped; there was no other way.

Next, nobody would cook; it was considered a degradation; so we had no dinner. We lazied the rest of the pleasant afternoon away, some dozing under the trees, some smoking cob-pipes and talking sweethearts and war, some playing games. By late supper-time all hands were famished; and to meet the difficulty all hands turned to, on equal footing, and gathered wood, built fires, and cooked the meal. Afterward everything was smooth for a while; then trouble broke out between the corporal and the sergeant, each claiming to rank the other. Nobody knew which was the higher office; so Lyman had to settle the matter by making the rank of both officers equal.

For a time life was idly delicious, it was perfect; there was nothing to mar it. Then came some farmers with an alarm one day. They said it was rumored that the enemy were advancing in our direction from over Hyde's prairie. The result was a sharp stir among us, and general consternation. It was a rude awakening from our pleasant trance. The rumor was simply a rumor—nothing definite about it; so, in the confusion, we did not know which way to retreat. Lyman was for not retreating at all in these uncertain circumstances; but he found that if he tried to maintain that attitude he would fare badly, for the command were in no humor to put up with insubordination. So he yielded the point and called a council of war—to consist of himself and the three other officers; but the privates made such a fuss about being left out that we had to allow them to remain, for they were already present, and doing the most of the talking too. The question was, which way to retreat; but all were so flurried that nobody seemed to have even a guess to offer. Except Lyman. He explained in a few calm words that, inasmuch as the enemy were approaching from over Hyde's prairie, our course was simple: all we had to do was not to retreat *toward* him; any other direction would answer our needs perfectly. Everybody saw in a moment how true this was, and how wise; so Lyman got a great many compliments. It was now decided that we should fall back on Mason's farm.

It was after dark by this time, and as we could not know how soon the enemy might arrive, it did not seem best to try to take the horses and things with us; so we only took the guns and ammunition, and started at once. The route was very rough and hilly and rocky, and presently the night grew very black and rain began to fall; so we had a troublesome time of it, struggling and stumbling along in the dark; and soon some person slipped and fell, and then the next person behind stumbled over him and fell, and so did the rest, one after the other; and then Bowers came, with the keg of powder in his arms, while the command were all mixed together, arms and legs, on the muddy slope; and so he fell, of course, with the keg, and this started the whole detachment down the hill in a body, and they landed in the brook at the bottom in a pile, and each that was undermost pulling the hair and scratching and biting those that were on top of him; and those that were being scratched and bitten scratching and biting the rest in their turn, and all saying they would die before they would ever go to war again if they ever got out of this brook this time, and the invader might rot for all they cared, and the country along with him—and all such talk as that, which was dismal to hear and take part in, in such smothered, low voices, and such a grisly dark place and so wet, and the enemy, maybe, coming any moment.

The keg of powder was lost, and the guns, too; so the growling and complaining continued straight along while the brigade pawed around the pasty hillside and slopped around in the brook hunting for these things; consequently we lost considerable time at this; and then we heard a sound, and held our breath and listened, and it seemed to be the enemy coming, though it could have been a cow, for it had a cough like a cow; but we did not wait, but left a couple of guns behind and struck out for Mason's again as briskly as we could scramble along in the dark. But we got lost presently among the rugged little ravines, and wasted a deal of time finding the way again, so it was after nine when we reached Mason's stile at last; and then before we could open our mouths to give the countersign several dogs came bounding over the fence, with great riot and noise, and each of them took a soldier by the slack of his trousers and began to back away with him. We could not shoot the dogs without endangering the persons they were attached to; so we had to look on helpless at what was perhaps the most mortifying spectacle of the Civil War. There was light enough, and to spare, for the Masons had now run out on the porch with candles in their hands. The old man and his son came and undid the dogs without difficulty, all but Bowers's; but they couldn't undo his dog, they didn't know his combination; he was of the bull kind, and seemed to be set with a Yale time-lock; but they got him loose at last with some scalding water, of which Bowers got his share and returned thanks. Peterson Dunlap afterward made up a fine name for this engagement, and also for the night march which preceded it, but both have long ago faded out of my memory.

We now went into the house, and they began to ask us a world of questions, whereby it presently came out that we did not know anything concerning who or what we were running from; so the old gentleman made himself very frank, and said we were a curious breed of soldiers, and guessed we could be depended on to end up the war in time, because no government could stand the expense of the shoe leather we should cost it trying to follow us around. "Marion *Rangers*! good name, b'gosh!" said he. And wanted to know why we hadn't had a picket-guard at the place where the road entered the prairie, and why we hadn't sent out a scouting party to spy out the enemy and bring us an account of his strength, and so on, before jumping up and stampeding out of a strong position upon a mere vague rumor—and so on, and so forth, till he made us all feel shabbier than the dogs had done, not half so enthusiastically welcomed. So we went to bed shamed and low-spirited; except Stevens. Soon Stevens began to devise a garment for Bowers which could be made to automatically display his battle-scars to the grateful, or conceal them from the envious, according to his occasions; but Bowers was in no humor for this, so there was a fight, and when it was over Stevens had some battle-scars of his own to think about.

Then we got a little sleep. But after all we had gone through, our activities were not over for the night; for about two o'clock in the morning we heard a shout of warning from down the lane, accompanied by a chorus from all the dogs, and in a moment everybody was up and flying around to find out what the alarm was about. The alarmist was a horseman who gave notice that a detachment of Union soldiers was on its way from Hannibal with orders to capture and hang any bands like ours which it could find, and said we had no time to lose. Farmer Mason was in a flurry this time himself. He hurried us out of the house with all haste, and sent one of his Negroes with us to show us where to hide ourselves and our telltale guns among the ravines half a mile away. It was raining heavily.

We struck down the lane, then across some rocky pasture-land which offered good advantages for stumbling; consequently we were down in the mud most of the time, and every time a man went down he blackguarded the war, and the people that started it, and everybody connected with it, and gave himself the master dose of all for being so foolish as to go into it. At last we reached the wooded mouth of a ravine, and there we huddled ourselves under the streaming trees, and sent the Negro back home. It was a dismal and heartbreaking time. We were like to be drowned with the rain, deafened with the howling wind and the booming thunder, and blinded by the lightning. It was, indeed, a wild night.

The drenching we were getting was misery enough, but a deeper misery still was the reflection that the halter might end us before we were a day older. A death of this shameful sort had not occurred to us as being among the possibilities of war. It took the romance all out of the campaign, and turned our dreams of glory into a repulsive nightmare. As for doubting that so barbarous an order had been given, not one of us did that.

The long night wore itself out at last, and then the Negro came to us with the news that the alarm had manifestly been a false one, and that breakfast would soon be ready. Straightway we were light-hearted again, and the world was bright, and life as full of hope and promise as ever.

The mongrel child of philology named this night's refuge Camp Devastation, and not a soul objected. The Masons gave us a Missouri country breakfast, in Missourian abundance, and we needed it: hot biscuits; hot "wheat bread," prettily criss-crossed in a lattice pattern on top; hot corn-pone; fried chicken; bacon, coffee, eggs, milk, buttermilk, etc.; and the world may be confidently challenged to furnish the equal of such a breakfast, as it is cooked in the South.

We stayed several days at Mason's; and after all these years the memory of the dullness, and still-ness, and lifelessness of that slumberous farm-house still oppresses my spirit as with a sense of the presence of death and mourning. There was nothing to do, nothing to think about; there was no interest in life. So at last it was with something very like joy that we received news that the enemy were on our track again. With a new birth of the old warrior spirit we sprang to our places in line of battle and fell back on Camp Ralls.

Captain Lyman had taken a hint from Mason's talk, and he now gave orders that our camp should be guarded against surprise by the posting of pickets. I was ordered to place a picket at the forks of the road in Hyde's prairie. Night shut down black and threatening. I told Sergeant Bowers to go out to that place and stay till midnight; and, just as I was expecting, he said he wouldn't do it. I tried to get others to go, but all refused. This kind of thing sounds odd now, and impossible, but there was no surprise in it at the time. On the contrary, it seemed a perfectly natural thing to do. There were scores of little camps scattered over Missouri where the same thing was happening. These camps were composed of young men who had been born and reared to a sturdy independence, and who did not know what it meant to be ordered around by Tom, Dick, and Harry, whom they had known familiarly all their lives, in the village or on the farm. It is quite within the probabilities that this same thing was happening all over the South. We never tried to establish a watch at night again, as far as I remember, but we generally kept a picket out in the daytime.

In that camp the whole command slept on the

corn in the big corn-crib; and there was usually a general row before morning, for the place was full of rats, and they would scramble over the boys' bodies and faces, annoying and irritating everybody; and now and then they would bite someone's toe, and the person who owned the toe would start up and magnify his English and begin to throw corn in the dark. The ears were half as heavy as bricks, and when they struck they hurt. The persons struck would respond, and inside of five minutes every man would be locked in a death-grip with his neighbor. There was a grievous deal of blood shed in the corn-crib, but this was all that was spilt while I was in the war.

Our scares were frequent. Every few days rumors would come that the enemy were approaching. In these cases we always fell back on some other camp of ours; we never stayed where we were. But the rumors always turned out to be false.

The rest of my war experience was of a piece with what I have already told of it. We kept monotonously falling back upon one camp or another, and eating up the farmers and their families. They ought to have shot us; on the contrary, they were as hospitably kind and courteous to us as if we had deserved it.

The last camp which we fell back upon was in a hollow near to the village of Florida, where I was born—in Monroe County. Here we were warned one day that a Union colonel was sweeping down on us with a whole regiment at his heel. This looked decidedly serious. Our boys went apart and consulted; then we went back and told the other companies present that the war was a disappointment to us, and we were going to disband. They were getting ready themselves to fall back on some place or other, and we were only waiting for our commanding officer in Missouri, General Tom Harris, who was expected to arrive at any moment; so they tried to persuade us to wait a little while, but the majority of us said no, we were accustomed to falling back, and didn't need any of Tom Harris's help; we could get along perfectly well without him—and save time, too. So about half of our fifteen, including myself, left on the instant; the others yielded to persuasion and stayed—stayed through the war.

An hour later we met General Harris on the road, with two or three people in his company—his staff, probably, but we could not tell; none of them were in uniform; uniforms had not come into vogue among us yet. Harris ordered us back; but we told him there was a Union colonel coming with a whole regiment in his wake, and it looked as if there was going to be a disturbance; so we had concluded to go home. He raged a little, but it was of no use; our minds were made up. We had done our share.

IN TIME I came to know that Union colonel whose coming frightened me out of the war and crippled

the Southern cause to that extent—General Grant.[1]
I came within a few hours of seeing him when he
was as unknown as I was myself; at a time when
anybody could have asked, "Grant?—Ulysses S.
Grant? I don't recall hearing that name before."

The thoughtful will not throw this war paper of
mine lightly aside as being valueless. It has this value: it is a not unfair picture of what went on in
many and many a militia camp in the first months
of the rebellion, when the green recruits were without discipline, without the steadying and hearten-
ing influence of trained leaders; when all their circumstances were new and strange, and charged with
exaggerated terrors, and before the invaluable experience of actual collision in the field had turned
them from rabbits into soldiers. If this side of the
picture of that early day has not before been put
into history, then history has been to that degree
incomplete, for it had and has its rightful place
there. There was more Bull Run material scattered
through the early camps of this country than exhibited itself at Bull Run. And yet it learned its trade
presently, and helped to fight the great battles later.
I could have become a soldier myself if I had waited. I had got part of it learned; I knew more about
retreating than the man that invented retreating.

[1]The fact was that Grant didn't arrive in the Salt River
area until three weeks after the Marion Rangers had left it.

# XI

## *Across Plains and Deserts*

THE CAMPAIGN that failed ended in June, 1861. Later the same summer, that old St. Louis friend of Orion, Edward Bates, then a member of Lincoln's first Cabinet, got him the place of Secretary of the new Territory of Nevada, and Orion and I cleared for that country in the overland stagecoach, I paying the fares. We crossed the plains and deserts and mountains of the West, two thousand miles of ceaseless rush and rattle and clatter, by night and by day, and never a lapse of interest!

Orion's office was of such majesty that it concentrated in itself the duties and dignities of Treasurer, Comptroller, Secretary of State, and Acting Governor in the Governor's absence. A salary of eighteen hundred dollars a year and the title of "Mr. Secretary," gave to the great position an air of wild and imposing grandeur. I was young and ignorant, and I envied my brother. I coveted his distinction and his financial splendor, but especially the long, strange journey he was going to make. He was going to travel! I never had been away from home,[1] and that word

[1] As earlier chapters of the present book have made clear, Sam Clemens had visited New York, Washington, D.C., St. Louis, Cincinnati, and points between, and had for several years piloted on the Mississippi River.

"travel" had a seductive charm for me. Pretty soon he would be hundreds and hundreds of miles away on the great plains and deserts, and among the mountains of the Far West, and would see buffaloes and Indians, and prairie-dogs, and antelopes, and have all kinds of adventures, and maybe get hanged or scalped, and have ever such a fine time, and write home and tell us all about it, and be a hero. And he would see the gold-mines and the silver-mines, and maybe go about of an afternoon when his work was done, and pick up two or three pailfuls of shining slugs and nuggets of gold and silver on the hillside. And by and by he would become very rich, and return home by sea, and be able to talk as calmly about San Francisco and the ocean and "the isthmus" as if it was nothing of any consequence to have seen those marvels face to face. What I suffered in contemplating his happiness, pen cannot describe. And so, when he offered me, in cold blood, the sublime position of private secretary under him, it appeared to me that the heavens and the earth passed away, and the firmament was rolled together as a scroll! I had nothing more to desire. My contentment was complete. At the end of an hour or two I was ready for the journey. Not much packing up was necessary, because we were going in the overland stage from the Missouri frontier to Nevada, and passengers were only allowed a small quantity of baggage apiece. There was no Pacific railroad in those fine times—not a single rail of it.

I only proposed to stay in Nevada three months—
I had no thought of staying longer than that. I
meant to see all I could that was new and strange,
and then hurry home to business. I little thought
that I would not see the end of that three-month
pleasure excursion for six or seven uncommonly
long years!

I dreamed all night about Indians, deserts, and
silver bars, and in due time, next day, we took shipping at the St. Louis wharf on board a steamboat
bound up the Missouri River.

WE WERE six days going from St. Louis to "St.
Joe"—a trip that was so dull, and sleepy, and event-
less that it left no more impression on my memory
than if its duration had been six minutes instead of
that many days. No record is left in my mind, now,
concerning it, but a confused jumble of savage-
looking snags, which we deliberately walked over
with one wheel or the other; and of the reefs which
we butted and butted, and then retired from and
climbed over in some softer place; and of sand-bars
which we roosted on occasionally, and rested, and
then got out our crutches and sparred over.

The first thing we did on that glad evening that
landed us at St. Joseph was to find the stage-office,
and pay a hundred and fifty dollars apiece for tickets per overland coach to Carson City, Nevada.

The next morning, bright and early, we took a
hasty breakfast, and hurried to the starting-place.

Then an inconvenience presented itself which we had not properly appreciated before, namely, that one cannot make a heavy traveling trunk stand for twenty-five pounds of baggage—because it weighs a good deal more. But that was all we could take— twenty-five pounds each. So we had to snatch our trunks open, and make a selection in a good deal of a hurry. We put our lawful twenty-five pounds apiece all in one valise, and shipped the trunks back to St. Louis again. It was a sad parting, for now we had no swallow-tail coats and white kid gloves to wear at Pawnee receptions in the Rocky Mountains, and no stove-pipe hats nor patent-leather boots, nor anything else necessary to make life calm and peaceful. We were reduced to a war-footing. Each of us put on a rough, heavy suit of clothing, woolen army shirt and "stogy" boots included; and into the valise we crowded a few white shirts, some underclothing and such things. My brother, the Secretary, took along about four pounds of United States statutes and six pounds of Unabridged Dictionary; for we did not know—poor innocents—that such things could be bought in San Francisco on one day and received in Carson City the next. I was armed to the teeth with a pitifully small Smith & Wesson's seven-shooter, which carried a ball like a homeopathic pill, and it took the whole seven to make a dose for an adult. But I thought it was grand. It appeared to me to be a dangerous weapon. It only had one fault—you could not hit anything with it. One of our "conductors" practiced awhile on a cow with it, and as long as she stood still and behaved herself she was safe; but as soon as she went to moving about, and he got to shooting at other things, she came to grief. The Secretary had a small-sized Colt's revolver strapped around him for protection against the Indians, and to guard against accidents he carried it uncapped. Mr. George Bemis was dismally formidable. George Bemis was our fellow traveler. We had never seen him before. He wore in his belt an old original "Allen" revolver, such as irreverent people called a "pepper-box." Simply drawing the trigger back, cocked and fired the pistol. As the trigger came back, the hammer would begin to rise and the barrel to turn over, and presently down would drop the hammer, and away would speed the ball. To aim along the turning barrel and hit the thing aimed at was a feat which was probably never done with an "Allen" in the world. But George's was a reliable weapon, nevertheless, because, as one of the stage-drivers afterward said, "If she didn't get what she went after, she would fetch something else."

By eight o'clock everything was ready to go, and we were on the other side of the river. We jumped into the stage, the driver cracked his whip, and we bowled away and left "the States" behind us. It was a superb summer morning, and all the landscape was brilliant with sunshine. There was a freshness and breeziness, too, and an exhilarating sense of emancipation from all sorts of cares and responsibilities, that almost made us feel that the years we had spent in the close, hot city, toiling and slaving, had been wasted and thrown away. We were spinning along through Kansas, and in the course of an hour and a half we were fairly abroad on the Great Plains. Just here the land was rolling—a grand sweep of regular elevations and depressions as far as the eye could reach—like the stately heave and swell of the ocean's bosom after a storm. And everywhere were corn fields, accenting with squares of deeper green this limitless expanse of grassy land. But presently this sea upon dry ground was to lose its "rolling" character and stretch away for seven hundred miles as level as a floor!

Our coach was a great swinging and swaying stage, of the most sumptuous description—an imposing cradle on wheels. It was drawn by six handsome horses, and by the side of the driver sat the "conductor," the legitimate captain of the craft; for it was his business to take charge and care of the mails, baggage, express matter, and passengers. We three were the only passengers, this trip. We sat on the back seat, inside. About all the rest of the coach was full of mail-bags—for we had three days' delayed mails with us. Almost touching our knees, a perpendicular wall of mail matter rose up to the roof. There was a great pile of it strapped on top of the stage, and both the fore and hind boots were full. We had twenty-seven hundred pounds of it aboard, the driver said—"a little for Brigham, and Carson, and 'Frisco, but the heft of it for the Injuns, which is powerful troublesome 'thout they get plenty of truck to read." But as he just then got up a fearful convulsion of his countenance which was suggestive of a wink being swallowed by an earthquake, we guessed that his remark was intended to be facetious, and to mean that we would unload the most of our mail matter somewhere on the Plains and leave it to the Indians, or whosoever wanted it.

We changed horses every ten miles, all day long, and fairly flew over the hard, level road. We jumped out and stretched our legs every time the coach stopped, and so the night found us still vivacious and unfatigued.

About an hour and a half before daylight we were bowling along smoothly over the road—so smoothly that our cradle only rocked in a gentle, lulling way, that was gradually soothing us to sleep, and dulling our consciousness—when something gave away under us! We were dimly aware of it, but indifferent to it. The coach stopped. We heard the driver and conductor talking together outside, and rummaging for a lantern, and swearing because they could not find it—but we had no interest in whatever had happened, and it only added to our comfort to think of those people out there at work in the murky night, and we snug in our nest. But presently, by the sounds, there seemed to be an examination going on, and then the driver's voice said:

"By George, the thoroughbrace is broke!"

This startled me broad awake—as an undefined sense of calamity is always apt to do. I said to myself: "Now, a thoroughbrace is probably part of a horse; and doubtless a vital part, too, from the dismay in the driver's voice. Leg, maybe—and yet how could he break his leg waltzing along such a road as this? No, it can't be his leg. That is impossible, unless he was reaching for the driver. Now, what could be the thoroughbrace of a horse, I wonder? Well, whatever comes, I shall not air my ignorance in this crowd, anyway."

Just then the conductor's face appeared at a lifted curtain, and his lantern glared in on us and our wall of mail matter. He said:

"Gents, you'll have to turn out a spell. Thoroughbrace is broke."

We climbed out into a chill drizzle, and felt ever so homeless and dreary. When I found that the thing they called a "thoroughbrace" was the massive combination of belts and springs which the coach rocks itself in, I said to the driver:

"I never saw a thoroughbrace used up like that, before, that I can remember. How did it happen?"

"Why, it happened by trying to make one coach carry three days' mail—that's how it happened," said he. "And right here is the very direction which is wrote on all the newspaper-bags which was to be put out for the Injuns for to keep 'em quiet. It's most uncommon lucky, becuz it's so nation dark I

should 'a' gone by unbeknowns if that thoroughbrace hadn't broke."

I knew that he was in labor with another of those
winks of his, though I could not see his face, because he was bent down at work; and wishing him a
safe delivery, I turned to and helped the rest get out
the mail-sacks. It made a great pyramid by the road-
side when it was all out. When they had mended
the thoroughbrace we filled the two boots again, but
put no mail on top, and only half as much inside as
there was before. The conductor bent all the seat-
backs down, and then filled the coach just half full
of mail-bags from end to end. We objected loudly
to this, for it left us no seats. But the conductor was
wiser than we, and said a bed was better than seats,
and, moreover, this plan would protect his tho-
roughbraces. We never wanted any seats after that.
The lazy bed was infinitely preferable. I had many
an exciting day, subsequently, lying on it reading
the statutes and the dictionary, and wondering how
the characters would turn out.

The conductor said he would send back a guard
from the next station to take charge of the abandoned mail-bags, and we drove on.

It was now just dawn; and as we stretched our
cramped legs full length on the mail sacks, and
gazed out through the windows across the wide
wastes of greensward clad in cool, powdery mist, to
where there was an expectant look in the eastern
horizon, our perfect enjoyment took the form of a

tranquil and contented ecstasy. The stage whirled along at a spanking gait, the breeze flapping curtains and suspended coats in a most exhilarating way; the cradle swayed and swung luxuriously, the pattering of the horses' hoofs, the cracking of the driver's whip, and his "Hi-yi! g'lang!" were music; the spinning ground and the waltzing trees appeared to give us a mute hurrah as we went by, and then slack up and look after us with interest, or envy, or something; and as we lay and smoked the pipe of peace and compared all this luxury with the years of tiresome city life that had gone before it, we felt that there was only one complete and satisfying happiness in the world, and we had found it.

After breakfast, at some station whose name I have forgotten, we three climbed up on the seat behind the driver, and let the conductor have our bed for a nap. And by and by, when the sun made me drowsy, I lay down on my face on top of the coach, grasping the slender iron railing, and slept for an hour more. That will give one an appreciable idea of those matchless roads. Instinct will make a sleeping man grip a fast hold of the railing when the stage jolts, but when it only swings and sways, no grip is necessary. Overland drivers and conductors used to sit in their places and sleep thirty or forty minutes at a time, on good roads, while spinning along at the rate of eight or ten miles an hour. I saw them do it, often. There was no danger about it; a sleeping man *will* seize the irons in time when the coach jolts. These men were hard worked, and it was not possible for them to stay awake all the time.

By and by we passed through Marysville, and over the Big Blue and Little Sandy; thence about a mile, and entered Nebraska. About a mile further on, we came to the Big Sandy—one hundred and eighty miles from St. Joseph.

As the sun was going down, we saw the first specimen of an animal known familiarly over two thousand miles of mountain and desert—from Kansas clear to the Pacific Ocean—as the "jackass rabbit." He is well named. He is just like any other rabbit except that he is from one-third to twice as large, has longer legs in proportion to his size, and has the most preposterous ears that ever were mounted on any creature *but* a jackass. When he is sitting quiet, thinking about his sins, or is absent minded or unapprehensive of danger, his majestic ears project above him conspicuously; but the breaking of a twig will scare him nearly to death, and then he tilts his ears back gently and starts for home. All you can see, then, for the next minute, is his long gray form stretched out straight and "streaking it" through the low sagebrush, head erect, eyes right, and ears just canted a little to the rear, but showing you where the animal is, all the time, the same as if he carried a jib. Now and then he makes a marvelous spring with his long legs, high over the stunted sagebrush, and scores a leap that would make a horse envious. Then, shortly, he settles down to a long, graceful "lope," and shortly he mysteriously disappears. He has crouched behind a sagebush, and will sit there and listen and tremble until you get within six feet of him, when he will get under way again. But one must shoot at this creature once, if he wishes to see him throw his heart into his heels, and do the best he knows how. He is frightened clear through, now, and he lays his long ears down on his back, straightens himself out like a yardstick every spring he makes, and scatters miles behind him with an easy indifference that is enchanting.

Our party made this specimen "hump himself," as the conductor said. The Secretary started him with a shot from the Colt; I commenced spitting at him with my weapon; and all in the same instant the old "Allen's" whole broadside let go with a rattling crash, and it is not putting it too strong to say that the rabbit was frantic! He dropped his ears, set up his tail, and left for San Francisco at a speed which can only be described as a flash and a vanish!

I do not remember where we first came across "sagebrush," but as I have been speaking of it I may as well describe it. This is easily done, for if the reader can imagine a gnarled and venerable live oak tree reduced to a little shrub two feet high, with its rough bark, its foliage, its twisted boughs, all complete, he can picture the "sagebrush" exactly. Often, on lazy afternoons in the mountains I have lain on the ground with my face under a sagebush, and entertained myself with fancying that the gnats among its foliage were lilliputian birds, and that the ants marching and countermarching about its base were lilliputian flocks and herds, and myself some vast loafer from Brobdingnag waiting to catch a little citizen and eat him.

It is an imposing monarch of the forest in exquisite miniature, is the "sagebrush." Its foliage is a grayish green, and gives that tint to mountain and desert. It smells like our domestic sage, and "sage-tea" made from it tastes like the sage-tea which all boys are so well acquainted with. The sagebrush is a singularly hardy plant, and grows right in the midst of deep sand, and among barren rocks where nothing else in the vegetable world would try to grow, except "bunch-grass." The sagebushes grow from three to six or seven feet apart, all over the mountains and deserts of the Far West, clear to the borders of California. There is not a tree of any kind in the deserts, for hundreds of miles—there is no vegetation at all in a regular desert, except the sagebrush and its cousin the "greasewood," which is so much like the sagebrush that the difference amounts to little. Campfires and hot suppers in the deserts would be impossible but for the friendly sagebrush. Its trunk is as large as a boy's wrist (and from that up to a man's arm), and its crooked branches are half as large as its trunk—all good, sound, hard wood, very like oak.

When a party camps, the first thing to be done is to cut sagebrush; and in a few minutes there is an opulent pile of it ready for use. A hole a foot wide, two feet deep, and two feet long, is dug, and sagebrush chopped up and burned in it till it is full to the brim with glowing coals; then the cooking begins, and there is no smoke, and consequently no swearing. Such a fire will keep all night, with very little replenishing; and it makes for a very sociable campfire, and one around which the most impossible reminiscences sound plausible, instructive, and profoundly entertaining.

Sagebrush is very fair fuel, but as a vegetable it is a distinguished failure. Nothing can abide the taste of it but the jackass and his illegitimate child, the mule. But their testimony to its nutritiousness is worth nothing, for they will eat pine-knots, or anthracite coal, or brass filings, or lead pipe, or old bottles, or anything that comes handy, and then go off looking as grateful as if they had had oysters for dinner.

I was about to say, when diverted from my subject, that occasionally one finds sagebushes five or six feet high, and with a spread of branch and foliage in proportion, but two or two and a half feet is the usual height.

# XII

## *On Toward the Setting Sun*

As the sun went down and the evening chill came
on, we made preparation for bed. We stirred
up the hard leather letter sacks, and also the knotty
canvas bags of printed matter (knotty and uneven
because of projecting ends and corners of magazines,
boxes and books). We stirred them up and redis-
posed them in such a way as to make our bed as
level as possible. And we *did* improve it, too,
though after all our work it had an upheaved and
billowy look about it, like a little piece of a stormy
sea. Next we hunted up our boots from odd nooks
among the mailbags where they had settled, and
put them on. Then we got down our coats, vests,
pantaloons and heavy woolen shirts, from the arm-
loops where they had been swinging all day, and
clothed ourselves in them—for, there being no ladies either at the stations or in the coach, and the
weather being hot, we had looked to our comfort by
stripping to our underclothing, at nine o'clock in
the morning. Then we smoked a final pipe, and
swapped a final yarn; after which, we put the pipes,
tobacco, and bag of coin in snug holes and caves
among the mailbags, and then fastened down the
coach curtains all around and made the place as

"dark as the inside of a cow," as the conductor phrased it in his picturesque way. It was certainly as dark as anyplace could be; nothing was even dimly visible in it. And finally, we rolled ourselves up like silkworms, each person in his own blanket, and sank peacefully to sleep.

Whenever the stage stopped to change horses, we would wake up, and then try to recollect where we were—and succeed—and in a minute or two the stage would be off again, and we likewise. We began to get into country, now, threaded here and there with little streams. These had high, steep banks on each side, and every time we flew down one bank and scrambled up the other, our party inside got mixed somewhat. First we would all be down in a pile at the forward end of the stage, nearly in a sitting posture, and in a second we would shoot to the other end, and stand on our heads. And we would sprawl and kick, too, and ward off ends and corners of mailbags that came lumbering over us and about us; and as the dust rose from the tumult, we would all sneeze in chorus, and the majority of us would grumble, and probably say some hasty thing, like: "Take your elbow out of my ribs!—can't you quit crowding?"

Still, all things considered, it was a very comfortable night. It wore gradually away, and when at last a cold gray light was visible through the puckers and the chinks in the curtains, we yawned and stretched with satisfaction, shed our cocoons, and felt that we had slept as much as was necessary. By and by, as the sun rose up and warmed the world, we pulled off our clothes and got ready for breakfast. We were just pleasantly in time, for five minutes afterward the driver sent the weird music of his bugle winding over the grassy solitudes, and presently we detected a low hut or two in the distance. Then the rattling of the coach, the clatter of our six horses' hoofs, and the driver's crisp commands, awoke to a louder emphasis, and we went sweeping down on the station at our smartest speed.

We jumped out in undress uniform. The driver tossed his gathered reins out on the ground, gaped and stretched complacently, drew off his heavy buckskin gloves with great deliberation and insufferable dignity—taking not the slightest notice of a dozen solicitous inquiries after his health, and humbly facetious and flattering accostings, and obsequious tenders of service, from five or six hairy and half-civilized station keepers and hostlers who were nimbly unhitching our steeds and bringing the fresh team out of the stables—for, in the eyes of the stage-driver of that day, station keepers and hostlers were a sort of good enough low creatures, useful in their place, but not the kind of beings which a person of distinction could afford to concern himself with; while, on the contrary, in the eyes of the station keeper and the hostler, the stage driver was a hero— a great and shining dignitary, the world's favorite son, the envy of the people.

The station buildings were long, low huts, made of sun-dried, mud-colored bricks, laid up without mortar (*adobes*, the Spaniards call these bricks, and Americans shorten it to '*dobies*). The roofs, which had no slant to them worth speaking of, were thatched and then sodded or covered with a thick layer of earth, and from this sprung a pretty rank growth of weeds and grass. It was the first time we had ever seen a man's front yard on top of his house. The buildings consisted of barns, stable-room for twelve or fifteen horses, and a hut for an eating-room for passengers. This latter had bunks in it for the station keeper and a hostler or two.

By the door of the station-keeper's den, outside, was a tin washbasin, on the ground. Near it was a pail of water and a piece of yellow bar-soap, and from the eaves hung a hoary blue woolen shirt, significantly—but this latter was the station-keeper's private towel, and only two persons in all the party might venture to use it—the stage-driver and the conductor. The latter would not, from a sense of decency; the former would not, because he did not choose to encourage the advances of a station keeper. We had towels—in the valise; they might as well have been in Sodom and Gomorrah. We (and the conductor) used our handkerchiefs, and the driver his pantaloons and sleeves.

The furniture of the hut was neither gorgeous nor much in the way. The rocking chairs and sofas were not present, and never had been, but they were represented by two three-legged stools, a pine-board bench four feet long, and two empty candle-boxes. The table was but a greasy board on stilts, and the tablecloth and napkins had not come—and they were not looking for them, either. A battered tin platter, a knife and fork, and a tin pint cup, were at each man's place, and the driver had a queens-ware saucer that had seen better days. Of course, this duke sat at the head of the table.

The station-keeper up-ended a disk of last week's bread, of the shape and size of an old-time cheese, and carved some slabs from it which were as good as Nicholson pavement, and tenderer.

He sliced off a piece of bacon for each man, but only the experienced old hands made out to eat it, for it was condemned army bacon.

Then he poured for us a beverage which he called *"Slumgullion,"* and it is hard to think he was not inspired when he named it. It really pretended to be tea, but there was too much dish-rag, and sand, and old bacon-rind in it to deceive the intelligent traveler. He had no sugar and no milk—not even a spoon to stir the ingredients with.

We could not eat the bread or the meat, nor drink the *"Slumgullion."*

We gave up the breakfast, and paid our dollar apiece and went back to our mailbag bed in the coach, and found comfort in our pipes. Yet, right here we suffered the first diminution of our princely state. We left our six fine horses and took six mules in their place. But they were wild Mexican fellows, and a man had to stand at the head of each of them and hold him fast while the driver gloved and got himself ready. And when, at last, he grasped the reins and gave the word, the men sprung suddenly away from the mules' heads and the coach shot from the station as if it had issued from a cannon. How the frantic animals did scamper! It was a fierce gallop; and the gait never altered for a moment till we reeled off ten or twelve miles and swept up to the next collection of little station huts and stables.

So we flew along all day. At 2 P.M. the belt of timber that fringes the North Platte and marks its windings through the vast level floor of the Plains came in sight. At 4 P.M. we crossed a branch of the river, and at 5 P.M. we crossed the Platte itself, and landed at Fort Kearney, *fifty-six hours out from St. Joe*—THREE HUNDRED MILES!

Another night of alternate tranquillity and turmoil. But morning came, by and by. It was another glad awakening to fresh breezes, vast expanses of level greensward, bright sunlight, an impressive solitude utterly without visible human beings or human habitations, and an atmosphere of such amazing magnifying properties that trees that seemed close at hand were more than three miles away. We resumed undress uniform, climbed atop of the flying coach, dangled our legs over the side, shouted occasionally at our frantic mules, only to see them lay their ears back and scamper faster, tied our hats

on to keep our hair from blowing away, and level-
ed an outlook over the world-wide carpet about us
for things new and strange to gaze at. Even at this
day it thrills me through and through to think of
the life, the gladness and the wild sense of freedom
that used to make the blood dance in my veins on
those fine overland mornings!

Along about an hour after breakfast we saw the
first prairie-dog villages, the first antelope, and the
first wolf. If I remember rightly, this latter was a
regular *coyote* (pronounced "ky-*o*-te") of the farther
deserts. And if it *was*, he was not a pretty creature,
or respectable either, for I got well acquainted with
his race afterward, and can speak with confidence.
The coyote is a long, slim, sick and sorry-looking
skeleton with a gray wolf-skin stretched over it; a
bushy tail that forever sags down with a despairing
expression of forsakenness and misery; a furtive and
evil eye, and a long, sharp face with slightly lifted
lip and exposed teeth. He has a general slinking expression all over. The coyote is a living, breathing
allegory of Want. He is *always* hungry. He is always
poor, out of luck and friendless. The meanest creatures despise him. He is so spiritless and cowardly
that even while his exposed teeth are pretending a
threat, the rest of his face is apologizing for it. And
he is *so* homely!—so scrawny, and ribby, and coarse-
haired, and pitiful. When he sees you he lifts his lip
and lets a flash of his teeth out, and then turns a
little out of the course he was pursuing, depresses

his head a bit, and strikes a long, soft-footed trot through the sage-brush, glancing over his shoulder at you, from time to time, till he is about out of easy pistol range, and then he stops and takes a deliberate survey of you; he will trot fifty yards and stop again—another fifty and stop again; and finally the gray of his gliding body blends with the gray of the sagebrush, and he disappears. All this is when you make no demonstration against him; but if you do, he develops a livelier interest in his journey, and instantly electrifies his heels and puts such a deal of real estate between himself and your weapon, that by the time you have raised the hammer you see that you need a minie rifle, and by the time you have got him in line you need a rifled cannon, and by the time you have "drawn a bead" on him you see well enough that nothing but an unusually long-winded streak of lightning could reach him where he is now. But if you start a swift-footed dog after him, you will enjoy it ever so much—especially if it is a dog that has a good opinion of himself, and has been brought up to think he knows something about speed. The coyote will go swinging gently off on that deceitful trot of his, and every little while he will smile a fraudful smile over his shoulder that will fill that dog entirely full of encouragement and worldly ambition, and make him lay his head still lower to the ground, and stretch his neck further to the front, and pant more fiercely, and stick his tail out straighter behind, and move his furious legs with a yet wilder frenzy, and leave a broader and broader, and higher and denser cloud of desert sand smoking behind, and marking his long wake across the level plain! And all this time the dog is only a short twenty feet behind the coyote, and to save the soul of him he cannot understand why it is that he cannot get perceptibly closer; and he begins to get aggravated, and it makes him madder and madder to see how gently the coyote glides along and never pants or sweats or ceases to smile; and he grows still more and more incensed to see how shamefully he has been taken in by an entire stranger, and what an ignoble swindle that long, calm, soft-footed trot is; and next he notices that he is getting fagged, and that the coyote actually has to slacken speed a little to keep from running away from him—and *then* that town dog is mad in earnest, and he begins to strain and weep and swear, and paw the sand higher than ever, and reach for the coyote with concentrated and desperate energy. This "spurt" finds him six feet behind the gliding enemy, and two miles from his friends. And then, in the instant that a wild new hope is lighting up his face, the coyote turns and smiles blandly upon him once more, and with a something about it which seems to say: "Well, I shall have to tear myself away from you, bub—business is business, and it will not do for me to be fooling along this way all day"—and forthwith there is a rushing sound, and the sudden splitting of a long crack through the atmosphere, and behold that dog is solitary and alone in the midst of a vast solitude!

It makes his head swim. He stops, and looks all around; climbs the nearest sand mound, and gazes into the distance; shakes his head reflectively, and then, without a word, he turns and jogs along back to his train, and takes up a humble position under the hindmost wagon, and feels unspeakably mean, and looks ashamed, and hangs his tail at half-mast for a week. And for as much as a year after that, whenever there is a great hue and cry after a coyote, that dog will merely glance in that direction without emotion, and apparently observe to himself, "I believe I do not wish any of the pie."

We soon learned to recognize the sharp, vicious bark of the coyote as it came across the murky plain at night to disturb our dreams among the mail-sacks; and remembering his forlorn aspect and his hard fortune, made shift to wish him the blessed novelty of a long day's good luck and a limitless larder on the morrow.

Our new conductor (just shipped) had been without sleep for twenty hours. Such a thing was very frequent. From St. Joseph, Missouri, to Sacramento, California, by stagecoach, was close to nineteen hundred miles, and the trip was often made in fifteen days, but the time specified in the mail contracts, and required by the schedule, was eighteen or nineteen days, if I remember rightly. This was to make fair allowance for winter storms and snows, and all other unavoidable causes of detention. The stage company had everything under strict discipline and good system. Over each two hundred and fifty miles of road they placed an agent or superintendent, and invested him with great authority. His beat or jurisdiction of two hundred and fifty miles was called a "division." He purchased the horses, mules, harness, and food for men and beasts, and distributed these things among his stage stations, from time to time, according to his judgment of what each station needed. He erected station buildings and dug wells. He attended to the paying of the station keepers, hostlers, drivers, and blacksmiths, and discharged them whenever he chose. He was a very, very great man in his "division."

Next in rank and importance to the division agent came the "conductor." His beat was the same length as the agent's—two hundred and fifty miles. He sat with the driver, and (when necessary) rode that fearful distance, night and day, without other rest or sleep than what he could get perched thus on top of the flying vehicle. Think of it! He had absolute charge of the mails, express matter, passengers, and stagecoach, until he delivered them to the next conductor. Consequently he had to be a man of intelligence and real executive ability.

Next in *real* and official rank and importance, *after* the conductor, came my delight, the driver— next in real but not in *apparent* importance—for we have seen that in the eyes of the common herd the driver was to the conductor as an admiral is to the captain of the flagship. The driver's beat was pretty long, and his sleeping time at the stations pretty short, sometimes; and so, but for the grandeur of his position his would have been a sorry life, as well as a hard and a wearing one. We took a new driver every day or every night (for they drove backward and forward over the same piece of road all the time), and therefore we never got as well acquainted with them as we did with the conductors; and besides, they would have been above being familiar with such rubbish as passengers, anyhow, as a general thing. Still, we were always eager to get a sight of each and every new driver as soon as the watch changed, for each and every day we were either anxious to get rid of an unpleasant one, or loath to part with a driver we had learned to like.

The stationkeepers, hostlers, etc., were low, rough characters; and from western Nebraska to Nevada a considerable sprinkling of them might be fairly set down as outlaws—fugitives from justice, criminals whose best security was a section of country which was without law or even the pretense of it. When the "division agent" issued an order to one of these parties he did it with the full understanding that he might have to enforce it with a navy six-shooter.

At noon on the fifth day out, we arrived at the "Crossing of the South Platte," *alias* "Julesburg," *alias* "Overland City," four hundred and seventy miles from St. Joseph—the strangest, quaintest, fun-

niest frontier town that our untraveled eyes had
ever stared at and been astonished with.

It did seem strange enough to see a town again
after what appeared to us such a long acquaintance
with deep, still, almost lifeless and houseless solitude! We tumbled out into the busy street feeling
like meteoric people crumbled off the corner of
some other world, and wakened up suddenly in
this. For an hour we took as much interest in Overland City as if we had never seen a town before.
The reason we had an hour to spare was because we
had to change our stage (for a less sumptuous affair,
called a "mud wagon") and transfer the mail.

Presently we got under way again. We came to
the shallow, yellow, muddy South Platte, with its
low banks and its scattering flat sandbars and pygmy islands—a melancholy stream straggling through
the center of the enormous flat plain, and only
saved from being impossible to find with the naked
eye by its sentinel rank of scattering trees standing
on either bank. The Platte was "up," they said—
which made me wish that I could see it when it was
down, if it could look any sicker and sorrier. They
said it was a dangerous stream to cross now, because its quicksands were liable to swallow up horses, coach, and passengers if any attempt was made
to ford it. But the mails had to go, and we made the
attempt. Once or twice in midstream the wheels
sunk into the yielding sands so threateningly that
we half believed we had dreaded and avoided the

sea all our lives only to be shipwrecked in a "mud wagon" in the middle of a desert at last. But we dragged through and sped away toward the setting sun.

Next morning just before dawn, when about five hundred and fifty miles from St. Joseph, our mud-wagon broke down. We were delayed five hours.

In a little while all interest was taken up in stretching our necks and watching for the "pony rider"—the fleet messenger who sped across the continent from St. Joe to Sacramento, carrying letters nineteen hundred miles in eight days! Think of that for perishable horse and human flesh and blood to do! The pony rider was usually a little bit of a man, brimful of spirit and endurance. No matter what time of the day or night his watch came on, and no matter whether it was winter or summer, raining, snowing, hailing, or sleeting, or whether his "beat" was a level straight road or a crazy trail over mountain crags and precipices, or whether it led through peaceful regions or regions that swarmed with hostile Indians, he must be always ready to leap into the saddle and be off like the wind! There was no idling time for a pony rider when on duty. He rode fifty miles without stopping, by daylight, moonlight, starlight, or through the blackness of darkness—just as it happened. He rode a splendid horse that was born for a racer and fed and lodged like a gentleman; kept him at his utmost speed for ten miles, and then, as he came crashing up to the station where stood two men holding fast a fresh, impatient steed, the transfer of rider and mailbag was made in the twinkling of an eye, and away flew the eager pair and were out of sight before the spectator could get hardly the ghost of a look. Both rider and horse went "flying light." The rider's dress was thin, and fitted close; he wore a "roundabout," and a skullcap, and tucked his pantaloons into his boot-tops like a race-rider. He carried no arms—he carried nothing that was not absolutely necessary, for even the postage on his literary freight was worth *five dollars a letter*. He got but little frivolous correspondence to carry—his bag had business letters in it, mostly. His horse was stripped of all unnecessary weight, too. He wore a little wafer of a racing saddle, and no visible blanket. He wore light shoes, or none at all. The little flat mail pockets strapped under the rider's thighs would each hold about the bulk of a child's primer. They held many and many an important business chapter and newspaper letter, but these were written on paper as airy and thin as gold leaf, nearly, and thus bulk and weight were economized. The stagecoach traveled about a hundred to a hundred and twenty-five miles a day (in twenty-four hours), and the pony rider about two hundred and fifty. There were about eighty pony riders in the saddle night and day, stretching in a long, scattering procession from Missouri to California, forty flying eastward and forty to the west, and among them making four hundred gallant horses earn a stirring livelihood.

We had had a consuming desire, from the beginning, to see a pony rider, but somehow or other all that passed us and all that met us managed to streak by in the night, and so we heard only a whiz and a hail, and the swift phantom of the desert was gone before we could get our heads out of the windows. But now we were expecting one along every moment, and would see him in broad daylight. Presently the driver exclaims:

"HERE HE COMES!"

Every neck is stretched further, and every eye strained wider. Away across the endless dead level of the prairie a black speck appears against the sky, and it is plain that it moves. Well, I should think so! In a second or two it becomes a horse and rider, rising and falling, rising and falling—sweeping on toward us, nearer and nearer—growing more and more distinct, more and more sharply defined—nearer and still nearer, and the flutter of the hoofs comes faintly to the ear—another instant a whoop and a hurrah from our upper deck, a wave of the rider's hand, but no reply, and man and horse burst past our excited faces, and go swinging away like a belated fragment of a storm!

So sudden is it all, and so like a flash of unreal fancy, that but for the flake of white foam left quivering and perishing on a mail sack after the vision had flashed by and disappeared, we might have doubted whether we had seen any actual horse and man at all, maybe.

We rattled through Scott's Bluffs Pass, by and by. It was along here somewhere that we first came across genuine and unmistakable alkali water in the road, and we cordially hailed it as a first-class curiosity, and a thing to be mentioned with éclat in letters to the ignorant at home. This water gave the road a soapy appearance, and in many places the ground looked as if it had been whitewashed. I think the strange alkali water excited us as much as any wonder we had come upon yet, and I know we felt very conceited, and better satisfied with life after we had added it to our list of things which *we* had seen and some other people had not.

We passed Fort Laramie in the night, and on the seventh morning out we found ourselves in the Black Hills, with Laramie Peak at our elbow (apparently) looming vast and solitary—a deep, dark, rich indigo blue in color, so portentously did the old colossus frown under his beetling brows of storm-cloud. He was thirty or forty miles away, in reality, but he only seemed removed a little beyond the low ridge at our right. We breakfasted at Horse Shoe Station, six hundred and seventy-six miles out from St. Joseph. We had now reached hostile Indian country, and during the afternoon we passed Laparelle Station, and enjoyed great discomfort all the time we were in the neighborhood, being aware that many of the trees we dashed by at arm's length concealed a lurking Indian or two. During the preceding night an ambushed savage had sent a bullet through the pony rider's jacket, but he had ridden on, just the same, because pony riders were not allowed to stop and inquire into such things except when killed. As long as they had life enough left in them they had to stick to the horse and ride, even if the Indians had been waiting for them a week, and were entirely out of patience. About two hours and a half before we arrived at Laparelle Station, the keeper in charge of it had fired four times at an Indian, but he said with an injured air that the Indian had "skipped around so's to spile everything— and ammunition's blamed skurse, too." The most natural inference conveyed by his manner of speaking was, that in "skipping around," the Indian had taken an unfair advantage. The coach we were in had a neat hole through its front—a reminiscence of its last journey through this region. The bullet that made it wounded the driver slightly, but he did not mind it much. He said the place to keep a man "huffy" was down on the south Overland Trail, among the Apaches, before the company moved the stage line up on the northern route. He said the Apaches used to annoy him all of the time down there, and that he came as near as anything to starving to death in the midst of abundance, because they kept him so leaky with bullet holes that he "couldn't hold his vittles." This person's statements were not generally believed.

# XIII

## *The End of Our Long Journey*

WE SHUT the blinds down very tightly that first night in the hostile Indian country, and lay on our arms. We slept on them some, but most of the time we only lay on them. We did not talk much, but kept quiet and listened. It was an inky-black night, and occasionally it rained. We were among woods and rocks, hills and gorges—so shut in, in fact, that when we peeped through a chink in a curtain, we could discern nothing. The driver and conductor on top were still, too, or only spoke at long intervals, in low tones, as is the way of men in the midst of invisible dangers. We listened to rain-drops pattering on the roof; and the grinding of the wheels through the muddy gravel; and the low wailing of the wind; and all the time we had that absurd sense upon us, inseparable from travel at night in a close-curtained vehicle, the sense of remaining perfectly still in one place, notwithstanding the jolting and swaying of the vehicle, the trampling of the horses, and the grinding of the wheels. We listened a long time, with intent faculties and bated breath; every time one of us would relax, and draw a long sigh of relief and start to say something, a comrade would be certain to utter a sudden "Hark!" and instantly the experimenter was rigid and listening again. So the tiresome minutes and the decades of minutes dragged away, until at last our intense forms filmed over with a dulled consciousness, and we slept, if one might call such a condition by so strong a name—for it was a sleep set with a hair trigger. It was a sleep seething and teeming with such a weird and distressful confusion of shreds and fag ends of dreams—a sleep that was a chaos. Presently, dreams and sleep and the sullen hush of the night were startled by a ringing report, and cloven by *such* a long, wild, agonizing shrick! Then we heard—ten steps from the stage—

"Help! help! help!" It was our driver's voice.

"Kill him! Kill him like a dog!"

"I'm being murdered! Will no man lend me a pistol?"

"Look out! head him off! head him off!"

Two pistol shots; a confusion of voices and the trampling of many feet, as if a crowd were closing and surging together around some object; several heavy, dull blows, as with a club; a voice that said appealingly, "Don't, gentlemen, please don't—I'm a dead man!" Then a fainter groan, and another blow, and away sped the stage into the darkness, and left the grisly mystery behind us.

What a startle it was! Eight seconds would amply cover the time it occupied—maybe even five would do it. We only had time to plunge at a curtain and unbuckle and unbutton part of it in an awkward and hindering flurry, when our whip cracked sharply overhead, and we went rumbling and thundering away, down a mountain "grade."

We fed on that mystery the rest of the night—what was left of it, for it was waning fast. It had to remain a present mystery, for all we could get from the conductor in answer to our hails was something that sounded, through the clatter of the wheels, like, "Tell you in the morning!"

So we lit our pipes and opened the corner of a curtain for a chimney, and lay there in the dark, listening to each other's story of how he first felt and how many thousand Indians he first thought had hurled themselves upon us, and what his remembrance of the subsequent sounds was, and the order of their occurrence. And we theorized, too, but there was never a theory that would account for our driver's voice being out there, nor yet account for his Indian murderers talking such good English, if they *were* Indians.

So we chatted and smoked the rest of the night comfortably away, our boding anxiety being somehow marvelously dissipated by the real presence of something to be anxious *about*.

We never did get much satisfaction about that dark occurrence. All that we could make out of the odds and ends of the information we gathered in the morning, was that the disturbance occurred at a station; that we changed drivers there, and that the driver that got off there had been talking roughly about some of the outlaws that infested the region ("for there wasn't a man around there but had a price on his head and didn't dare show himself in the settlements," the conductor said); he had talked roughly about these characters, and ought to have "drove up there with his pistol cocked and ready on the seat alongside of him, and begun business himself, because any softy would know they would be laying for him."

That was all we could gather, and we could see that neither the conductor nor the new driver were much concerned about the matter. They plainly had little respect for a man who would deliver offensive opinions of people and then be so simple as to come into their presence unprepared to "back his judgment," as they pleasantly phrased the killing of any fellow-being who did not like said opinions. And likewise they plainly had a contempt for the man's poor discretion in venturing to rouse the wrath of such utterly reckless wild beasts as those outlaws—and the conductor added:

"I tell you it's as much as Slade himself wants to do!"

This remark created an entire revolution in my curiosity. I cared nothing now about the Indians, and I even lost interest in the murdered driver. There was much magic in that name, SLADE! Day or night, now, I stood always ready to drop any subject in hand, to listen to something new about Slade and his ghastly exploits. Even before we got to Overland

City, we had begun to hear about Slade and his "division" (for he was a "division agent") on the Overland; and from the hour we had left Overland City we had heard the drivers and conductors talk about only three things—"Californy," the Nevada silver mines, and this desperado Slade. Most of the talk was about Slade. We had gradually come to have a realizing sense of the fact that Slade was a man whose heart and hands and soul were steeped in the blood of offenders against his dignity; a man who awfully avenged all injuries, affronts, insults or slights, of whatever kind—on the spot if he could, years afterward if lack of earlier opportunity compelled it; a man whose hate tortured him day and night till vengeance appeased it—and not an ordinary vengeance either, but his enemy's absolute death—nothing less; a man whose face would light up with a terrible joy when he surprised a foe and had him at a disadvantage. A high and efficient servant of the Overland, an outlaw among outlaws and yet their relentless scourge, Slade was at once the most bloody, the most dangerous, and the most valuable citizen that inhabited the savage fastnesses of the mountains.

Slade was born in Illinois, of good parentage. At about twenty-six years of age he killed a man in a quarrel and fled the country. At St. Joseph, Missouri he joined one of the early California-bound emigrant trains, and was given the post of trainmaster. One day on the plains he had an angry dispute with one of his wagon drivers, and both drew their revolvers. But the driver was the quicker artist, and had his weapon cocked first. So Slade said it was a pity to waste life on so small a matter, and proposed that the pistols be thrown on the ground and the quarrel settled by a fistfight. The unsuspecting driver threw down his pistol—whereupon Slade laughed at his simplicity, and shot him dead!

He made his escape, and lived a wild life for a while, dividing his time between fighting Indians and avoiding an Illinois sheriff, who had been sent to arrest him for his first murder. It is said that in one Indian battle he killed three with his own hand, and afterward cut their ears off and sent them, with his compliments, to the chief of the tribe.

From a bloodthirstily interesting little Montana book[1] I take this paragraph:

While on the road, Slade held absolute sway. He would ride down to a station, get into a quarrel, turn the house out of windows, and maltreat the occupants most cruelly. The unfortunates had no means of redress, and were compelled to recuperate as best they could. On one of these occasions, it is said he killed the father of the fine little half-breed boy Jemmy, whom he adopted, and who lived with his widow after his execution. Stories of Slade's innumerable assaults, shootings, stabbings, and beatings, in which he was a principal actor, form part of the legends of the stage line. As for minor quarrels and shootings, it is absolutely certain that a minute history of Slade's life would be one long record of such practices.

[1] *The Vigilantes of Montana*, by Prof. Thos. J. Dimsdale.

In due time we rattled up to a stage station, and sat down to breakfast with a half-savage, half-civilized company of armed and full-bearded mountaineers, ranchmen and station employees. The most gentlemanly appearing, quiet, and affable officer we had yet found along the road in the Overland Company's service was the person who sat at the head of the table, at my elbow. Never youth stared and shivered as I did when I heard them call him SLADE![2]

Here was romance, and I sitting face to face with it!—looking upon it—touching it—hobnobbing with it, as it were! Here, right by my side, was the actual ogre who, in fights and brawls and various ways, *had taken the lives of twenty-six human beings*, or all men lied about him! I suppose I was the proudest stripling that ever traveled to see strange lands and wonderful people.

He was so friendly and so gentle-spoken that I warmed to him in spite of his awful history. It was hardly possible to realize that this pleasant person was the pitiless scourge of the outlaws, the raw-head-and-bloody-bones the nursing mothers of the mountains terrified their children with. And to this day I cannot remember anything remarkable about Slade except that his face was rather broad across

[2]True, the Clemens brothers' party did encounter "Captain" J. A. Slade, although they did so rather later in the journey than is indicated. Mark Twain based details in his account on his memories, a letter that Orion wrote him in 1871 reminiscing about the trip, and the book by Prof. Thos. J. Dimsdale which he has just quoted.

the cheekbones, and that the cheekbones were low and the lips peculiarly thin and straight. But that was enough to leave something of an effect upon me, for since then I seldom see a face possessing those characteristics without fancying that the owner of it is a dangerous man.

The coffee ran out. At least it was reduced to one tin cupful, and Slade was about to take it when he saw that my cup was empty. He politely offered to fill it, but although I wanted it, I politely declined. I was afraid he had not killed anybody that morning, and might be needing diversion. But still with firm politeness he insisted on filling my cup, and said I had traveled all night and better deserved it than he—and while he talked he placidly poured the fluid, to the last drop. I thanked him and drank it, but it gave me no comfort, for I could not feel sure that he would not be sorry, presently, that he had given it away, and proceed to kill me to distract his thoughts from the loss. But nothing of the kind occurred. We left him with only twenty-six dead people to account for, and I felt a tranquil satisfaction in the thought that in so judiciously taking care of No. 1 at that breakfast table I had pleasantly escaped being No. 27. Slade came out to the coach and saw us off, first ordering certain rearrangements of the mailbags for our comfort, and then we took leave of him, satisfied that we should hear of him again, and wondering in what connection.

And sure enough, two or three years afterward,

we did hear of him again. News came to the Pacific coast that the Vigilance Committee in Montana (whither Slade had removed from Rocky Ridge) had hanged him.

JUST beyond the breakfast station, we overtook a Mormon emigrant train of thirty-three wagons; and tramping wearily along while driving their herds of loose cows, were dozens of coarse-clad and sad-appearing men, women, and children, who had walked as they were walking now, day after day for eight lingering weeks, and in that time had compassed the distance our stage had come in *eight days and three hours*—seven hundred and ninety-eight miles! They were dusty and uncombed, hatless, bonnetless, and ragged, and they did look so tired!

After breakfast, we bathed in Horse Creek, a (previously) limpid, sparkling stream—an appreciated luxury, for it was very seldom that our furious coach halted long enough for an indulgence of that kind. We changed horses ten or twelve times in every twenty-four hours—changed mules, rather—six mules—and did it nearly every time in *four minutes*. It was lively work. As our coach rattled up to each station six harnessed mules stepped gaily from the stable; and in the twinkling of an eye, the old team was out and the new one in and we were off and away again.

During the afternoon we passed Devil's Gate, Independence Rock, Sweetwater Creek, and the

Devil's Gap. The latter were wild specimens of rugged scenery, and full of interest—*we were in the heart of the Rocky Mountains, now.*

In the night we sailed by a most notable curiosity, and one we had been hearing a good deal about for a day or two, and were suffering to see. This was what might be called a natural icehouse. It was August, now, and sweltering weather in the daytime, yet at one of the stations the men could scrape the soil on the hillside under the lee of a range of boulders, and at a depth of about six inches cut out pure blocks of ice—hard, compactly frozen, and clear as crystal!

Toward dawn we got under way again, and presently, as we sat with raised curtains enjoying our early morning smoke and contemplating the first splendor of the rising sun as it swept down the long array of mountain peaks, flushing and gilding crag after crag and summit after summit, as if the invisible Creator reviewed his gray veterans and they saluted with a smile, we hove in sight of South Pass City. The hotelkeeper, the postmaster, the blacksmith, the mayor, the constable, the city marshal, and the principal citizen and property holder, all came out and greeted us cheerily, and we gave him good day.

Two miles beyond South Pass City we saw for the first time that mysterious marvel which all Western untraveled boys have heard of and fully believe in, but are sure to be astounded at when they see it with their own eyes, nevertheless—banks of snow in dead summertime. We were now far up toward the sky, and knew all the time that we must presently encounter lofty summits clad in the "eternal snow" which was so commonplace a matter of mention in books, and yet when I did see it glittering in the sun on stately domes in the distance and knew the month was August and that my coat was hanging up because it was too warm to wear it, I was full as much amazed as if I never had heard of snow in August before.

In a little while quite a number of peaks swung into view with long claws of glittering snow clasping them; and with here and there, in the shade, down the mountainside, a little solitary patch of snow looking no larger than a lady's pocket handkerchief but being in reality as large as a "public square."

And now, at last, we were fairly in the renowned South Pass, and whirling gaily along high above the common world. We were perched on top of the extreme summit of the great range of the Rocky Mountains, toward which we were climbing, patiently climbing, ceaselessly climbing, for days and nights together.

We bowled along cheerily, and presently, at the very summit (though it had been all summit to us, and all equally level, for half an hour or more), we came to a spring which spent its water through two outlets and sent it in opposite directions. The con-

ductor said that one of those streams which we were
looking at was just starting on a journey westward
to the Gulf of California and the Pacific Ocean,
through hundreds and even thousands of miles of
desert solitudes. He said that the other was just
leaving its home among the snow peaks on a similar
journey eastward—and we knew that long after we
should have forgotten the simple rivulet it would
still be plodding its patient way down the mountainsides, and cañon beds, and between the banks
of the Yellowstone; and by and by would join the
broad Missouri and flow through unknown plains
and deserts and unvisited wildernesses; and add a
long and troubled pilgrimage among snags and
wrecks and sandbars; and enter the Mississippi.

We had been climbing up the long shoulders of
the Rocky Mountains for many tedious hours—we
started *down* them, now. And we went spinning
away at a round rate, too.

We left the snowy Wind River Mountains and
the Uinta Mountains behind, and sped away, always
through splendid scenery, but occasionally through
long ranks of white skeletons of mules and oxen—
monuments of the huge emigration of other days—
and here and there were up-ended boards or small
piles of stones which the driver said marked a resting place of more precious remains. It was the lone-
liest land for a grave! A land given to the coyote and
the raven—which is but another name for desolation
and utter solitude. On damp, murky nights, these

scattered skeletons gave forth a soft, hideous glow, like very faint spots of moonlight starring the vague desert. It was because of the phosphorus in the bones. But no scientific explanation could keep a body from shivering when he drifted by one of those ghostly lights and knew that a skull held it.

At midnight it began to rain, and I never saw anything like it—indeed, I did not even see this, for it was too dark. Meantime the stage was wandering about a plain with gaping gullies in it, for the driver could not see an inch before his face nor keep the road, and the storm pelted so pitilessly that there was no keeping the horses still. With the first abatement the conductor turned out with lanterns to look for the road, and the first dash he made was into a chasm about fourteen feet deep, his lantern following like a meteor. As soon as he touched bottom he sang out frantically:

"Don't come here!"

To which the driver, who was looking over the precipice where he had disappeared, replied, with an injured air: "Think I'm a dam' fool?"

The conductor was more than an hour finding the road—a matter which showed us how far we had wandered and what chances we had been taking. He traced our wheel tracks to the imminent verge of danger, in two places. I have always been glad that we were not killed that night. I do not know any particular reason, but I have always been glad.

In the morning, the tenth day out, we crossed

Green River, a fine, large, limpid stream—stuck in it, with the water just up to the top of our mail bed. At four in the afternoon we arrived on the summit of Big Mountain, fifteen miles from Salt Lake City, when all the world was glorified with the setting sun, and the most stupendous panorama of mountain peaks yet encountered burst on our sight. We looked out upon this sublime spectacle from under the arch of a brilliant rainbow! Even the Overland stage driver stopped his horses and gazed!

Half an hour or an hour later, we changed horses, and took supper with a Mormon "Destroying Angel." "Destroying Angels," as I understand it, are Latter-Day Saints who are set apart by the Church to conduct permanent disappearances of obnoxious citizens. I had heard a deal about these Mormon Destroying Angels and the dark and bloody deeds they had done, and when I entered this one's house I had my shudder all ready. But alas for all our romances, he was nothing but a loud, profane, offensive old blackguard! A lot of slatternly women flitted hither and thither in a hurry, with coffee-pots, plates of bread, and other appurtenances to supper, and these were said to be the wives of the Angel—or some of them at least. We did not tarry long, but hurried on to the home of the Latter-Day Saints, the stronghold of the prophets, the capital of the only absolute monarchy in America—Great Salt Lake City. As the night closed in we took sanctuary in the Salt Lake House and unpacked our baggage.

At the end of two days' sojourn, we left Great Salt Lake City hearty and well fed and happy. The accustomed coach life began again, now, and by midnight it almost seemed as if we never had been out of our snuggery among the mail sacks at all. We had made one alteration, however. We had provided enough bread, boiled ham, and hard-boiled eggs to last double the six hundred miles of staging we had still to do.

And it was comfort in those succeeding days to sit up and contemplate the majestic panorama of mountains and valleys spread out below us and to eat ham and hard-boiled eggs while our spiritual natures reveled alternately in rainbows, thunderstorms, and peerless sunsets. Nothing helps scenery like ham and eggs. Ham and eggs, and after these a pipe—an old, rank, delicious pipe—ham and eggs and scenery, a "down grade," a flying coach, a fragrant pipe and a contented heart—these make happiness. It is what all the ages have struggled for.

At eight in the morning we reached the remnant and ruin of what had been the important military station of "Camp Floyd," some forty-five or fifty miles from Salt Lake City. At 4 P.M. we had doubled our distance and were ninety or a hundred miles from Salt Lake. And now we entered upon one of that species of deserts whose concentrated hideousness shames the diffused and diluted horrors of Sahara—an "*alkali*" desert. For sixty-eight miles there was but one break in it. I do not remember that this was really a break; indeed, it seems to me that it was nothing but a watering depot *in the midst* of the stretch of sixty-eight miles. If my memory serves me, there was no well or spring at this place, but the water was hauled there by mule and ox teams. There was a stage station there. It was forty-five miles from the beginning of the desert, and twenty-three from the end of it.

We plowed and dragged and groped along, the whole livelong night, and at the end of this uncomfortable twelve hours we finished the forty-five-mile part of the desert and got to the stage station where the imported water was. The sun was just rising. It was easy enough to cross a desert in the night while we were asleep; and it was pleasant to reflect, in the morning, that we in actual person *had* encountered an absolute desert and could always speak knowingly of deserts in presence of the ignorant thenceforward. And it was pleasant also to reflect that this was not an obscure, back-country desert, but a very celebrated one, the metropolis itself, as you may say. All this was very well and very comfortable and satisfactory—but now we were to cross a desert in *daylight*. This was fine—novel—romantic—dramatically adventurous—*this*, indeed, was worth living for, worth traveling for!

This enthusiasm, this stern thirst for adventure, wilted under the sultry August sun and did not last above one hour. One poor little hour—and then we were ashamed that we had "gushed" so. The poetry was all in the anticipation—there is none in the reality. Imagine a vast, waveless ocean stricken dead and turned to ashes; imagine this solemn waste tufted with ash-dusted sage bushes; imagine the lifeless silence and solitude that belong to such a place; imagine a coach, creeping like a bug through the midst of this shoreless level, and sending up tumbled volumes of dust as if it were a bug that went by steam; imagine this aching monotony of toiling and plowing kept up hour after hour, and the shore still as far away as ever, apparently; imagine team, driver, coach, and passengers so deeply coated with ashes that they are all one colorless color; imagine ash drifts roosting above mustaches and eyebrows like snow accumulations on boughs and bushes. This is the reality of it.

Two miles and a quarter an hour for ten hours—that was what we accomplished. It was hard to bring the comprehension away down to such a snail-pace as that, when we had been used to making eight and ten miles an hour.

On the morning of the sixteenth day out from St. Joseph we arrived at the entrance of Rocky Cañon, two hundred and fifty miles from Salt Lake.

On the seventeenth day we passed the highest mountain peaks we had yet seen, and although the day was very warm the night that followed was wintry cold and blankets were next to useless.

On the eighteenth day we encountered the east-bound telegraph constructors at Reese River station and sent a message to his Excellency, Governor Nye at Carson City.

On the nineteenth day we crossed the Great American Desert—forty memorable miles of bottomless sand, into which the coach wheels sunk from six inches to a foot. We worked our passage most of the way across. That is to say, we got out and walked. It was a dreary pull and a long and thirsty one, for we had no water. From one extremity of this desert to the other, the road was white with the bones of oxen and horses.

Along the border of the desert lies Carson Lake, or the "Sink" of the Carson, a shallow, melancholy sheet of water some eighty or a hundred miles in circumference. Carson River empties into it and is lost—sinks mysteriously into the earth and never appears in the light of the sun again—for the lake has no outlet whatever.

There are several rivers in Nevada, and they all have this mysterious fate. They end in various lakes or "sinks" and that is the last of them.

We were approaching the end of our long journey. At noon of the twentieth day we would reach Carson City, the capital of Nevada Territory. We were not glad, but sorry. It had been a fine pleasure trip; we had fed fat on wonders every day; we were now well accustomed to stage life, and very fond of it; so the idea of coming to a standstill and settling down to a humdrum existence in a village was not agreeable, but on the contrary depressing.

Visibly our new home was a desert, walled in by barren, snow-clad mountains. There was not a tree in sight. There was no vegetation but the endless sagebrush and greasewood. All nature was gray with it. We were plowing through great deeps of powdery alkali dust that rose in thick clouds and floated across the plain like smoke from a burning house. We were coated with it like millers; so were the coach, the mules, the mailbags, the driver—we and the sagebrush and the other scenery were all one monotonous color. Long trains of freight wagons in the distance enveloped in ascending masses of dust suggested pictures of prairies on fire. These teams and their masters were the only life we saw. Otherwise we moved in the midst of solitude, silence, and desolation. Every twenty steps we passed the skeleton of some dead beast of burthen, with its dust-coated skin stretched tightly over its empty ribs. Frequently a solemn raven sat upon the skull or the hips and contemplated the passing coach with meditative serenity.

By and by Carson City was pointed out to us. It nestled in the edge of a great plain and was a sufficient number of miles away to look like an assemblage of mere white spots in the shadow of a grim range of mountains overlooking it, whose summits seemed lifted clear out of companionship and consciousness of earthly things.

We arrived, disembarked, and the stage went on.

# XIV

## *Landowners*

CARSON CITY was a "wooden" town; its population two thousand souls. The main street consisted of four or five blocks of little white frame
stores which were too high to sit down on, but not
too high for various other purposes; in fact, hardly
high enough. They were packed close together, side
by side, as if room were scarce in that mighty plain.
The sidewalk was of boards that were more or less
loose and inclined to rattle when walked upon. In
the middle of the town, opposite the stores, was the
"plaza," which is native to all towns beyond the
Rocky Mountains—a large, unfenced, level vacancy,
with a liberty pole in it, and very useful as a place
for public auctions, horse trades, and mass meet-
ings; and for teamsters to camp in. Two other sides
were faced by stores, offices, and stables. The rest of
Carson City was pretty scattering.

We were introduced to several citizens, at the
stage office and on the way up to the Governor's
from the hotel—among others, to a Mr. Harris, who
was on horseback; he began to say something, but
interrupted himself with the remark:

"I'll have to get you to excuse me a minute; yonder is the witness that swore I helped to rob the

California coach—a piece of impertinent intermeddling, sir, for I am not even acquainted with him."

Then he rode on over and began to rebuke the stranger with a six-shooter, and the stranger began to explain with another. When the pistols were emptied, the stranger resumed his work (mending a whiplash), and Mr. Harris rode on by with a polite nod, homeward bound, with a bullet through one of his lungs, and several through his hips; and from them ran little rivulets of blood that coursed down the horse's sides and made the animal look quite picturesque. I never saw Harris shoot a man after that but it recalled to mind my first day in Carson.

This was all we saw that day, for it was two o'clock, now, and according to custom the daily "Washoe Zephyr" set in; a soaring dust drift about the size of the United States set up edgewise came with it, and the capital of Nevada Territory disappeared from view. Still, there were sights to be seen which were not wholly uninteresting to newcomers; for the vast dust cloud was thickly freckled with things strange to the upper air—things living and dead, that flitted hither and thither, going and coming, appearing and disappearing among the rolling billows of dust—hats, chickens, and parasols sailing in the remote heavens; blankets, tin signs, sagebrush, and shingles a shade lower; doormats and buffalo robes lower still; shovels and coal scuttles on the next grade; glass doors, cats, and little children on the next; disrupted lumber yards, light

*Overland Stage stop, Carson City, Nevada.*
Courtesy of the Mark Twain Papers, The Bancroft Library

buggies, and wheelbarrows on the next; and down only thirty or forty feet above ground was a scurrying storm of emigrating roofs and vacant lots.

It was something to see that much. I could have seen more, if I could keep the dust out of my eyes.

The "Washoe Zephyr" (Washoe is a pet nickname for Nevada) is a peculiarly Scriptural wind, in that no man knoweth "whence it cometh." That is to say, where it *originates*. It comes right over the mountains from the West, but when one crosses the ridge he does not find any of it on the other side! It probably is manufactured on the mountaintop for the occasion, and starts from there. It is a pretty regular wind, in the summertime. Its office hours are from two in the afternoon until two the next morning; and anyone venturing abroad during those twelve hours needs to allow for the wind or he will bring up a mile or two to leeward of the point he is aiming at. And yet the first complaint a Washoe visitor to San Francisco makes, is that the sea winds blow so, there! There is a good deal of human nature in that.

We found the state palace of the Governor of Nevada Territory[1] to consist of a white frame one story house with two small rooms and a stanchion

[1]This was James W. Nye (1814–1876). He had served as president of the New York City police force from 1857 to 1860 before President Lincoln appointed him governor of Neveda Territory. He held the office until 1864, when Nevada was granted statehood, and he was elected to the United States Senate. He served until 1873.

supported shed in front—for grandeur; it compelled the respect of the citizen and inspired the Indians with awe. The newly arrived Chief and Associate Justices of the Territory, and other machinery of the government, were domiciled with less splendor. They were boarding around privately, and had their offices in their bedrooms.

The Secretary and I took quarters in the "ranch" of a worthy French lady by the name of Bridget O'Flannigan,[2] a camp follower of his Excellency the Governor. She had known him in his prosperity as commander-in-chief of the Metropolitan Police of New York, and she would not desert him in his adversity as Governor of Nevada. Our room was on the lower floor, facing the plaza; and when we had got our bed, a small table, two chairs, the government fireproof safe, and the unabridged dictionary into it, there was still room for a visitor; maybe two, but not without straining the walls.

We had a carpet and a genuine queen's-ware washbowl. Consequently we were hated without reserve by the other tenants of the O'Flannigan "ranch." When we added a painted oilcloth window curtain, we simply took our lives into our own hands. To prevent bloodshed I removed upstairs and took up quarters with the untitled plebeians in one of the fourteen white pine cot-bedsteads that stood

---

[2]"Bridget" was actually Mrs. M. Murphy. Her boarding house on the north side of the plaza, as Mark Twain says, housed a number of officials.

*Orion Clemens, when he was Secretary of
Nevada Territory.*
Courtesy of The Nevada Historical Society

in two long ranks in the one sole room of which the second story consisted.

It was a jolly company, the fourteen. They were principally voluntary camp followers of the Governor, who had joined his retinue by their own election at New York and San Francisco, and came along, feeling that in the scuffle for little territorial crumbs and offices they could not make their condition more precarious than it was, and might reasonably expect to make it better. They were popularly known as the "Irish Brigade," though there were only four or five Irishmen among all the Governor's retainers. Mrs. O'Flannigan was boarding and lodging them at ten dollars a week apiece.

It was the end of August, and the skies were cloudless and the weather superb. In two or three weeks I had grown wonderfully fascinated with the curious new country, and concluded to put off my return to "the States" awhile. I had grown well accustomed to wearing a damaged slouch hat, blue woolen shirt, and pants crammed into boot tops; and gloried in the absence of coat, vest, and braces. I felt quite rowdyish and "bully" (as the historian Josephus phrases it, in his fine chapter upon the destruction of the Temple). It seemed to me that nothing could be so fine and so romantic. I had become an officer of the government, but that was for mere sublimity. The office was an unique sinecure. I had nothing to do and no salary. I was the private secretary to his majesty the Secretary, and there was not yet writing enough for two of us. So Johnny Kinney and I devoted our time to amusement. He was the young son of an Ohio nabob and was out there for recreation. He got it. We had heard a world of talk about the marvelous beauty of Lake Tahoe, and finally curiosity drove us thither to see it. Three or four members of the Brigade had been there and located some timberlands on its shores and stored up a quantity of provisions in their camp. We strapped a couple of blankets on our shoulders and took an ax apiece and started— for we intended to take up a wood ranch or so ourselves and become wealthy. We were on foot. The reader will find it advantageous to go horseback. We were told that the distance was eleven miles. We tramped a long time on level ground, and then toiled laboriously up a mountain about a thousand miles high and looked over. No lake there. We descended on the other side, crossed the valley and toiled up another mountain three or four thousand miles high, apparently, and looked over again. No lake yet. We sat down tired and perspiring, and hired a couple of Chinamen to curse those people who had beguiled us. Thus refreshed, we presently resumed the march with renewed vigor and determination. We plodded on, two or three hours longer, and at last the lake burst upon us—a noble sheet of blue water lifted six thousand three hundred feet above the level of the sea, and walled in by a rim of snow-clad mountain peaks that towered aloft full three thousand feet higher still! It was a vast oval, and one would have to use up eighty or a hundred good miles in traveling around it. As it lay there with the shadows of the mountains brilliantly photographed upon its still surface I thought it must surely be the fairest picture the whole earth affords.

We found the small skiff belonging to the Brigade boys, and without loss of time set out across a deep bend of the lake toward the landmarks that signified the locality of the camp. I got Johnny to row—not because I mind exertion myself, but because it makes me sick to ride backward when I am at work. But I steered. A three-mile pull brought us to the camp just as the night fell, and we stepped ashore very tired and wolfishly hungry. In a "cache" among the rocks we found the provisions and the cooking utensils, and then, all fatigued as I was, I sat down upon a boulder and superintended while Johnny gathered wood and cooked supper. Many a man who had gone through what I had, would have wanted to rest.

It was a delicious supper—hot bread, fried bacon, and black coffee. It was a delicious solitude we were in, too. Three miles away was a sawmill and some workmen, but there were not fifteen other human beings throughout the wide circumference of the lake. As the darkness closed down and the stars came out and spangled the great mirror with jewels, we smoked meditatively in the solemn hush and forgot our troubles and our pains. In due time we spread our blankets in the warm sand between two large boulders and soon fell asleep, careless of the procession of ants that passed in through rents in our clothing and explored our persons. Nothing could disturb the sleep that fettered us, for it had been fairly earned, and if our consciences had any sins upon them they had to adjourn court for that night, anyway.

It is always very cold on that lakeshore in the night, but we had plenty of blankets and were warm enough. We never moved a muscle all night, but waked at early dawn in the original positions, and got up thoroughly refreshed, free from soreness, and brim full of friskiness. There is no end of wholesome medicine in such an experience. That morning we could have whipped ten such people as we were the day before—sick ones at any rate.

I superintended again, and as soon as we had eaten breakfast we got in the boat and skirted along the lakeshore about three miles and disembarked. We liked the appearance of the place, and so we claimed some three hundred acres of it and stuck our "notices" on a tree. It was yellow pine timberland—a dense forest of trees a hundred feet high and from one to five feet through at the butt. It was necessary to fence-in our property or we could not hold it. That is to say, it was necessary to cut down trees here and there and make them fall in such a way as to form a sort of inclosure (with pretty wide gaps in it). We cut down three trees apiece, and

found it such heartbreaking work that we decided
to "rest our case" on those; if they held the property, well and good; if they didn't, let the property
spill out through the gaps and go; it was no use to
work ourselves to death merely to save a few acres
of land. Next day we came back to build a house—
for a house was also necessary, in order to hold the
property. We decided to build a substantial log
house and excite the envy of the Brigade boys; but
by the time we had cut and trimmed the first log it
seemed unnecessary to be so elaborate, and so we
concluded to build it of saplings. However, two saplings, duly cut and trimmed, compelled recognition
of the fact that a still modester architecture would
satisfy the law, and so we concluded to build a
"brush" house. We devoted the next day to this
work, but we did so much "sitting around" and discussing, that by the middle of the afternoon we had
achieved only a halfway sort of affair which one of
us had to watch while the other cut brush, lest if
both turned our backs we might not be able to find
it again; it had such a strong family resemblance to
the surrounding vegetation. But we were satisfied.

We were landowners now, duly seized and possessed, and within the protection of the law. Therefore we decided to take up our residence on our
own domain and enjoy that large sense of independence which only such an experience can bring.
The next afternoon, after a long rest, we sailed away
from the Brigade camp with all the provisions and

cooking-utensils we could carry off—borrow is the
more accurate word—and just as the night was falling we beached the boat at our own landing.

If there is any life that is happier than the life we
led on our timber ranch for the next two or three
weeks, it must be a sort of life which I have not read
of in books or experienced in person. We did not
see a human being but ourselves during the time, or
hear any sounds but those that were made by the
wind and the waves, the sighing of the pines, and
now and then the far-off thunder of an avalanche.
The forest about us was dense and cool, the sky
above us was cloudless and brilliant with sunshine,
the broad lake before us was glassy and clear, or
rippled and breezy, or black and storm-tossed, according to Nature's mood; and its circling border of
mountain domes, clothed with forests, scarred with
landslides, cloven by cañons and valleys, and hel-
meted with glittering snow, fitly framed and finished the noble picture. The view was always fascinating, bewitching, entrancing. The eye was never
tired of gazing, night or day, in calm or storm; it
suffered but one grief, and that was that it could not
look always, but must close sometimes in sleep.

We slept in the sand close to the water's edge,
between two protecting boulders, which took care
of the stormy night winds for us. We never took any
paregoric to make us sleep. At the first break of
dawn we were always up and running footraces to
tone down excess of physical vigor and exuberance

of spirits. That is, Johnny was—but I held his hat. While smoking the pipe of peace after breakfast we watched the sentinel peaks put on the glory of the sun, and followed the conquering light as it swept down among the shadows, and set the captive crags and forests free. We watched the tinted pictures grow and brighten upon the water till every detail of forest, precipice, and pinnacle was wrought in and finished, and the miracle of the enchanter complete. Then to "business."

That is, drifting around in the boat. We were on the north shore. There, the rocks on the bottom are sometimes gray, sometimes white. This gives the marvelous transparency of the water a fuller advantage than it has elsewhere on the lake. We usually pushed out a hundred yards or so from the shore, and then lay down on the thwarts in the sun, and let the boat drift by the hour whither it would. We seldom talked. It interrupted the Sabbath stillness.

We fished a good deal, but we did not average one fish a week. We could see trout by the thousand in the emptiness under us, or sleeping in shoals on the bottom, but they would not bite; they could see the line too plainly, perhaps. We frequently selected the trout we wanted, and rested the bait patiently and persistently on the end of his nose at a depth of eighty feet, but he would only shake it off with an annoyed manner, and shift his position.

We bathed occasionally, but the water was rather chilly for all it looked so sunny.

We never slept in our "house." It never occurred to us, for one thing; and besides, it was built to hold ground, and that was enough. We did not wish to strain it.

By and by our provisions began to run short, and we went back to the old camp and laid in a new supply. We were gone all day, and reached home again about nightfall, pretty done in and hungry. While Johnny was carrying the main bulk of the provisions up to our "house" for future use, I took the loaf of bread, some slices of bacon, and the coffeepot ashore, set them by a tree, lit a fire, and went back to the boat to get the frying pan. While I was at this, I heard a shout from Johnny, and looking up I saw that my fire was galloping all over the premises!

Johnny was on the other side of it. He had to run through the flames to get to the lakeshore, and then we stood helpless and watched the devastation.

The ground was deeply carpeted with dry pine-needles, and the fire touched them off as if they were gunpowder. It was wonderful to see with what fierce speed the tall sheet of flame traveled! My coffeepot was gone, and everything with it. In a minute and a half the fire seized upon a dense growth of dry manzanita chapparal six or eight feet high, and then the popping and crackling was something terrific. We were driven to the boat by the intense heat, and there we remained, spellbound.

Within half an hour all before us was a tossing,

blinding tempest of flame! It went surging up adjacent ridges—surmounted them and disappeared in the cañons beyond—burst into view upon higher and farther ridges, presently—shed a grander illumination abroad, and dove again—flamed out again, directly, still higher up the mountainside—threw out skirmishing parties of fire here and there, and sent them trailing their crimson spirals away among remote ramparts and ribs and gorges, till as far as the eye could reach the lofty mountain-fronts were webbed as it were with a tangled network of red lava streams. Away across the water the crags and domes were lit with a ruddy glare, and the firmament above was a reflected hell!

Every feature of the spectacle was repeated in the glowing mirror of the lake! Both pictures were sublime, both were beautiful; but that in the lake had a bewildering richness about it that enchanted the eye and held it with the stronger fascination.

We sat absorbed and motionless through four long hours. We never thought of supper, and never felt fatigue. But at eleven o'clock the conflagration had traveled beyond our range of vision, and then darkness stole down upon the landscape again.

Hunger asserted itself now, but there was nothing to eat. The provisions were all cooked, no doubt, but we did not go to see. We were homeless wanderers again, without any property. Our fence was gone, our house burned down; no insurance. Our pine forest was well scorched, the dead trees all burned up, and our broad acres of manzanita swept away. Our blankets were on our usual sand bed, however, and so we lay down and went to sleep. The next morning we started back to the old camp but while a long way from shore, so great a storm came up that we dared not try to land. So I bailed out the seas we shipped, and Johnny pulled heavily through the billows till we had reached a point three or four miles beyond the camp. The storm was increasing, and it became evident that it was better to take the hazard of beaching the boat than go down in a hundred fathoms of water; so we ran in, with tall whitecaps following, and I sat down in the stern sheets and pointed her head-on to the shore. The instant the bow struck, a wave came over the stern that washed crew and cargo ashore, and saved a deal of trouble. We shivered in the lee of a boulder all the rest of the day, and froze all the night through. In the morning the tempest had gone down, and we paddled down to the camp without any unnecessary delay. We were so starved that we ate up the rest of the Brigade's provisions, and then set out to Carson to tell them about it and ask their forgiveness. It was accorded, upon payment of damages.

We made many trips to the lake after that, and had many a hairbreadth escape and bloodcurdling adventure which will never be recorded.

# XV

## *Silver Fever*

BY AND BY I was smitten with the silver fever. "Prospecting parties" were leaving town for the mountains every day, and discovering and taking possession of rich, silver-bearing lodes and ledges of quartz. Plainly this was the road to fortune. The great "Gould and Curry" mine was held at three or four hundred dollars a foot when we arrived; but in two months it had sprung up to eight hundred. The "Ophir" had been worth only a mere trifle, a year gone by, and now it was selling at nearly *four thousand dollars a foot*! Not a mine could be named that had not experienced an astonishing advance in value within a short time. Everybody was talking about these marvels. Go where you would, you heard nothing else, from morning till far into the night. Tom So-and-So had sold out from the "Amanda Smith" for $40,000—hadn't a cent when he "took up" the ledge six months ago. John Jones had sold half his interest in the "Bald Eagle and Mary Ann" for $65,000, gold coin, and gone to the States for his family. The widow Brewster had "struck it rich" in the "Golden Fleece" and sold ten feet for $18,000— but hadn't money enough to buy a crepe bonnet when Sing-Sing Tommy killed her husband at Baldy

Johnson's wake last spring. The "Last Chance" had found a "clay casing" and knew they were "right on the ledge"—consequence, "feet" that went begging yesterday were worth a brick house apiece today, and seedy owners who could not get trusted for a drink at any bar in the country yesterday were roaring drunk on champagne today and had hosts of warm personal friends in a town where they had forgotten how to bow or shake hands from long-continued want of practice. Johnny Morgan, a common loafer, had gone to sleep in the gutter and waked up worth a hundred thousand dollars, in consequence of the decision in the "Lady Franklin and Rough and Ready" law-suit. And so on—day in and day out the talk pelted our ears and the excitement waxed hotter and hotter around us.

I would have been more or less than human if I had not gone mad like the rest. Cartloads of solid silver bricks, as large as pigs of lead, were arriving from the mills every day, and such sights as that gave substance to the wild talk about me. I succumbed and grew as frenzied as the craziest.

Every few days news would come of the discovery of a brand-new mining region; immediately the papers would teem with accounts of its richness, and away the surplus population would scamper to take possession. By the time I was fairly inoculated with the disease, "Esmeralda"[1] had just had a run

---

[1] A district surrounding Aurora, Nevada, about 100 miles southeast of Carson City.

and "Humboldt"[2] was beginning to shriek for attention. "Humboldt! Humboldt!" was the new cry, and straightway Humboldt, the newest of the new, the richest of the rich, the most marvelous of the marvelous discoveries in Silverland, was occupying two columns of the public prints to "Esmeralda's" one. I was on the point of starting to Esmeralda, but turned with the tide and got ready for Humboldt. The instant we had finished reading the article, four of us decided to go to Humboldt. We commenced getting ready at once. And we also commenced upbraiding ourselves for not deciding sooner—for we were in terror lest all the rich mines would be found and secured before we got there, and we might have to put up with ledges that would not yield more than two or three hundred dollars a ton, maybe. An hour before, I would have felt opulent if I had owned ten feet in a Gold Hill mine whose ore produced twenty-five dollars to the ton; now I was already annoyed at the prospect of having to put up with mines the poorest of which would be a marvel in Gold Hill.

Hurry, was the word! We wasted no time. Our party consisted of four persons—a blacksmith sixty years of age, two young lawyers, and myself. We bought a wagon and two miserable old horses. We put eighteen hundred pounds of provisions and mining tools in the wagon and drove out of Carson

[2]A district around Unionville, about 175 miles northeast of Carson City.

on a chilly December afternoon. The horses were so weak and old that we soon found that it would be better if one or two of us got out and walked. It was an improvement. Next, we found that it would be better if a third man got out. That was an improvement also. It was at this time that I volunteered to drive, although I had never driven a harnessed horse before, and many a man in such a position would have felt fairly excused from such a responsibility. But in a little while longer it was found that it would be a fine thing if the driver got out and walked also. It was at this time that I resigned the position of driver, and never resumed it again. Within the hour, we found that it would not only be better, but was absolutely necessary, that we four, taking turns, two at a time, should put our hands against the end of the wagon and push it through the sand, leaving the feeble horses little to do but keep out of the way and hold up the tongue. Perhaps it is well for one to know his fate at first, and get reconciled to it. We had learned ours in one afternoon. It was plain that we had to walk through the sand and shove that wagon and those horses two hundred miles. So we accepted the situation, and from that time forth we never rode. More than that, we stood regular and nearly constant watches pushing up behind.

We made seven miles, and camped in the desert. Young Claggett (later a member of Congress from Montana) unharnessed and fed and watered the horses. A couple of us cut sagebrush, built the fire and brought water to cook with; and old Mr. Ballou, the blacksmith, did the cooking. This division of labor, and this appointment, was adhered to throughout the journey. We had no tent, and so we slept under our blankets out on the open plain. We were so tired that we slept soundly.

We were fifteen days making the trip—two hundred miles; thirteen, rather, for we lay by a couple of days, in one place, to let the horses rest. We could really have accomplished the journey in ten days if we had towed the horses behind the wagon, but we did not think of that until it was too late, and so went on shoving the horses and the wagon too when we might have saved half the labor. Parties who met us, occasionally, advised us to put the horses *in* the wagon, but Mr. Ballou, through whose ironclad earnestness no sarcasm could pierce, said that that would not do, because the provisions were exposed and would suffer; the horses being "bituminous from long deprivation." The reader will excuse me from translating. What Mr. Ballou customarily meant, when he used a long word, was a secret between himself and his Maker. He was one of the finest and kindest-hearted men that ever graced a humble sphere of life. He was gentleness and simplicity itself—and unselfishness, too. Although he was more than twice as old as the eldest of us, he never gave himself any airs, privileges, or exemptions on that account. He did a *young* man's share of the work; and did his share of conversing and entertaining from the general standpoint of *any* age—not from the arrogant, overawing summit-height of sixty years. His one striking peculiarity was his Partingtonian fashion[3] of loving and using big words *for their own sakes,* and independent of any bearing they might have upon the thought he was purposing to convey. He always let his ponderous syllables fall with an easy unconsciousness that left them wholly without offensiveness. In truth, his air was so natural and so simple that one was quite often catching himself accepting his stately sentences as meaning something, when they really meant nothing in the world. If a word was long and grand and resonant, that was sufficient to win the old man's love, and he would drop that word into the most out-of-the-way place in a sentence, and be as pleased with it as if it were perfectly luminous with meaning.

We four always spread-out our common stock of blankets together on the frozen ground, and slept side by side; and after finding that our foolish, long-legged hound pup had a deal of animal heat in him, Oliphant got to admitting him to the bed, between himself and Mr. Ballou, hugging the dog's warm back to his breast and finding great comfort in it. But during the night the pup would get stretchy and

[3]Mrs. Partington, B. P. Shillaber's very popular comic Yankee character from the 1840s to the last decade of the century, sprinkled her monologues with malapropisms, e.g., "if you give anybody power of eternity . . . you won't never see the final conclusion of it."

brace his feet against the old man's back and shove, grunting complacently the while; and now and then, being warm and snug, grateful and happy, he would paw the old man's back simply in excess of comfort; and at yet other times he would dream of the chase and in his sleep tug at the old man's back hair and bark in his ear. The old gentleman complained mildly about these familiarities, at last, and when he got through with his statement he said that such a dog as that was not a proper animal to admit to bed with tired men, because he was "so meretricious in his movements and so organic in his emotions." We turned the dog out.

It was a hard, wearing, toilsome journey, but it had its bright side; for after each day was done and our wolfish hunger appeased with a hot supper of fried bacon, bread, molasses, and black coffee, the pipe-smoking, song-singing, and yarn-spinning time around the evening camp fire in the still solitudes of the desert was a happy, carefree sort of recreation that seemed the very summit and culmination of earthly luxury.

Once we made twenty-five miles in a day, and once we made forty miles (through the Great American Desert), and ten miles beyond—fifty in all—in twenty-three hours, without halting to eat, drink, or rest. To stretch out and go to sleep, even on stony and frozen ground, after pushing a wagon and two horses fifty miles, is a delight so supreme that for the moment it almost seems cheap at the price.

We camped two days in the neighborhood of the "Sink of the Humboldt." We tried to use the strong alkaline water of the Sink, but it would not answer. It was like drinking lye, and not weak lye, either. It left a taste in the mouth, bitter and every way execrable, and a burning in the stomach that was very uncomfortable. We put molasses into it, but that helped it very little; we added a pickle, yet the alkali was the prominent taste, and so it was unfit for drinking. The coffee we made of this water was the meanest compound man has yet invented. It was really viler to the taste than the unameliorated water itself. Mr. Ballou, being the architect and builder of the beverage, felt constrained to indorse and uphold it, and so drank half a cup, by little sips, making shift to praise it faintly the while, but finally threw out the remainder, and said frankly it was "too technical for *him*."

But presently we found a spring of fresh water, which was quite convenient, and then, with nothing to mar our enjoyment, and no stragglers to interrupt it, we entered into our rest.

After leaving the Sink, we traveled along the Humboldt River a little way. People accustomed to the monsterous, mile-wide Mississippi, grow accustomed to associating the term "river" with a high degree of watery grandeur. Consequently, such people feel rather disappointed when they stand on the shores of the Humboldt or the Carson and find that a "river" in Nevada is a sickly rivulet which is just the counterpart of the Erie canal in all respects save that the canal is twice as long and four times as deep. One of the pleasantest and most invigorating exercises one can contrive is to run and jump across the Humboldt River till he is overheated, and then drink it dry.

On the fifteenth day we completed our march of two hundred miles and entered Unionville, Humboldt County, in the midst of a driving snowstorm. Unionville consisted of eleven cabins and a liberty pole. Six of the cabins were strung along one side of a deep cañon, and the other five faced them. The rest of the landscape was made up of bleak mountain walls that rose so high into the sky from both sides of the cañon that the village was left, as it were, far down in the bottom of a crevice. It was always daylight on the mountaintops a long time before the darkness lifted and revealed Unionville.

We built a small, rude cabin in the side of the crevice and roofed it with canvas, leaving a corner open to serve as a chimney, through which the cattle used to tumble occasionally, at night, and mash our furniture and interrupt our sleep. It was very cold weather and fuel was scarce.

I confess, without shame, that I expected to find masses of silver lying all about the ground. I expected to see it glittering in the sun on the mountain summits. I said nothing about this, for some instinct told me that I might possibly have an exaggerated idea about it, and so if I betrayed my thought I might bring derision upon myself. Yet I was as perfectly satisfied in my own mind as I could be of anything, that I was going to gather up, in a day or two, or at furthest a week or two, silver enough to make me satisfactorily wealthy—and so my fancy was already busy with plans for spending this money. The first opportunity that offered, I sauntered carelessly away from the cabin, keeping an eye on the other boys, and stopping and contemplating the sky when they seemed to be observing me; but as soon as the coast was manifestly clear, I fled away as guiltily as a thief might have done and never halted till I was far beyond sight and call. Then I began my search with a feverish excitement that was brimful of expectation—almost of certainty. I crawled about the ground, seizing and examining bits of stone, blowing the dust from them or rubbing them on my clothes, and then peering at them with anxious hope. Presently I found a bright fragment and my heart bounded! I hid behind a boulder and polished it and scrutinized it with a nervous eagerness and a delight that was more pronounced than absolute certainty itself could have afforded. The more I examined the fragment the more I was convinced that I had found the door to fortune. I marked the spot and carried away my specimen. Up and down the rugged mountainside I searched, with always increasing interest and always augmenting gratitude that I had come to Humboldt and come in time. Of the many experiences of my life, this secret search

among the hidden treasures of Silverland was the
nearest to unmarred ecstasy. It was a delirious revel.
By and by, in the bed of a shallow rivulet, I found a
deposit of shining yellow scales, and my breath almost forsook me! A gold mine, and in my simplicity I had been content with vulgar silver! I was so
excited that I half believed my overwrought imagination was deceiving me. Then a fear came upon
me that people might be observing me and would
guess my secret. Moved by this thought, I made a
circuit of the place, and ascended a knoll to recon-
noiter. Solitude. No creature was near. Then I returned to my mine, fortifying myself against any
disappointment, but my fears were groundless—the
shining scales were still there. I set about scooping
them out, and for an hour I toiled down the windings of the stream and robbed its bed. But at last the
descending sun warned me to give up the quest,
and I turned homeward laden with wealth.

As I walked along I could not help smiling at the
thought of my being so excited over my fragment of
silver when a nobler metal was almost under my
nose. In this little time the former had so fallen in
my estimation that once or twice I was on the point
of throwing it away.

The boys were as hungry as usual, but I could eat
nothing. Neither could I talk. I was full of dreams
and far away. Their conversation interrupted the
flow of my fancy somewhat, and annoyed me a bit.
I despised the sordid and commonplace things they

talked about. But as they proceeded, it began to amuse me. It grew to be rare fun to hear them planning their poor little economies and sighing over possible privations and distresses when a gold mine, all our own, lay within sight of the cabin, and I could point it out at any moment. Smothered hilarity began to oppress me, presently. It was hard to resist the impulse to burst out with exultation and reveal everything; but I did resist. I said within myself that I would filter the great news through my lips calmly and be serene as a summer morning while I watched its effect in their faces. I said:

"Where have you all been?"

"Prospecting."

"What did you find?"

"Nothing."

"Nothing? What do you think of the country?"

"Can't tell, yet," said Mr. Ballou, who was an old gold miner, and had considerable experience among the silver mines.

"Well, haven't you formed any sort of opinion?"

"Yes, a sort of a one. It's fair enough here, maybe, but overrated. Seven-thousand-dollar ledges are scarce, though. That Sheba may be rich enough, but we don't own it; and, besides, the rock is so full of base metals that all the science in the world can't work it. We'll not starve here, but we'll not get rich, I'm afraid."

"So you think the prospect is pretty poor?"

"No name for it!"

"Well, we'd better go back, hadn't we?"

"Oh, not yet—of course not. We'll try it a riffle, first."

"Suppose, now—this is merely a supposition, you know—suppose you could find a ledge that would yield, say, a hundred and fifty dollars a ton—would that satisfy you?"

"Try us once!" from the whole party.

"Or suppose—merely a supposition, of course—you were to find a ledge that would yield two thousand dollars a ton—would *that* satisfy you?"

"Here—what do you mean? What are you coming at? Is there some mystery behind all this?"

"Never mind. I am not saying anything. You know perfectly well there are no rich mines here—of course you do. Because you have been around and examined for yourselves. Anyone would know that, that had been around. But just for the sake of argument, suppose—in a kind of general way—some person were to tell you that two-thousand-dollar ledges were simply contemptible—contemptible, understand—and that right yonder in sight of this very cabin there were piles of pure gold and pure silver—oceans of it—enough to make you all rich in twenty-four hours! Come!"

"I should say he was as crazy as a loon!" said old Ballou, but wild with excitement, nevertheless.

"Gentlemen," said I, "I don't say anything—I haven't been around, you know, and of course don't know anything—but all I ask of you is to cast your eye on *that*, for instance, and tell me what you think of it!" and I tossed my treasure before them.

There was an eager scrabble for it, and a closing of heads together over it under the candle-light. Then old Ballou said:

"Think of it? I think it is nothing but a lot of granite rubbish and nasty glittering mica that isn't worth ten cents an acre!"

So vanished my dream. So melted my wealth away. So toppled my castle to the earth and left me stricken and forlorn.

Moralizing, I observed, then, that "all that glitters is not gold."

Mr. Ballou said I could go further than that, and lay it up among my treasures of knowledge, that *nothing* that glitters is gold. So I learned then, once and for all, that gold in its native state is but dull, unornamental stuff, and that only lowborn metals excite the admiration of the ignorant with an ostentatious glitter. However, like the rest of the world, I still go on underrating men of gold and glorifying men of mica. Commonplace human nature cannot rise above that.

True knowledge of the nature of silver mining came fast enough. We went out "prospecting" with Mr. Ballou. We climbed up the mountainsides, and clambered among sagebrush, rocks, and snow till we were ready to drop with exhaustion, but found no silver—nor yet any gold. Day after day we did this. Now and then we came upon holes burrowed a few feet into the declivities and apparently abandoned; and now and then we found one or two listless men still burrowing. But there was no appearance of silver. These holes were the beginnings of tunnels, and the purpose was to drive them hundreds of feet into the mountain, and some day tap the hidden ledge where the silver was. Some day! It seemed far enough away, and very hopeless and dreary. Day after day we toiled, and climbed, and searched, and then we younger partners grew sicker and still sicker of the promiseless toil. At last we halted under a beetling rampart of rock which projected from the earth high upon the mountain. Mr. Ballou broke off some fragments with a hammer, and examined them long and attentively with a small eyeglass; threw them away and broke off more; said this rock was quartz, and quartz was the sort of rock that contained silver. *Contained* it! I had thought that at least it would be caked on the outside of it like a kind of veneering. He still broke off pieces and critically examined them, now and then wetting the piece with his tongue and applying the glass. At last he exclaimed:

"We've got it!"

We were full of anxiety in a moment. The rock was clean and white, where it became broken, and across it ran a ragged thread of blue. He said that little thread had silver in it, mixed with base metals, such as lead and antimony, and other rubbish and that there was a speck or two of gold visible.

After a great deal of effort we managed to discern some little fine yellow specks, and judged that a couple of tons of them massed together might make a gold dollar, possibly. We were not jubilant, but Mr. Ballou said there were worse ledges in the world than that. He saved what he called the "richest" piece of the rock, in order to determine its value by the process called the "fire-assay." Then we named the mine "Monarch of the Mountains" (modesty of nomenclature is not a prominent feature in the mines), and Mr. Ballou wrote out and stuck up the following "notice," preserving a copy to be entered in the books of the mining recorder's office in the town.

### NOTICE

We the undersigned claim three claims, of three hundred feet each (and one for discovery), on this silver-bearing quartz lead or lode, extending north and south from this notice, with all its dips, spurs, and angles, variations and sinuosities, together with fifty feet of ground on either side for working the same.

We put our names to it and tried to feel that our fortunes were made. But when we talked the matter all over with Mr. Ballou, we felt depressed and dubious. He said that this surface quartz was not all there was of our mine; but that the wall or ledge of rock we called the "Monarch of the Mountains" extended down hundreds and hundreds of feet into the earth—he illustrated by saying that it was like a curbstone, and maintained a nearly uniform thickness—say twenty feet—away down into the bowels of earth, and was perfectly distinct from the casing rock on each side of it; and that it kept to itself, and maintained its distinctive character always, no matter how deep it extended into the earth or how far it stretched itself through and across the hills and valleys. He said it might be a mile deep and ten miles long, for all we knew; and that wherever we bored into it above ground or below, we would find gold and silver in it, but no gold or silver in the meaner rock it was cased between. And he said that down in the great depths of the ledge was its richness, and the deeper it went the richer it grew. Therefore, instead of working here on the surface, we must either bore down into the rock with a shaft till we came to where it was rich—say a hundred feet or so—or else we must go down into the valley and bore a long tunnel into the mountainside and tap the ledge far under the earth. To do either was plainly the labor of months; for we could blast and bore only a few feet a day—some five or six. But this was not all. He said that after we got the ore out it must be hauled in wagons to a distant silver mill, ground up, and the silver extracted by a tedious and costly process. Our fortune seemed a century away!

But we went to work. We decided to sink a shaft. So, for a week we climbed the mountain, laden with picks, drills, gads, crowbars, shovels, cans of blasting powder and coils of fuse, and strove with might and main. At first the rock was broken and loose, and we dug it up with picks and threw it out with shovels, and the hole progressed very well. But the rock became more compact, presently, and gads and crowbars came into play. But shortly nothing could make any impression but blasting powder. That was the weariest work! One of us held the iron drill in its place and another would strike with an eight-pound sledge—it was like driving nails on a large scale. In the course of an hour or two the drill would reach a depth of two or three feet, making a hole a couple of inches in diameter. We would put in a charge of powder, insert half a yard of fuse, pour in sand and gravel and ram it down, then light the fuse and run. When the explosion came and the rocks and smoke shot into the air, we would go back and find about a bushel of that hard, rebellious quartz jolted out. Nothing more. One week of this satisfied me. I resigned. Claggett and Oliphant followed. Our shaft was only twelve feet deep. We decided that a tunnel was the thing we wanted.

So we went down the mountainside and worked a week; at the end of which time we had blasted a tunnel about deep enough to hide a hogshead in, and judged that about nine hundred feet more of it would reach the ledge. I resigned again, and the other boys only held out one day longer. We decided that a tunnel was not what we wanted. We wanted a ledge that was already "developed." There were none in the camp.

We dropped the "Monarch" for the time being.

Meantime the camp was filling up with people, and there was a constantly growing excitement about our Humboldt mines. We fell victims to the epidemic and strained every nerve to acquire more "feet." We prospected and took up new claims, put "notices" upon them and gave them grandiloquent names. We traded some of our "feet" for "feet" in other people's claims. In a little while we owned largely in the "Gray Eagle," the "Columbiana," the "Branch Mint," the "Maria Jane," the "Universe," the "Root-Hog-or-Die," the "Samson and Delilah," the "Boomerang," the "Golconda," the "Sultana," the "Treasure Trove," the "Great Republic," the "Grand Mogul," and fifty other "mines" that had never been molested by a shovel or scratched with a pick. We had not less than thirty thousand "feet" apiece in the "richest mines on earth" as the frenzied cant phrased it—yet we owed the butcher. We were stark mad with excitement—drunk with happiness—smothered under mountains of prospective wealth—arrogantly compassionate toward the plodding millions who knew not our marvelous cañon but our credit was not good at the grocer's.

It was the strangest phase of life one can imagine. It was a beggars' revel. There was nothing doing in the district—no mining—no milling—no productive effort—no income—and not enough money in the entire camp to buy a corner lot in an eastern village, hardly; and yet a stranger would have supposed he was walking among bloated millionaires.

Prospecting parties swarmed out of town with the first flush of dawn, and swarmed in again at nightfall laden with spoil—rocks. Nothing but rocks. Every man's pockets were full of them; the floor of his cabin was littered with them; they were disposed in labeled rows on his shelves.

I met men at every turn who owned from one thousand to thirty thousand "feet" in undeveloped silver mines, every single foot[4] of which they believed would shortly be worth from fifty to a thousand dollars—and as often as any other way they were men who had not twenty-five dollars in the world. Every man you met had his new mine to boast of, and his "specimens" ready; and if the opportunity offered, he would infallibly back you into a corner and offer as a favor to *you*, not to him, to part with just a few feet in the "Golden Age," or the "Sarah Jane," or some other unknown stack of croppings, for money enough to get a "square meal" with, as the phrase went. And you were never to reveal that he had made you the offer at such a ruinous price, for it was only out of friendship for you that he was willing to make the sacrifice. Then he would fish a piece of rock out of his pocket, and after looking mysteriously around as if he feared he might be waylaid and robbed if caught with such wealth in his possession, he would then dab the rock against

[4] A foot was twelve inches in length in the lode, regardless of its width, and extending its entire depth toward the center of the earth.

his tongue, clap an eyeglass to it, and exclaim:

"Look at that! Right there in that red dirt! See it? See the specks of gold? And the streak of silver? That's from the 'Uncle Abe.' There's a hundred thousand tons just like that in sight! Right in sight, mind you! And when we get down on it and the ledge comes in solid, it will be the richest thing in the world! Look at the assay! I don't want you to believe *me*—look at the assay!"

Then he would get out a greasy sheet of paper which showed that the portion of rock assayed had given evidence of containing silver and gold in the proportion of so many hundreds or thousands of dollars to the ton. I little knew, then, that the custom was to hunt out the *richest* piece of rock and get it assayed! Very often, that piece, the size of a filbert, was the only fragment in a ton that had a particle of metal in it—and yet the assay made it pretend to represent the average value of the ton of rubbish it came from!

On such a system of assaying as that, the Humboldt world had gone crazy. From the authority of such assays its newspaper correspondents were frothing about rock worth four and seven thousand dollars a ton!

Everybody's head was full of such "calculations" as those—such raving insanity, rather. Few people took *work* into their calculations—or outlay of money either; except the work and expenditures of other people.

We never touched our tunnel or our shaft again. Why? Because we judged that we had learned the *real* secret of success in silver mining—which was, *not* to mine the silver ourselves by the sweat of our brows and the labor of our hands, but to *sell* the ledges to the dull slaves of toil and let them do the mining!

# XVI

## *City Editor*

UNFORTUNATELY, every now and then during the
months that followed, I misplaced that lesson
and had to relearn it. My comrade in one curious
episode—the most curious, I think, that had yet ac-
cented my slothful, valueless, heedless career—was
Calvin H. Higbie, an experienced miner. He figures
in a chapter of mine in *Roughing It*, where the tale
is told of how we discovered a rich blind lead in the
Wild West Mine in Aurora—or, as we called that
region then, Esmeralda—and how, instead of making our ownership of that exceedingly rich property
permanent by doing ten days' work on it, as required by the mining laws, he went off on a wild-
goose chase to search for the mysterious cement
mine; and how I went off nine miles to Walker
River to nurse Captain John Nye[1] through a violent
case of spasmodic rheumatism or blind staggers, or
some malady of the kind; and how Cal and I came
wandering back into Esmeralda one night just in
time to be too late to save our fortune from the
jumpers.

It reads like a wild fancy sketch, but the evidence

[1]Captain John Nye, the governor's brother and a fellow
prospector.

of many witnesses, and likewise that of the official records of Esmeralda District, is easily obtainable in proof that it is a true history. I can always have it to say that I was absolutely and unquestionably worth a million dollars, once, for ten days.

What to do next?

I yielded to Higbie's appeals and consented to try the mining once more. We climbed far up on the mountainside and went to work on a little rubbishy claim of ours that had a shaft on it eight feet deep. Higbie descended into it and worked bravely with his pick till he had loosened up a deal of rock and dirt, and then I went on down with a long-handled shovel (the most awkward invention yet contrived by man) to throw it out. You must brace the shovel forward with the side of your knee till it is full, and then, with a skilful toss, throw it backward over your left shoulder. I made the toss, and landed the mess just on the edge of the shaft and it all came back on my head and down the back of my neck. I never said one word, but climbed out and walked home. I inwardly resolved that I would starve before I would make a target of myself and shoot rubbish at it with a long-handled shovel. I sat down, in the cabin, and gave myself up to solid misery—so to speak. Now in pleasanter days I had amused myself with writing letters to the chief paper of the territory, the Virginia *Daily Territorial Enterprise*, and had always been surprised when they appeared in print. My good opinion of the editors had steadily declined; for it seemed to me that they might have found something better to fill up with than my literature. I had found a letter in the post office as I came home from the hillside, and finally I opened it. Eureka! (I never did know what Eureka meant, but it seems to be as proper a word to heave in as any when no other that sounds pretty offers.) It was a deliberate offer to me of Twenty-five Dollars a week to come up to Virginia and be city editor of the *Territorial Enterprise.*

I was to take the place of William H. Wright (pen name, Dan De Quille), and do Wright's work for three months while he crossed the plains to Iowa to visit his family.

Something over two years before, Joe Goodman[2] and another journeyman printer had borrowed forty dollars and set out from San Francisco to try their fortunes in the new city of Virginia. They found the *Enterprise*, a poverty-stricken weekly journal, gasping for breath and likely to die. They bought it, type, fixtures, good will, and all, for a thousand dollars, on long time. The editorial sanctum, newsroom, pressroom, publication office, bed-chamber, parlor, and kitchen were all compressed into one apartment, and it was a small one, too. The editors and printers slept on the floor, a Chinaman did their cooking, and the "imposing-stone" was the general dinner table. But things were changed. The paper

[2] Joseph T. Goodman, who became the editor-in-chief of the paper.

was a great daily, printed by steam; there were five editors and twenty-three compositors; the subscription price was sixteen dollars a year; the advertising rates were exorbitant, and the columns crowded. The paper was clearing from six to ten thousand dollars a month, and the "Enterprise Building" was finished and ready for occupation—a stately fireproof brick. Every day from five up to eleven columns of "live" advertisements were left out or crowded into spasmodic and irregular "supplements."

I would have challenged the publisher in the "blind lead" days—now I wanted to fall down and worship him. Twenty-five Dollars a week—it looked like bloated luxury—a fortune, a sinful and lavish waste of money. But my transports cooled when I thought of my inexperience and consequent unfitness for the position—and straightway, on top of this, my long array of failures rose up before me. Yet if I refused this place I must presently become dependent upon somebody for my bread, a thing necessarily distasteful to a man who had never experienced such a humiliation since he was thirteen years old. Not much to be proud of, since it is so common— but then it was all I had to *be* proud of. So I was scared into being a city editor. I would have declined, otherwise. Necessity is the mother of "taking a chance." I do not doubt that if, at that time, I had been offered a salary to translate the Talmud from the original Hebrew, I would have accepted—albeit with diffidence and some misgivings—and thrown

*"Territorial Enterprise"* building, Virginia City, Nevada.
Courtesy of the Mark Twain Papers, The Bancroft Library

as much variety into it as I could for the money.

I went up to Virginia and entered upon my new vocation. I was a rusty-looking city editor, I am free to confess—coatless, slouch hat, blue woolen shirt, pantaloons stuffed into boot tops, whiskered half down to the waist, and the universal navy revolver slung to my belt. But I secured a more Christian costume and discarded the revolver. I had never had occasion to kill anybody, nor ever felt a desire to do so, but had worn the thing in deference to popular sentiment, and in order that I might not, by its absence, be offensively conspicuous, and a subject of remark. But the other editors, and all the printers carried revolvers. I asked the chief editor and proprietor (Mr. Goodman, I will call him, since it describes him as well as any fictitious name could do) for some instructions with regard to my duties, and he told me to go all over town and ask all sorts of people all sorts of questions, then make notes of the information gained, and write them out for publication. And he added:

"Never say 'We learn' so-and-so, or 'It is reported,' or 'It is rumored,' or 'We understand', but go, to headquarters and get the absolute facts, and then speak out and say 'It *is* so-and-so.' Otherwise, people will not put confidence in your news. Unassailable certainty is the thing that gives a newspaper the firmest and most valuable reputation."

It was the whole thing in a nutshell; and to this day, when I find a reporter commencing his article with "We understand," I gather a suspicion that he has not taken as much pains to inform himself as he ought to have done. I moralize well, but I did not always practice well when I was a city editor; I let fancy get the upper hand of fact too often when there was a dearth of news. I can never forget my first day's experience as a reporter. I wandered about town questioning everybody, boring everybody, and finding out that nobody knew anything. At the end of five hours my reporter's notebook was still barren. I spoke to Mr. Goodman. He said:

"Dan used to make a good thing out of the hay-wagons in a dry time when there were no fires or inquests. Are there any haywagons in from the Truckee? If there are, you might speak of the renewed activity and all that sort of thing, in the hay business, you know. It isn't sensational or exciting, but it fills up and looks businesslike."

I canvassed the city again and found one wretched old hay truck dragging in from the country. But I made affluent use of it. I multiplied it by sixteen, brought it into town from sixteen different directions, made sixteen separate items of it, and got up such another sweat about hay as Virginia City had never seen in the world before.

This was encouraging. Two nonpareil columns had to be filled, and I was getting along. Presently, when things began to take on a dismal look again, a desperado killed a man in a saloon and great joy returned once more. I never was so glad over any mere trifle before in my life. I said to the murderer:

"Sir, you are a stranger to me, but you have done me a kindness this day which I can never forget. If whole years of gratitude can be to you any slight compensation, they shall be yours. I was in trouble and you have relieved me nobly and at a time when all seemed dark and drear. Count me as your friend, for I am not a man to forget a favor."

If I did not really say that to him I at least felt a sort of itching desire to do it. I wrote up the murder with a hungry attention to details and when it was finished experienced but one regret—namely, that they had not hanged my benefactor on the spot, so that I could work him up too.

Next I discovered some emigrant wagons going into camp on the plaza and found that they had lately come through the hostile Indian country and had fared rather roughly. I made the best of the item that the circumstances permitted, and felt that if I were not confined within rigid limits by the presence of the reporters of the other papers I could add particulars that would make the article much more interesting. However, I found one wagon that was going on to California, and made some judicious inquiries of the proprietor. When I learned, through his short and surly answers to my cross-questioning, that he was certainly going on and would not be in the city next day to make trouble, I got ahead of the other papers, for I took down his list of names and added his party to the killed and wounded. Having more scope here, I put this wagon through an Indian fight that to this day has no parallel in history.

My two columns were filled. When I read them over in the morning I felt that I had found my legitimate occupation at last. I reasoned within myself that news, and stirring news, too, was what a paper needed, and I felt that I was peculiarly endowed with the ability to furnish it. Mr. Goodman said that I was as good a reporter as Dan. I desired no higher commendation. With encouragement like that, I felt that I could take my pen and murder all the immigrants on the plains if need be, and the interests of the paper demanded it.

However, as I grew better acquainted with the business and learned the run of the sources of information I ceased to require the aid of fancy to any large extent, and became able to fill my columns without diverging noticeably from the domain of fact.

I struck up friendships with the reporters of the other journals, and we swapped "regulars" with each other and thus economized work. "Regulars" are permanent sources of news, like courts, bullion returns, "clean-ups" at the quartz mills, and inquests. Inasmuch as everybody went armed, we had an inquest about every day, and so this department was naturally set down among the "regulars." We had lively papers in those days.

Six months after my entry into journalism the

grand "flush times" of Silverland began, and they
continued with unabated splendor for three years.
All difficulty about filling up the "local department" ceased, and the only trouble now was how to
make the lengthened columns hold the world of
incidents and happenings that came to our literary
net every day. Virginia had grown to be the "livest"
town, for its age and population, that America had
ever produced. The sidewalks swarmed with people—to such an extent, indeed, that it was generally
no easy matter to stem the human tide. The streets
themselves were just as crowded with quartz wagons, freight teams, and other vehicles. The procession was endless. So great was the pack, that buggies
frequently had to wait half an hour for an opportunity to cross the principal street. Joy sat on every
countenance, and there was a glad, almost fierce,
intensity found in every eye, that told of the money-
getting schemes that were seething in every brain
and the hope that held sway in every heart. Money
was as plenty as dust; every individual considered
himself wealthy, and a melancholy countenance
was nowhere to be seen. There were fire companies,
military companies, big brass bands, banks, hotels,
theaters, "hurdy-gurdy houses," wide open gambling palaces, political pow wows, civic processions,
street fights, murders, inquests, riots, a whisky mill
every fifteen steps, a Board of Aldermen, a Mayor,
a City Surveyor, a City Engineer, a Chief of the
Fire Department, with First, Second, and Third

Assistants, a Chief of Police, City Marshal, and a large police force, two Boards of Mining Brokers, a dozen breweries, and half a dozen jails and station houses in full operation, and some talk of building a church. The "flush times" were in magnificent flower! Large fireproof brick buildings were going up in the principal streets, and the wooden suburbs were spreading out in every direction. Town lots soared up to prices that were amazing.

The great "Comstock lode" stretched its opulent length straight through the town from north to south, and every mine on it was in diligent process of development. One of these mines alone employed six hundred and seventy-five men, and in the matter of elections the old adage was, "as the 'Gould & Curry' goes, so goes the city." Laboring men's wages were four and six dollars a day, and they worked in three "shifts" or gangs, and the blasting and picking and shoveling went on without ceasing, night and day.

The "city" of Virginia roosted royally midway up the steep side of Mount Davidson, seven thousand two hundred feet above the level of the sea, and in the clear Nevada atmosphere was visible from a distance of fifty miles! It claimed a population of fifteen thousand to eighteen thousand, and all day long half of this little army swarmed the streets like bees and the other half swarmed among the drifts and tunnels of the "Comstock," hundreds of feet down in the earth directly under those same

*Virginia City, Nevada, as viewed from
Mount Davidson in 1861.*

Courtesy of the California State Library

299

streets. Often we felt our chairs jar, and heard the faint boom of a blast down in the bowels of the earth under the office.

The mountainside was so steep that the entire town had a slant to it like a roof. Each street was a terrace, and from each to the next street below the descent was forty or fifty feet. The fronts of the houses were level with the street they faced, but their rear first floors were propped on lofty stilts; a man could stand at a rear first floor window of a C Street house and look down the chimneys of the row of houses below him facing D Street. It was a laborious climb, in that thin atmosphere, to ascend from D to A Street, and you were panting and out of breath when you got there; but you could turn around and go down again like a house afire—so to speak. The atmosphere was so rarefied, on account of the great altitude, that one's blood lay near the surface always, and the scratch of a pin was a disaster worth worrying about, for the chances were that a grievous erysipelas would ensue. But to offset this, the thin atmosphere seemed to carry healing to gunshot wounds, and, therefore, to simply shoot your adversary through both lungs was something not likely to afford you any permanent satisfaction, for he would probably be around looking for you within the month, and not with an opera glass, either.

From Virginia's airy situation one could look out over a vast and far-reaching panorama of mountain ranges and deserts; and whether the day was bright or overcast, whether the sun was rising or setting, or flaming in the zenith, or whether night and the moon held sway, the spectacle was always impressive and beautiful. Over your head Mount Davidson lifted its gray dome, and before and below you a rugged cañon clove the battlemented hills, making a somber gateway through which a soft-tinted desert was glimpsed, with the silver thread of a river winding through it, bordered with trees which many miles of distance diminished to a delicate fringe; and still further away the snowy mountains rose up and stretched their long barrier to the filmy horizon—far enough beyond a lake that burned in the desert like a fallen sun, though that, itself, lay fifty miles removed. Look from your window where you would, there was fascination in the picture. At rare intervals—but very rare—there were clouds in our skies, and then the setting sun would gild and flush and glorify this mighty expanse of scenery with a bewildering pomp of color that held the eye like a spell and moved the spirit like music.

My salary was increased to forty dollars a week; but I rarely drew it. I had plenty of other resources, and what did two broad twenty-dollar gold pieces mean to a man who had his pockets full of such and a cumbersome abundance of bright half-dollars besides? (Paper money has never come into use on the Pacific coast.) Reporting was lucrative, and every man in the town was lavish with his money and his "feet." The city and all the great mountainside were riddled with mining shafts. There were more mines than miners. True, not ten of these mines were yielding rock worth hauling to a mill, but everybody said: "Wait till the shaft gets down where the ledge comes in solid, and then you will see!" So, nobody was discouraged. These were nearly all "wildcat" mines, and wholly worthless, but nobody believed it then.

New claims were taken daily, and it was the friendly custom to run straight to the newspaper offices, give the reporter forty or fifty "feet," and get him to go and examine the mine and publish a notice of it. They did not care a fig what you said about the property so you said something. Consequently we generally said a word or two to the effect that the "indications" were good, or that the ledge was "six feet wide," or that the rock "resembled the Comstock" (and so it did—but as a general thing the resemblance was not startling enough to knock you down).

There was *nothing* in the shape of a mining claim that was not salable. We received presents of "feet" every day. If we needed a hundred dollars or so, we sold some; if not, we hoarded it away, satisfied that it would ultimately be worth a thousand dollars a foot. I had a trunk about half full of "stock." When a claim made a stir in the market and went up to a high figure, I searched through my pile to see if I had any of its stock—and generally found it.

The prices rose and fell constantly; but still a fall

disturbed us little, because a thousand dollars a foot was our figure, and so we were content to let it fluctuate as much as it pleased till it reached it. My pile of stock was not all given to me by people who wished their claims "noticed." At least half of it was given me by persons who had no thought of such a thing, and looked for nothing more than a simple verbal "thank you"; and you were not even obliged by law to furnish that. If you are coming up the street with a couple of baskets of apples in your hands, and you meet a friend, you naturally invite him to take a few. That describes the condition of things in Virginia in the "flush times."

There were nabobs in those days—in the "flush times," I mean. Every rich strike in the mines created one or two. I call to mind several of these. They were careless, easy going fellows, as a general thing, and the community at large was as much benefited by their riches as they were themselves—possibly more, in some cases.

Two cousins, teamsters, did some hauling for a man and had to take a small segregated portion of a silver mine in lieu of three hundred dollars cash. They gave an outsider a third to open the mine, and they went on teaming. But not long. Ten months afterward the mine was out of debt and paying each owner eight to ten thousand dollars a month—say one hundred thousand dollars a year.

One of the earliest nabobs that Nevada was delivered of wore six thousand dollars' worth of diamonds, and swore he was unhappy because he could not spend his money as fast as he made it.

Another Nevada nabob boasted an income that often reached sixteen thousand dollars a month; and he used to love to tell how he had worked in the very mine that yielded it, for five dollars a day, when he first came to the country.

The silver and sagebrush state has knowledge of another of these pets of fortune—lifted from actual poverty to affluence almost in a single night—who was able to offer one hundred thousand dollars for a position of high official distinction, shortly afterward, and did offer it—but failed to get it, his politics not being as sound as his bank account.

Then there was John Smith. He was a good, honest, kindhearted soul, born and reared in the lower ranks of life, and miraculously ignorant. He drove a team, and owned a small ranch—a ranch that paid him a comfortable living, for although it yielded but little hay, what little it did yield was worth from two hundred and fifty to three hundred dollars in gold per ton in the market. Presently Smith traded a few acres of the ranch for a small undeveloped silver mine in Gold Hill. He opened the mine and then built a little unpretending ten-stamp mill. Eighteen months afterward he retired from the hay business, for his mining income had reached a most comfortable figure. Some people said it was thirty thousand dollars a month, and others said it was sixty thousand dollars. He was very rich, at any rate.

And then he went to Europe and traveled. And when he came back he was never tired of telling about the fine hogs he had seen in England, and the gorgeous sheep he had seen in Spain, and the fine cattle he had noticed in the vicinity of Rome. He was full of the wonders of the Old World, and advised everybody to travel. He said a man never imagined what surprising things there were in the world till he had traveled.

The Gould & Curry claim comprised twelve hundred feet, and it all belonged originally to the two men whose names it bears. Mr. Curry owned two-thirds of it—and he said that he sold it out for twenty-five hundred dollars in cash, and an old plug horse that ate up his market value in hay and barley in seventeen days by the watch. And he said that Gould sold out for a pair of secondhand government blankets and a bottle of whisky that killed nine men in three hours, and that an unoffending stranger that smelt the cork was disabled for life. Four years afterward the mine thus disposed of was worth in the San Francisco market seven million six hundred thousand dollars in gold coin.

In the early days a poverty-stricken Mexican who lived in a cañon directly back of Virginia City, had a stream of water as large as a man's wrist trickling from the hillside on his premises. The Ophir Company segregated a hundred feet of their mine and traded it to him for the stream of water. The hundred feet proved to be the richest part of the mine;

and four years after the swap, its market value (including its mill) was one and a half million dollars.

An individual who owned twenty feet in the Ophir mine before its great riches were revealed to men, traded it for a horse, and a very sorry-looking brute he was, too. A year or so afterward, when Ophir stock went up to three thousand dollars a foot, this man, who had not a cent, used to say he was the most startling example of magnificence and misery the world had ever seen—because he was able to ride on a sixty-thousand-dollar horse—yet could not scrape up cash enough to buy a saddle, and was obliged to borrow one or ride bareback. He said if fortune were to give him another sixty-thousand-dollar horse it would ruin him.

A youth of nineteen, who was a telegraph operator in Virginia on a salary of a hundred dollars a month, and who, when he could not make out German names in the list of San Francisco steamer arrivals, used to ingeniously select substitutes for them out of an old Berlin city directory, made himself rich by watching the mining telegrams that passed through his hands and buying and selling stocks accordingly, through a friend in San Francisco. Once when a private dispatch was sent from Virginia City announcing a rich strike in a prominent mine and advising that the matter be kept secret till a large amount of the stock could be secured, he bought forty "feet" of the stock at twenty dollars a foot, and afterward sold half of it at eight hundred dollars a foot and the rest at double that figure. In three months he was worth one hundred and fifty thousand dollars and resigned his telegraphic position.

But why go on? The traditions of Silverland are filled with instances like these, and I would never get through enumerating them were I to attempt to do it.

I was personally acquainted with the majority of the nabobs I have referred to, and so, for old acquaintance' sake, I have shifted their occupations and experiences around in such a way as to keep the Pacific public from recognizing these once notorious men. Years later they were no longer notorious for the majority of them have drifted back into poverty and obscurity again.

THE first twenty-six graves in the Virginia City cemetery were occupied by *murdered* men. So everybody said, so everybody believed, and so they will always say and believe. The reason why there was so much slaughtering done, was, that in a new mining district the rough element predominates, and a person is not respected until he has "killed his man." That was the very expression used.

If an unknown individual arrived, they did not inquire if he was capable, honest, industrious, but— had he killed his man? If he had not, he gravitated to his natural and proper position, that of a man of small consequence; if he had, the cordiality of his reception was graduated according to the number of his dead. It was tedious work struggling up to a position of influence with bloodless hands; however when a man came with the blood of half a dozen men on his soul, his worth was recognized at once and his acquaintance sought.

In Nevada, for a time, the lawyer, the editor, the banker, the chief desperado, the chief gambler, and the saloonkeeper, occupied the same level in society, and it was the highest. The cheapest and easiest way to become an influential man and be looked up to by the community at large, was to stand behind a bar, wear a cluster-diamond pin, and sell whisky. I am not sure but that the saloonkeeper held a shade higher rank than any other member of society. His opinion had weight. It was his privilege to say how the elections should go. No great movement could succeed without the countenance and direction of the saloonkeepers. It was a high favor when the chief saloonkeeper consented to serve in the legislature or the board of aldermen. Youthful ambition hardly aspired so much to the honors of the law, or the army and navy as to the dignity of proprietorship in a saloon. To be a saloonkeeper and kill a man was to be illustrious. Hence the reader will not be surprised to learn that more than one man was killed in Nevada under hardly the pretext of provocation, so impatient was the slayer to achieve reputation and throw off the galling sense of being held in indifferent repute by his associates. I knew two youths who tried to "kill their men" for no other reason—and got killed themselves for their pains. "There goes the man that killed Bill Adams" was higher praise and a sweeter sound in the ears of this sort of people than any other speech that admiring lips could utter.

Vice flourished luxuriantly during the heyday of our "flush times." The saloons were overburdened with custom; so were the police courts, the gambling dens, the brothels, and the jails—unfailing signs of high prosperity in a mining region—in any region, for that matter. Is it not so? A crowded police court docket is the surest of all signs that trade is brisk and money plenty.

# XVII

# *A Pair of Hoaxes*

"PETRIFIED MAN", published on October 4, 1862,
and "A Bloody Massacre," published on October 18, 1863, were my pieces for the *Enterprise* that
made the biggest stir. My experiences with both
shows how really hard it is to foist a moral or a
truth upon an unsuspecting public through a burlesque without entirely missing one's mark.

In the fall of 1862, in Nevada and California, the
people got to running wild about extraordinary petrifactions and other natural marvels. One could
scarcely pick up a paper without finding in it one or
two glorified discoveries of this kind. The mania
was becoming a little ridiculous. I was a brand new
local editor, and I felt called upon to destroy this
growing evil; we all have our benignant, fatherly
moods at one time or another, I suppose. I chose to
kill the petrifaction mania with a delicate, a very
delicate satire. But maybe it was altogether too delicate, for nobody ever perceived the satire part of it
at all. I put my scheme in the shape of the discovery of a remarkably petrified man.

I had had a temporary falling out with Mr. G. T.
Sewall, the new coroner and justice of the peace of
Humboldt, and thought I might as well touch him

up a little at the same time and make him ridiculous; and thus combine pleasure with business. So I told, in patient, belief-compelling detail, all about the finding of a petrified man at Gravelly Ford (exactly a hundred and twenty miles, over a breakneck mountain trail from where Sewall lived); how all the savants from the immediate neighborhood had been to examine it (it was notorious that there was not a living creature within fifty miles of there, except a few starving Indians, some crippled grasshoppers, and four or five buzzards out of meat and too feeble to get away); how all those savants then pronounced the petrified man to have been in a state of complete petrifaction for over ten generations; and then, with a seriousness that I ought to have been ashamed to assume, I stated that as soon as Mr. Sewell heard the news he summoned a jury, mounted his mule, and posted off, with noble reverence for official duty, on that terrible five days' journey, through alkali, sagebrush, peril of body, and imminent starvation, to *hold an inquest* on this man that had been dead and turned to everlasting stone for more than three hundred years![1] And because my

[1] Although Londoners and Easterners may have missed the satire, nearer home, California journalists called attention to it. For instance, San Francisco editors headed a reprint "A Washoe Joke." For citations of other incorrect claims in this account, and a suggestion that Rabelais may have been a source for some details, see Walter Blair, "The Petrified Man and His French Ancestor," *Mark Twain Journal*, Vol. 19 (Winter, 1977–78), 1–3.

*Artist's conception of "The Petrified Man" from the first
edition of* Sketches, New and Old.

hand was "in," so to say, I went on, with the same unflinching gravity, to state that the jury returned a verdict that deceased came to his death from *protracted exposure*. This only moved me to higher flights of imagination, and I said that the jury, with that charity so characteristic of pioneers, then dug a grave, and were about to give the petrified man Christian burial, when they found that for ages a limestone sediment had been trickling down the face of the stone against which he was sitting, and this stuff had run under him and cemented him fast to the "bedrock;" that the jury (they were all silver miners) canvassed the difficulty a moment, and then got out their powder and fuse, and proceeded to drill a hole under him, in order to *blast him from his position*, when Mr. Sewall, "with that delicacy so characteristic of him, forbade them, observing that it would be little less than sacrilege to do such a thing."

From the beginning to end the "Petrified Man" squib was a string of roaring absurdities, albeit they were told with an unfair pretense of truth that even imposed upon me to some extent, and I was in some danger of believing in my own fraud. But I really had no desire to deceive anybody, and no expectation of doing it. I depended on the way the petrified man was *sitting* to explain to the public that he was a swindle. Yet I purposely mixed that up with other things, hoping to make it obscure— and I did. I would describe the position of one foot, and then say his right thumb was against the side of his nose; then talk about his other foot, and presently come back and say the fingers of his right hand were spread apart; then talk about the back of his head a little, and return and say the left thumb was hooked into the right little finger; then ramble off about something else, and then by and by drift back again and remark that the fingers of the left hand were spread like those of the right. But I was too ingenious. I mixed it up rather too much; and so all that description of the attitude, as a key to the humbuggery of the article, was entirely lost, for nobody but me ever discovered and comprehended the peculiar and suggestive position of the petrified man's hands.

As a *satire* on the petrifaction mania, or anything else, my Petrified Man was a disheartening failure; for everybody received him in innocent good faith, and I was stunned to see the creature I had begotten to pull down the wonder-business with, and bring derision upon it, calmly exalted to the grand chief place in the list of the genuine marvels our Nevada had produced. I was so disappointed at the curious miscarriage of my scheme, that at first I was angry, and did not like to think about it; but by and by, when the exchanges began to come in with the Petrified Man copied and guilelessly glorified, I began to feel a soothing secret satisfaction; and as my gentleman's field of travels broadened, and by the exchanges I saw that he steadily and implacably penetrated territory after territory, state after state, and land after land, till he swept the great globe and culminated in sublime and unimpeached legitimacy in the august London *Lancet*, my cup was full, and I said I was glad I had done it. I think that for about eleven months, as nearly as I can remember, Mr. Sewall's daily mailbag continued to be swollen by the addition of half a bushel of newspapers hailing from many climes with the Petrified Man in them, marked around with a prominent belt of ink. I sent them to him. I did it for spite, not for fun. He used to shovel them into his back yard and curse. And every day during all those months the miners, his constituents (for miners never quit joking a person when they get started), would call on him and ask if he could tell them where they could get hold of a paper with the Petrified Man in it. He could have accommodated a continent with them. I hated Sewall in those days, and these things pacified me and pleased me. I could not have gotten more real comfort out of him without killing him.

The other burlesque I have referred to was my fine satire upon the financial expedients of "cooking dividends," a thing which became shamefully frequent on the Pacific coast for a while. Once more, in my self-complacent simplicity I felt that the time had arrived for me to rise up and be a reformer. I put this reformatory satire in the shape of a fearful "Massacre at Empire City." The San Francisco papers were making a great outcry about the iniquity of the Daney Silver Mining Company, whose directors had declared a "cooked" or false dividend, for the purpose of increasing the value of their stock, so that they could sell out at a comfortable figure, and then scramble from under the tumbling concern. And while abusing the Daney, those papers did not forget to urge the public to get rid of all their silver stocks and invest in sound and safe San Francisco stocks, such as the Spring Valley Water Company, etc. But right at this unfortunate juncture, behold the Spring Valley cooked a dividend too! And so, under the insidious mask of an invented "bloody massacre," I stole upon the public unawares with my scathing satire upon the dividend-cooking system. In about half a column of imaginary human carnage I told how a citizen had murdered his wife and nine children, and then committed suicide. And I said slyly, at the bottom, that the sudden madness of which this melancholy massacre was the result had been brought about by his having allowed himself to be persuaded by the California papers to sell his sound and lucrative Nevada silver stocks, and buy into Spring Valley just in time to get cooked along with that company's fancy dividend, and sink every cent he had in the world.

Ah, it was a deep, deep satire, and most ingeniously contrived. But I made the horrible details so carefully and conscientiously interesting that the public devoured *them* greedily, and wholly overlooked the following distinctly stated facts, to wit: The murderer was perfectly well known to every creature in the land as a *bachelor* and consequently he could not murder his wife and nine children; he murdered them "in his splendid dressed-stone mansion just in the edge of the great pine forest between Empire City and Dutch Nick's," when even the very pickled oysters that came on our tables knew that there was not a "dressed-stone mansion" in all Nevada Territory; also that, so far from there being a "great pine forest between Empire City and Dutch Nick's," there wasn't a solitary tree within fifteen miles of either place; and, finally, it was patent and notorious that Empire City and Dutch Nick's were one and the same place, and contained only six houses anyhow, and consequently there could be no forest *between* them; and on top of all these absurdities I stated that this diabolical murderer, after inflicting a wound upon himself that the reader ought to have seen would kill an elephant in the twinkling of an eye, jumped on his horse and rode *four miles*, waving his wife's reeking scalp in the air, and thus performing entered Carson City with tremendous *éclat*, and dropped dead in front of the chief saloon, the envy and admiration of all beholders.

Well, in all my life I never saw anything like the sensation that little satire created. It was the talk of the town, it was the talk of the territory. Most of the citizens dropped gently into it at breakfast, and they never finished their meal. There was something about those minutely faithful details that was a sufficing substitute for food. Few people that were able to read took food that morning. Dan and I (Dan was my reportorial associate) took our seats on either side of our customary table in the "Eagle Restaurant," and, as I unfolded the shred they used to call a napkin in that establishment, I saw at the next table two stalwart innocents with that sort of vegetable dandruff sprinkled about their clothing which was the sign and evidence that they were in from the Truckee with a load of hay. The one facing me had the morning paper folded to a long, narrow strip, and I knew, without any telling, that that strip represented the column that contained my pleasant financial satire. From the way he was excitedly mumbling, I saw that the heedless son of a haymow was skipping with all his might, in order to get to the bloody details as quickly as possible; and so he was missing the guideboards I had set up to warn him that the whole thing was a fraud. Presently his eyes spread wide open, just as his jaws swung asunder to take in a potato approaching it on a fork; the potato halted, the face lit up redly, and the whole man was on fire with excitement. Then he broke into a disjointed checking off of the particulars—his potato cooling in midair meantime, and his mouth making a reach for it occasionally, but always bringing up suddenly against a new and still more direful performance of my hero. At last he looked his stunned and rigid comrade impressively in the face, and said, with an expression of concentrated awe:

"Jim, he b'iled his baby, and he took the old 'oman's skelp. Cuss'd if *I* want any breakfast!"

And he laid his lingering potato reverently down, and he and his friend departed from the restaurant empty but satisfied.

He *never got down* to where the satire part of it began. Nobody ever did.[2] They found the thrilling particulars sufficient. To drop in with a poor little moral at the fag end of such a gorgeous massacre was like following the expiring sun with a candle and hope to attract the world's attention to it.

The idea that anybody could ever take my massacre for a genuine occurrence never once suggested itself to me, hedged about as it was by all those telltale absurdities and impossibilities concerning the "great pine forest," and the "dressed-stone mansion," etc. But I found out then, and never have forgotten since, that we never *read* the dull explanatory surroundings of marvelously exciting things when we have no occasion to suppose that some irresponsible scribbler is trying to defraud us; we skip all that, and hasten to revel in the bloodcurdling particulars and be happy.

[2]The Virginia *Evening Bulletin* immediately labeled the story "as baseless as the fabric of a dream," and scolded the author. But other newspapers were less skeptical.

No. 10 - $20 enclosed                    Virginia, July 18.

My Dear Mother & Sister

Ma, you are slinging incin-
erations at me again. Such as "where
did I get the money?" and "The company
I kept" in San Francisco." Why it
sold "wildcat" mining ground that
was given me, & my credit was always good at the bank for two or
three thousand dollars, & is yet.
I _never_ gamble, in any shape or
manner, and never drink anything
stronger than claret or lager beer,
which conduct is regarded as miraculously temperate in this country.
As for my company, Ma, I went
into the very best society to be found
in San Francisco, & to do that, you
must know, of course, that I had
to keep myself mighty straight.
I also move in the best society
of Virginia, & actually have a reputation to preserve.

As for money, I manage to
make a living, but if I had any business tact the office of reporter here
would be worth $30,000 a year —
whereas, if I get 4 or $5,000 out of it,
it will be as much as I expect. I have
stock in my possession, which, if I had
sold when it was first given me, from
time to time, in the last 9 months,

*Letter from Mark Twain to his Mother and Sister, Pamela.*

would have brought me $10,000 — but I have carelessly let it go down to nothing again. I don't think I am any account, anyhow. Now, I raised the price of "South Ophir" from $15 got to $45 a foot, to-day, & they re me five feet. That will go the wa of all the rest. I shall probably mislay it or throw it in my trunk & never get a dollar out of it. But I am telling you too many secrets, & I'll stop. One more. A gentleman in San Francisco told me to call at his office, & he would give me five feet of "Overman". Well, do you know I never went after it? The stock is worth $400 a foot, now — $2,000 thrown away. I don't care a straw, for myself, but I ought to have had more thought for you. Never mind, though, Ma — I will be more careful in future. I will take care that your expenses are paid— sure.

You and Pamela only pay $8 a week apiece for board (& lodging too?) Well, you are not in a very expensive part of the world, certainly. My room-mate & I pay, together, $90 a month for our bedchamber, & $50 a month, each, for board besides. Put in my washing, & it costs me $100 a month to live.

Affectionately, Mark

# XVIII

## *Exiled from Nevada by Request*

EVERY now and then I got away from Virginia
City for trips to San Francisco. Also I had to go
to Carson City, the capital, and report the proceedings of the legislature. Every Sunday I wrote a letter
to the newspaper, in which I made a resumé of the
week's legislative work, and in order that it might
be readable I put no end of seasoning into it. My
home base continued to be Virginia City until I was
exiled from Nevada by request in the early summer
of 1864.

Dueling suddenly became quite a fashion in the
new territory of Nevada, and by 1864 everybody was
anxious to have a chance in the new sport, mainly
for the reason that he was not able to thoroughly
respect himself so long as he had not killed or crippled somebody in a duel or been killed or crippled
in one himself.

At that time I had been serving as city editor on
Mr. Goodman's Virginia City *Enterprise* for a matter of two years. I was twenty-nine years old. I was
ambitious in several ways, but I had entirely escaped that particular fashion. I had had no desire to
fight a duel. I had no intention of provoking one. I
did not feel respectable, but I got a certain amount

of satisfaction out of feeling safe. I was ashamed of myself, the rest of the staff were ashamed of me—but I got along well enough. Since I had always been accustomed to feeling ashamed of myself, for one thing or another, there was no novelty for me in the situation. I bore it very well. Plunkett was on the staff. R. M. Daggett was on the staff. These had tried to get into duels, but, for the present, had failed and were waiting. Goodman was the only one of us who had done anything to shed credit upon the paper. The rival paper was the Virginia *Union*. Its editor for a little while was named Fitch, called the "silver-tongued orator of Wisconsin"—that was where he came from. He tuned up his oratory in the editorial columns of the *Union*, and Mr. Goodman invited him out and modified him with a bullet. I remember the joy of the staff when Goodman's challenge was accepted by Fitch. We ran late that night, and made much of Joe Goodman. He was only twenty-four years old; he lacked the wisdom which a person has at twenty-nine, and he was as glad of being *it* as I was that I wasn't. He chose Major Graves for his second (that name is not right, but it's close enough, I don't remember the major's name). Graves came over to instruct Joe in the dueling art. He had been a major under Walker, the "gray-eyed man of destiny," and had fought all the way through that remarkable man's filibustering campaign in Central America. That fact gauges the major. To say that a man was a major under Walker, and came out of that struggle ennobled by Walker's praise, is to say that the major was not merely a brave man, but that he was brave to the very utmost limit of that word. All of Walker's men were like that. I knew the Gillis family intimately. The father made the campaign under Walker, and with him one son. They were in the memorable Plaza fight, and stood it out to the last against overwhelming odds, as did also all of the Walker men. The son was killed at the father's side. The father received a bullet through the eye. The old man—for he was an old man at the time—wore spectacles, and the bullet and one of the glasses went into his skull, and the bullet remained there. There were some other sons—Steve, George, and Jim, very young chaps— the merest lads—who wanted to be in the Walker expedition, for they had their father's dauntless spirit. But Walker wouldn't have them; he said it was a serious expedition, and no place for children.

The major was a majestic creature, with a most stately and dignified and impressive military bearing, and he was by nature and training courteous, polite, graceful, winning; and he had that quality which I think I have encountered in only one other man—Bob Howland—that quality which resides in the eye; and when that eye is turned upon an individual or a squad, in warning, that is enough. The man that has that eye doesn't need to go armed; he can move upon an armed desperado and quell him and take him prisoner without saying a single word.

I saw Bob Howland do that once—a slender, good-natured, amiable, gentle, kindly little skeleton of a man, with a sweet blue eye that would win your heart when it smiled upon you, or turn cold and freeze it, according to the nature of the occasion.

The major stood Joe up straight; stood Steve Gillis up fifteen paces away; made Joe turn his right side toward Steve, cock his navy six-shooter—that prodigious weapon—and hold it straight down against his leg; told him that *that* was the correct position for the gun—that the position ordinarily in use at Virginia City (that is to say, the gun straight up in the air, bring it slowly down to your man) was all wrong. At the word "One," you must raise the gun slowly and steadily to the place on the other man's body that you desire to convince. "One, two, three—fire—Stop!" At the word "stop," you may fire—but not earlier. You may give yourself as much time as you please *after* that word. Then, when you fire, you may advance and go on firing at your leisure and pleasure, if you can get any pleasure out of it. And, in the meantime, the other man, if he has been properly instructed and is alive to his privileges, is advancing on *you*, and firing—and it is always likely that more or less trouble will result.

Naturally, when Joe's revolver had risen to a level it was pointing at Steve's breast, but the major said: "No, that is not wise. Take all the risks of getting murdered yourself, but don't run any risk of murdering the other man. If you survive a duel you want to survive it in such a way that the memory of it will not linger along with you through the rest of your life, and interfere with your sleep. Aim at your man's leg; not at the knee, not above the knee, for those are dangerous spots. Aim below the knee so as to cripple him, but leave the rest of him to his mother."

By the grace of these truly wise and excellent instructions, Joe tumbled his man down with a bullet through his lower leg, which furnished him a permanent limp. And Joe lost nothing but a lock of hair, which he could spare better then than he could now. For when I saw him here a year ago his crop was gone, and he had nothing much left but a fringe, with a dome rising above.

About a year later I got *my* chance. But I was not hunting for it. Goodman went off to San Francisco for a week's holiday, and left me to be chief editor. I had supposed that that was an easy berth, there being nothing to do but write one editorial per day; but I became disappointed in that superstition. I couldn't find anything to write an article about, the first day. Then it occurred to me that inasmuch as it was the twenty-second of April, 1864, the next morning would be the three-hundredth anniversary of Shakespeare's birthday—and what better subject could I want than that? I got the Cyclopædia and examined it, and found out who Shakespeare was and what he had done, and I borrowed all that and laid it before a community that could not have been better prepared for instruction about Shakespeare than if they had been prepared by art. There wasn't *enough* of what Shakespeare had done to make an editorial of the necessary length, but I filled it out with what he hadn't done; which in many respects was more important and striking and readable than the handsomest things he had really accomplished. But next day I was in trouble again. There were no more Shakespeares to work up. There was nothing in past history, or in the world's future possibilities, to make an editorial out of suitable to that community; so there was but one theme left. That theme was Mr. Laird, proprietor of the Virginia *Union. His* editor had gone off to San Francisco, too, and Laird was trying his hand at editing. I woke up Mr. Laird with some courtesies of the kind that were fashionable among newspaper editors in that region, and he came back at me the next day in a most vitriolic way. So we expected a challenge from Mr. Laird, because according to the rules—according to the etiquette of dueling as reconstructed and reorganized and improved by the duelists of that region—whenever you said a thing about another person that he didn't like, it wasn't sufficient for him to talk back in the same, or a more offensive spirit; etiquette required him to send a challenge. So we waited for a challenge—waited all day. It didn't come. And as the day wore along, hour after hour, and no challenge came, the boys grew depressed. They lost heart. But I was cheerful; I felt better and better all the time. They couldn't understand it, but *I* could understand it. It was my *make* that enabled me to be cheerful when other people were despondent. So then it became necessary for us to waive etiquette and challenge Mr. Laird. When we reached that decision, they began to cheer up, but *I* began to lose some of my animation. However, in enterprises of this kind you are in the hands of your friends; there is nothing for you to do but to abide by what they consider to be the best course. Daggett wrote a challenge for me, for Daggett had the language—the correct language—the convincing language—and I lacked it. Daggett poured out a stream of unsavory epithets upon Mr. Laird, charged with a vigor and venom of a strength calculated to persuade him; and Steve Gillis, my second, carried the challenge and came back to wait for the return. But it didn't come. The boys were exasperated, but I kept my temper. Steve carried another challenge, hotter than the other, and we waited again. Nothing came of it. I began to feel quite comfortable. I began to take an interest in the challenges myself. I had not felt any before; but it seemed to me that I was accumulating a great and valuable reputation at no expense, and my delight in this grew and grew as challenge after challenge was declined, until by midnight I was beginning to think that there was nothing in the world so much to be desired as a chance to fight a duel. So I hurried Daggett up; made him keep on sending challenge after challenge. Oh, well, I overdid it. I might have suspected that would happen—Laird was a man you couldn't depend on.

The boys were jubilant beyond expression. They helped me make my will, which was another discomfort—and I already had enough. Then they took me home. I didn't sleep any—didn't want to sleep. I had plenty of things to think about, and less than four hours to do it in—because five o'clock was the hour appointed for the tragedy, and I should have to use about one hour—beginning at four—in practicing with the revolver and finding out which end of it to level at the adversary. At four we went down into a little gorge, about a mile from town, and borrowed a barn door for a mark—borrowed it of a man who was over in California on a visit—and we set the barn door up and stood a fence rail up against the middle of it. The rail was no proper representative of Mr. Laird, for he was longer than a rail and thinner. Nothing would ever fetch him but a line shot, and then, as like as not, he would split the bullet—the worst material for dueling purposes that could be imagined. I began on the rail, but I couldn't hit the rail; I couldn't hit the barn door. There was nobody in danger except for stragglers around on the flanks of that mark. I was thoroughly discouraged, and I didn't cheer up any when we presently heard pistol shots over in the next little ravine. I knew what that was—that was Laird's gang out practicing him. They would hear my shots, and of course they would come up over the ridge to see what kind of a record I was making—see what their chances were against me. Well, I hadn't any record; and I knew that if Laird came over that ridge and looked at my barn door without a scratch on it, he would be as anxious to fight as I was—or as I had been at midnight, before that acceptance came.

Now just at this moment a little bird, no bigger than a sparrow, flew along by and lit on a sage bush about thirty yards away. Steve whipped out his revolver and shot its head off. Oh, he was a marksman—much better than I was. We ran down there to pick up the bird, and just then, sure enough, Mr. Laird and his people came over the ridge, and they joined us. And when Laird's second saw that bird with its head shot off, he lost color, and you could see that he was interested.

He said:

"Who did that?"

Before I could answer, Steve spoke up and said quite calmly, and in a matter-of-fact way, "Clemens did it."

The second said, "Why, that is wonderful! How far off was that bird?"

Steve said, "Oh, not far—about thirty yards."

The second then said, "Well, that is astonishing shooting. How often can he do that?"

Steve said, languidly, "Oh, about four times out of five!"

I knew the little rascal was lying, but I didn't say anything. The second said:

"Why, that is *wonderful* shooting! Why, I suppose he couldn't hit a church!"

He was supposing very sagaciously, but I didn't say anything. Well, they then said good morning. The second took Mr. Laird home, a little tottery on his legs, to be sure, and Laird sent back a note in his own hand declining to fight a duel with me on any terms whatever.

Well, my life was saved—saved by that accident. I don't know what the bird thought about that interposition of Providence, but I felt very, very comfortable over it—satisfied and content. Now we found out, later, that Laird had hit *his* mark four times out of six, right along. If the duel had come off, he would have so filled my skin with bullet holes that it wouldn't have held my principles.

By breakfast time the news was all over town that I had sent a challenge and Steve Gillis had carried it. Now that would entitle us to two years apiece in the penitentiary, according to the brand-new law. Governor North sent us no message as coming from himself, but a message *came* from a close friend of his. He said it would be a good idea for us to leave the territory by the first stagecoach. This would sail next morning at four o'clock—and in the meantime we would be looked for, but not with avidity; and if we stayed in the territory after that stagecoach left, we would be the first victims of the new law. Judge North was anxious to have some victims for that law, and he would absolutely keep us in the prison the full two years. He wouldn't pardon us out to please anybody.

Well, it seemed to me that our society was no longer desirable in Nevada; so we stayed in our quarters and observed proper caution all day—except that one time Steve went over to the hotel to attend to another customer of mine. That was a Mr. Cutler. You see, Laird was not the only person whom I had tried to reform during my occupancy of the editorial chair. I had looked around and selected several other people, and delivered a new zest of life into them through warm criticism and disapproval—so that when I laid down my editorial pen I had four horsewhippings and two duels owing to me. We didn't care for the horsewhippings; there was no glory in them; they were not worth the trouble of collecting. But honor required that some notice should be taken of that other duel. Mr. Cutler had come up from Carson City, and sent a man over with a challenge from the hotel. Steve went over to pacify him. Steve weighed only ninety-five pounds, but it was well known throughout the territory that with his fists he could whip anybody that walked on two legs, let his weight and science be what they might. Steve was a Gillis, and when a Gillis confronted a man and had a proposition to make, the proposition always contained business. When Cutler found out that Steve was my second he cooled down; he became calm and rational, and was ready to listen. Steve gave him fifteen minutes to get out of the hotel, and half an hour to get out of town, or there would be results. So *that* duel went off with success, because Mr. Cutler went off toward Carson, a convinced and reformed man.

I have never had anything to do with duels since. I thoroughly disapprove of duels. I consider them unwise, and I know they are dangerous. Still, I have always taken a great interest in other people's duels. One always feels an abiding interest in any heroic thing which has entered into his own experience.[1]

In 1878, fourteen years after my unmaterialized duel, Messieurs Fortu and Gambetta fought a duel which made heroes of both of them in France, and made them ridiculous throughout the rest of the world. I was living in Munich that fall and winter, and I was so interested in that duel that I wrote a long account of it, and it is in one of my books, *A Tramp Abroad*—an account which had some inaccuracies in it, but as an exhibition of the *spirit* of that duel I think it was correct and trustworthy.

[1]Paul Fatout in *Mark Twain in Virginia City* (Blooming-ton, 1964), p. 213, calls this account of an abortive duel "a mistaken recollection in old age," and persuasively argues for "the inference that he (Mark Twain) was ashamed" of his less creditable performance.

# XIX

## *San Francisco Reporter*

I HAD begun to get tired, anyhow, of staying in one place so long. There was no longer any satisfying variety in going down to Carson to report the proceedings of the legislature once a year, and horse-races and pumpkin shows once in three months (they had got to raising pumpkins and potatoes in Washoe Valley, and, of course, one of the first achievements of the legislature was to institute a ten-thousand-dollar agricultural fair to show off forty dollars' worth of those pumpkins in—however, the territorial legislature was usually spoken of as the "asylum"). I wanted to see San Francisco. I wanted to go somewhere. I wanted—I did not know *what* I wanted. I had the "spring fever" and wanted a change, principally, no doubt. Besides, a convention had framed a state constitution; nine men out of every ten wanted an office; I believed that these gentlemen would "treat" the moneyless and the irresponsible among the population into adopting the constitution and thus well-nigh killing the country (it could not well carry such a load as a state government, since it had nothing to tax that could stand a tax, for undeveloped mines could not, and there were not fifty developed ones in the land, there was but little realty to tax, and it did seem as if nobody was ever going to think of the simple salvation of inflicting a money penalty on murder). I believed that a state government would destroy the "flush times," and I wanted to get away. I believed that the mining stocks I had on hand would soon be worth one hundred thousand dollars, and thought if they reached that before the constitution was adopted, I would sell out and make myself secure from the crash the change of government was going to bring. I considered one hundred thousand dollars sufficient to go home with decently, though it was but a small amount compared to what I had been expecting to return with. I felt rather downhearted about it, but I tried to comfort myself with the reflection that with such a sum I could not fall into want. About this time a schoolmate of mine, whom I had not seen since boyhood, came tramping in on foot from Reese River, a very allegory of Poverty. The son of wealthy parents, here he was, in a strange land, hungry, bootless, mantled in an ancient horse blanket, roofed with a brimless hat, and so generally and so extravagantly dilapidated that he could have "taken the shine out of the Prodigal Son himself," as he pleasantly remarked. He wanted to borrow forty-six dollars—twenty-six to take him to San Francisco, and twenty for something else; to buy some soap with, maybe, for he needed it. I found I had but little more than the amount wanted, in my pocket; so I stepped in and borrowed forty-six dollars of a banker (on twenty days' time, without the formality of a note), and gave it to him, rather than walk half a block to the office, where I had some specie laid up. If anybody had told me that it would take me two years to pay back that forty-six dollars to the banker (for I did not expect it of the Prodigal Son, and was not disappointed), I would have felt injured. And so would the banker.

It was not without regret that I took a last look at the tiny flag (it was thirty-five feet long and ten feet wide) fluttering like a lady's handkerchief from the topmost peak of Mount Davidson, two thousand feet above Virginia's roofs, and felt that doubtless I was bidding a permanent farewell to a city which had afforded me the most vigorous enjoyment of life I had ever experienced.

San Francisco, a truly fascinating city to live in, is stately and handsome at a fair distance, but close at hand one notes that the architecture is mostly old-fashioned, many streets are made up of decaying, smoke-grimed, wooden houses, and the barren sand hills toward the outskirts obtrude themselves too prominently. Even the kindly climate is sometimes pleasanter when read about than personally experienced, for a lovely, cloudless sky wears out its welcome by and by, and then when the longed-for rain does come it *stays*. Even the playful earthquake is better contemplated at a dis—

However, there are varying opinions about that. The climate of San Francisco is quite mild and

singularly equable. The thermometer usually reads
about seventy degrees all year. It hardly changes a
bit. You sleep under one or two light blankets summer and winter, and never use a mosquito bar. Nobody ever wears summer clothing. You wear black
broadcloth—if you have it—in August and January,
just the same. It is no colder, and no warmer, in the
one month than the other. You do not use overcoats
and you do not use fans. It is as pleasant a climate as
could well be contrived, take it all around, and is
doubtless the most unvarying in the whole world.
The wind blows there a good deal in the summer
months, but then you can go over to Oakland, if
you choose—three or four miles away—it does not
blow there. It has only snowed twice in San Francisco in nineteen years, and then it only remained on
the ground long enough to astound the children, and
set them to wondering what the feathery stuff was.

During eight months of the year, straight along,
the skies are bright and cloudless, and never a drop
of rain falls. But when the other four months come
along, you will need to go and steal an umbrella.
Because you will require it. Not just one day, but
one hundred and twenty days in hardly varying suc-
cession. When you want to go visiting, or attend
church, or the theater, you never look up at the
clouds to see whether it is likely to rain or not—you
look at the almanac. If it is winter, it will *rain*—and
if it is summer, it *won't* rain, and you cannot help it.
You never need a lightning rod, because it never

thunders and it never lightnings. And after you have listened for six or eight weeks, every night, to the dismal monotony of those quiet rains, you will wish in your heart the thunder *would* leap and crash and roar along those drowsy skies once, and make everything alive—you will wish the prisoned lightnings *would* cleave the dull firmament asunder and light it with a blinding glare for *one* little instant. You would give *anything* to hear the old familiar thunder again and see the lightning strike somebody. And along in the summer, when you have suffered about four months of lustrous, pitiless sunshine, you are ready to go down on your knees and plead for some rain—hail—snow—thunder and lightning—anything to break up the monotony—you will take an earthquake, if you cannot do any better.

San Francisco is built on sand hills, but they are prolific sand hills. They yield a generous vegetation. All the rare flowers which people in "the States" rear with such patient care in parlor flowerpots and greenhouses, flourish luxuriantly in the open air there all the year round. Calla lilies and all sorts of geraniums, passion flowers, moss roses— I do not know the names of a tenth part of them. I only know that while New Yorkers are burdened with banks and drifts of snow, Californians are burdened with banks and drifts of flowers, if they only keep their hands off and let them grow. And I have heard that they have also that rarest and most curious of all flowers, the beautiful *Espiritu Santo*, as

the Spaniards call it—or flower of the Holy Spirit—
though I thought it grew only in Central America—
down on the Isthmus. In its cup is the daintiest
little facsimile of a dove, as pure as the snow. The
Spaniards have a superstitious reverence for it. Now,
the blossom has been conveyed to the States, submerged in ether; and the bulb has been taken thither also, but every attempt to make it bloom after it
arrived, has failed.

For a few months I enjoyed what to me was a
completely new phase of existence—a butterfly idle-
ness; nothing to do, nobody to be responsible to,
and untroubled with financial uneasiness. I fell in
love with the most cordial and sociable city in the
Union. After the sagebrush and alkali deserts of
Washoe, San Francisco was Paradise to me. I lived
at the best hotel, exhibited my clothes in the most
conspicuous places, infested the opera, and learned
to seem enraptured with music which oftener afflicted my ignorant ear than enchanted it, if I had had
the vulgar honesty to confess it. However, I suppose
I was not greatly worse than the most of my coun-
trymen in that. I had longed to be a butterfly, and I
was one at last. I attended private parties in sumptuous evening dress, simpered and aired my graces
like a born beau, and polked and schottisched with
a step peculiar to myself—and the kangaroo. In a
word, I kept the due state of a man worth a hundred
thousand dollars (prospectively), and quite likely to
reach absolute affluence when that silver mine sale

should be ultimately achieved in the East. I spent money with a free hand, and meantime watched the stock sales with an interested eye and looked to see what might happen in Nevada.

Something very important happened. The property holders of Nevada voted against the state constitution; but the folks who had nothing to lose were in the majority, and carried the measure over their heads. But after all it did not immediately look like a disaster, though unquestionably it was one. I hesitated, calculated the chances, and then concluded not to sell. Stocks went on rising; speculation went mad; bankers, merchants, lawyers, doctors, mechanics, laborers, even the very servant girls and washer-women, were putting up their earnings on silver stocks, and every sun that rose in the morning went down on paupers enriched and rich men beggared. What a gambling carnival it was! Gould & Curry soared to six thousand dollars a foot! And then—all of a sudden, out went the bottom and everything and everybody went to ruin and destruction! The wreck was complete. The bubble scarcely left a microscopic moisture behind it. I was an early beggar and a thorough one. My hoarded stocks were not worth the paper they were printed on. I threw them all away. I, the cheerful idiot that had been squandering money like water, and thought myself beyond the reach of misfortune, had not now as much as fifty dollars when I gathered together my various debts and paid them. I removed from the hotel to a very private boarding-house. I took a berth and went to work as a reporter on the San Francisco *Morning Call*. I was more than that—I was *the* reporter. There was no other. There was enough work for one and a little over, but not enough for two—according to Mr. Barnes's idea, and he was the proprietor and therefore better situated to know about it than other people.

By nine in the morning I had to be at the police court for an hour and make a brief history of the squabbles of the night before. They were usually between Irishmen and Irishmen, and Chinamen and Chinamen, with now and then a squabble between the two races for a change. Each day's evidence was substantially a duplicate of the evidence of the day before, therefore the daily performance was killingly monotonous and wearisome. So far as I could see, there was only one person connected with it who found anything like a compensating interest in it, and that was the court interpreter. He was an Englishman who was glibly familiar with fifty-six Chinese dialects. He had to change from one to another of them every ten minutes and this exercise was so energizing that it kept him always awake, which was not the case with the reporters. Next we visited the higher courts and made notes of the decisions which had been rendered the day before. All the courts came under the heading of "regulars." They were sources of reportorial information which never failed. During the rest of the day we raked the town from end to end, gathering such material as we might, wherewith to fill our required column—and if there were no fires to report we started some on our own.

At night we visited the six theaters, one after the other: seven nights in the week, three hundred and sixty-five nights in the year. We remained in each of those places five minutes, got the merest passing glimpse of play and opera, and with that for a text we "wrote up" those plays and operas, as the phrase goes, torturing our souls every night from the beginning of the year to the end of it in the effort to find something to say about those performances which we had not said a couple of hundred times before. There has never been a time from that day to this, forty years, that I have been able to look at even the outside of a theater without a spasm of the dry gripes, as "Uncle Remus"[1] calls it—and as for the inside, I know next to nothing about that, for in all this time I have seldom had a sight of it nor ever had any desire in that regard which couldn't have been overcome by argument.

After having been hard at work from nine or ten in the morning until eleven at night scraping material together, I took the pen and spread this muck out in words and phrases and made it cover as much acreage as I could. It was fearful drudgery, soulless drudgery, and almost destitute of interest. It was an awful slavery for a lazy man, and I was born lazy.

[1] Joel Chandler Harris's popular black dialect storyteller.

Finally, there was an event. One Sunday afternoon I saw some hoodlums chasing and stoning a Chinaman who was heavily laden with the weekly wash of his Christian customers, and I noticed that a policeman was observing this performance with an amused interest—nothing more. He did not interfere. I reported on the incident with considerable warmth and holy indignation. Usually I didn't want to read in the morning what I had written the night before; it had come from a torpid heart. But this item had come from a live one. There was fire in it and I believed it was literature—and so I sought for it in the paper the next morning with eagerness. It wasn't there. It wasn't there the next morning, nor the next. I went up to the composing room and found it tucked away among condemned matter on the standing galley. I asked about it. The foreman said Mr. Barnes had found it in a galley proof and ordered its extinction. And Mr. Barnes furnished his reasons—either to me or to the foreman, I don't remember which; but they were all commercially sound. He said that the *Call* was like the New York *Sun* of that day: it was the washerwomen's paper—that is, it was the paper of the poor; it was the only cheap paper. It gathered its livelihood from the poor and must respect their prejudices or perish. The Irish were the poor. They were the stay and support of the *Morning Call*; without them the *Morning Call* could not survive a month—and they hated the Chinamen. The kind of assault as I had attempted could rouse the entire Irish hive, and seriously damage the paper. The *Call* could not afford to publish articles criticizing the hoodlums for stoning Chinamen.

I was lofty in those days. I have survived it. I was unwise, then. I am up-to-date now. A recent New York *Sun* has a paragraph or two from its London correspondent which enables me to locate myself. The correspondent mentions a few of our American events, such as the limitless rottenness of our great insurance companies, where theft has been carried on by our most distinguished commercial men as a profession; the exposures of conscienceless graft, colossal graft, in great municipalities like Philadelphia, St. Louis, and other large cities; the recent exposure of millionfold graft in the great Pennsylvania Railway system—with minor uncoverings of commercial swindles from one end of the United States to the other; and finally the lurid exposure, by Upton Sinclair, of the most titanic and death-dealing swindle of them all, the Beef Trust, an exposure which has moved the President to demand of a reluctant Congress a law which shall protect America and Europe from falling, in a mass, into the hands of the doctor and the undertaker.[2]

In the words of that correspondent, Europe had

[2]Upton Sinclair's popular novel, *The Jungle* (1906), contained exposures of unsanitary conditions in the Chicago stockyards which led to the passage of a Pure Food and Drugs Act.

begun to wonder if there was really an honest male human creature left in the United States. In 1905, I was satisfied that there was no such person existing upon American soil except myself. That exception was rubbed out in 1906, and now it is my belief that there isn't a single male human being in America who is honest. I held the belt all alone, until January, 1906, and then I went down, with Rockefeller and Carnegie and a group of Goulds and Vanderbilts and other professional grafters, and swore off my taxes like the most conscienceless of the lot. I was a great loss to America, because I was irreplaceable. It is my belief that it will take fifty years to produce my successor. I believe the entire population of the United States, exclusive of the women, to be rotten, as far as the dollar is concerned. Understand, I am saying these things as a dead person. I should consider it indiscreet in any live one to make these remarks publicly.

But, as I was saying, I was loftier when I was twenty-nine than I am now, and I felt a deep shame in being situated as I was—slave of such a journal as the *Morning Call*. If I had been still loftier I would have thrown up my berth and gone out and starved, like any other hero. But I had never had any experience. I had *dreamed* heroism, like everybody, but I had had no practice and I didn't know how to begin. I couldn't bear to begin with starving. I had already come near to that once or twice in my life, and found no real enjoyment out of remembering about it. I knew I couldn't get another berth if I resigned. I knew it perfectly well. Therefore I swallowed my humiliation and stayed where I was. But whereas there had been little enough interest attaching to my industries, before, there was none at all now. I continued my work but I took not the least interest in it, and naturally there were results. I got to neglecting it. As I have said, there was too much of it for one man. The way I was conducting it now, there was apparently work enough in it for two or three. Even Barnes noticed that, and told me to get an assistant, on half wages.

There was a great hulking creature down in the counting room—good-natured, obliging, unintellectual—and he was getting little or nothing a week and boarding himself. A graceless boy of the counting room force who had no reverence for anybody or anything was always making fun of this beachcomber, and he had a name for him which somehow seemed intensely apt and descriptive—I don't know why. He called him Smiggy McGlural. I offered the berth of assistant to Smiggy, and he accepted it with alacrity and gratitude. He went at his work with ten times the energy that was left in me. He was not intellectual but mentality was not required or needed in a *Morning Call* reporter, and so he conducted his office to perfection. I gradually got to leaving more and more of the work to McGlural. I grew lazier and lazier, and within thirty days he was doing almost the whole of it. It was also plain that he could accomplish the whole of it, and more, all by himself, and therefore had no real need of me.

It was at this crucial moment that that event happened which I mentioned a while ago. Mr. Barnes discharged me. It was the only time in my life that I have ever been discharged, and it hurts me yet—although I am in my grave. He did not discharge me rudely. It was not in his nature to do that. He was a large, handsome man, with a kindly face and courteous ways, and was faultless in his dress. He could not have said a rude, ungentle thing to anybody. He took me privately aside and advised me to resign. It was like a father advising a son for his good, and I obeyed.

I was on the world, now, with nowhere to go. By my Presbyterian training, I knew that the *Morning Call* had brought a disaster upon itself. I knew the ways of Providence, and I knew that this offense would have to be answered for. I could not foresee when the penalty would fall nor what shape it would take, but I was as certain that it would come, sooner or later, as I was of my very own existence. I could not tell whether it would fall upon Barnes or upon his newspaper. But Barnes was the guilty one, and I knew by my training that the punishment always falls upon the innocent one, consequently I felt sure that it was the newspaper that at some future day would suffer for Barnes's crime.

Sure enough! Among the very first pictures of the great San Francisco earthquake that arrived in the fourth week of April 1906—there stood the *Morning Call* building towering out of the wrecked city, like a Washington Monument; and the body of it was all gone, and nothing was left but the iron bones! It was then that I said, "How wonderful are the ways of Providence!" I had known it would happen. I had known it for forty years. I had never lost my confidence in Providence during all that time. It was put off longer than I was expecting but it was now comprehensive and satisfactory enough to make up for that. Some people would think it curious that Providence should destroy an entire city of four hundred thousand inhabitants to settle an account of forty years standing, between a mere discharged reporter and a newspaper, but to me there was nothing strange about that, because I was educated, I was trained, I was a Presbyterian, and I knew how these things are done. I knew that in Biblical times, if a man committed a sin, the extermination of the whole surrounding nation—cattle and all—was likely to happen. I knew that Providence was not particular about the rest, so that He got somebody connected with the one He was after. I remembered that in the *Magnalia*[3] a man who went home swearing from prayer meeting one night got his reminder within the next nine months. He had a wife and seven children, and all at once they

[3] *Magnalia Christi Americana* (1702) is an ecclesiastical history of New England by Cotton Mather (1663–1728), a Puritan religious leader in Massachusetts.

were attacked by a terrible disease, and one by one they died in agony till at the end of a week there was nothing left but the man himself. I knew that the idea was to punish the man, and I knew that if he had any intelligence he recognized that that intention had been carried out, although mainly at the expense of other people.

In those ancient times the counting room of the *Morning Call* was on the ground floor; the office of the Superintendent of the United States Mint was on the next floor above, with Bret Harte[4] as private secretary of the Superintendent. The quarters of the editorial staff and the reporter were on the third floor, and the composing room on the fourth and final floor. I spent a good deal of time with Bret Harte in his office after Smiggy McGlural came, but nothing before that. Harte was doing a good deal of writing for the *Californian*—contributing "Condensed Novels" and sketches to it and also acting as editor, I think. I was a contributor. So was Charles H. Webb; also Prentiss Mulford; also a young lawyer named Hastings, who gave promise of distinguishing himself in literature some day. Charles Warren Stoddard was also a contributor. Ambrose

[4]A contemporary (1836–1902) of Clemens whose local color writings about the Far West were remarkably popular. Harte had many dealings with the humorist and eventually won his lasting antipathy. For a detailed account of the relationship that is prejudiced in favor of Harte, see Margaret Duckett, *Mark Twain and Bret Harte* (Norman, Oklahoma, 1964).

Bierce,[5] who is still writing acceptably for the magazines today, was then employed on some paper in San Francisco—*The Golden Era*,[6] perhaps. We had very good times together—very social and pleasant times. But that was after Smiggy McGlural came to my assistance; there was no leisure time before that. Smiggy was a great advantage to me—during thirty days. Then he turned into a disaster.

It was Mr. Swain, Superintendent of the Mint, who discovered Bret Harte. Harte had arrived in California in the fifties, twenty-three or twenty-four years old, and had wandered up into the surface diggings of the camp at Yreka, a place which had acquired its curious name—when in its first days it much needed a name—through an accident. There was a bakeshop with a canvas sign which had not yet been put up but had been painted and stretched to dry in such a way that the word BAKERY, all but the "B", showed through and was reversed. A stranger read it wrong end first, YREKA, and supposed that was the name of the camp. The campers were satisfied with it and adopted it.

Harte taught school in that camp several months. He also edited the weekly rag which was doing duty as a newspaper. He spent a little time also in the

[5]Webb . . . Bierce, prominent Western authors who in time achieved national fame.
[6]A San Francisco literary journal which started publication in 1852, was quite successful in the 1860s, and which, though it survived until 1893, was less successful during its last decades.

pocket-mining camp of Jackass Gulch (where I tarried, some years later, during three months). It was at Yreka and Jackass Gulch that Harte learned to accurately observe and put with photographic exactness on paper the woodland scenery of California and the general country aspects—the stagecoach, its driver and its passengers, and the clothing and general style of the surface miner, the gambler, and their women; and it was also in these places that he learned, without the trouble of observing, all that he didn't know about mining, and how to make it read as if an expert were behind the pen. It was in those places that he also learned how to fascinate Europe and America with the quaint dialect of the miner—a dialect which no man in heaven or earth had ever used until Harte invented it. With Harte it died, but it was no loss. By and by he came to San Francisco. He was a compositor by trade, and got work in *The Golden Era* office at ten dollars a week.

Harte was paid for setting type only but he lightened his labors and entertained himself by contributing literature to the paper, uninvited. The editor and proprietor, Joe Lawrence, never saw Harte's manuscripts, because there weren't any. Harte spun his literature out of his head while at work at the case, and set it up as he spun. *The Golden Era* was ostensibly and ostentatiously a literary paper, but its literature was pretty feeble and sloppy and only exhibited the literary forms, without really being literature. Mr. Swain, the Superintendent of the Mint, noticed a new note in that *Golden Era* orchestra—a new and fresh and spirited note that rose above that orchestra's mumbling confusion and was recognizable as music. He asked Joe Lawrence who the performer was, and Lawrence told him. It seemed to Mr. Swain a shame that Harte should be wasting himself in such a place and on such a pittance so he took him away, made him his private secretary, on a very good salary, with little or nothing to do, and told him to follow his own bent and develop his talent. Harte was quite willing and the development began.

Bret Harte was one of the pleasantest men I have ever known. He was also one of the unpleasantest men I have ever known. He was showy, meretricious, insincere; and he constantly advertised these qualities in his dress. He was distinctly pretty, in spite of the fact that his face was badly pitted with smallpox. In the days when he could afford it—and in the days when he couldn't—his clothes always exceeded the fashion by a shade or two. He was always conspicuously a little more intensely fashionable than the fashionablest of the rest of the community. He had good taste in clothes. With all his conspicuousness there was never anything really loud nor offensive about them. They always had a single smart little accent, effectively located and that accent would have distinguished Harte from any other of the ultrafashionables. Oftenest it was his necktie. Always it was of a single color, and intense. Most frequently, perhaps, it was crimson—a flash of flame under his chin; or it was indigo blue and as hot and vivid as if one of those splendid and luminous Brazilian butterflies had lighted there. Harte's dainty self-complacencies extended to his carriage and gait. His carriage was graceful and easy, his gait was of the mincing sort, but was the right gait for him, for an unaffected one would not have harmonized with the man and the clothes.

He hadn't a sincere fiber in him. I think he was incapable of emotion, for I think he had nothing to feel with. I think his heart was merely a pump and had no other function. I am almost moved to say I *know* it had no other function. I knew him intimately in the days when he was private secretary on the second floor and I a fading and perishing reporter on the third, with Smiggy McGlural looming doomfully in the near distance. I knew him intimately when he came east five years later, in 1870, to take the editorship of the proposed *Lakeside Magazine*, in Chicago, and crossed the continent through such a prodigious blaze of national interest and excitement that one might have supposed he was the Viceroy of India on a progress, or Halley's comet come again after seventy-five years of absence.

I knew him pretty intimately thenceforth until he crossed the ocean to be consul, first at Crefeldt in Germany and afterwards in Glasgow. He never returned to America. When he died, in London, he had been absent from America and from his wife and daughters twenty-six years.

This is the Bret Harte whose pathetics, imitated from Dickens, used to be a godsend to the farmers of two hemispheres on account of the freshets of tears they compelled. He said to me once with a cynical chuckle that he thought he had mastered the art of pumping up the tear of sensibility. The idea conveyed was that the tear of sensibility was oil, and that by luck he had struck it.

C. H. Webb had established a very excellent literary weekly called the *Californian*, but high merit was no guaranty of success; it languished, and he sold out to three printers, and Bret Harte became editor at twenty dollars a week, and I was employed to contribute an article a week at twelve dollars. But the journal still languished, and the printers sold out to Captain Ogden, a rich man and also a pleasant gentleman who chose to amuse himself with such an expensive luxury without much caring about the cost of it. When he grew tired of the novelty, he resold to the printers, the paper presently died a peaceful death, and I was out of work again. I would not mention these things but for the fact that they so aptly illustrate the ups and downs that characterize life on the Pacific coast. A man could hardly stumble into such a variety of queer vicissitudes in any other country.

For two months my sole occupation was avoiding acquaintances; for during that time I did not earn a penny, or buy an article of any kind, or pay my board. I became very adept at "slinking." I slunk from back street, I slunk away from approaching faces that looked familiar, I slunk to my meals, ate them humbly and with a mute apology for every mouthful I robbed my generous landlady of, and at midnight, after wanderings that were but slinkings away from cheerfulness and light, I slunk to my bed. I felt meaner, and lowlier, and more despicable than the worms. During all this time I had but one piece of money—a silver ten-cent piece—and I held to it and would not spend it on any account, lest the consciousness coming strong upon me that I was *entirely* penniless, might suggest suicide. I had pawned everything but the clothes I had on; so I clung to my dime desperately, till it was smooth with handling.

# XX

# Jackass Gulch, Angel's Camp, and a Famous Frog

B<sup>Y AND BY</sup>, an old friend of mine, a miner named
Jim Gillis, came down from one of the decayed
mining camps of Tuolumne, California, and I went
back with him. He, his "pard" Dick Stoker, and I
lived in a small cabin on a verdant hillside, and
there were not five other cabins in view over the
wide expanse of hill and forest. Yet a flourishing
city of two or three thousand population had occupied this grassy dead solitude during the flush times
of twelve or fifteen years before, and where our cabin stood had once been the heart of the teeming
hive, the center of the city. When the mines gave
out the town fell into decay, and in a few years
wholly disappeared—streets, dwellings, shops, everything—and left no sign. The grassy slopes were
as green and smooth and desolate of life as if they
had never been disturbed. The mere handful of
miners still remaining had seen the town spring up,
spread, grow, and flourish in its pride; and they had
seen it sicken and die, and pass away like a dream.
With it their hopes had died, and their zest of life.
They had long ago resigned themselves to their exile, and ceased to correspond with their distant
friends or turn longing eyes toward their early

homes. They had accepted banishment, forgotten the world and been forgotten of the world. They were far from telegraphs and railroads, and they stood, as it were, in a living grave, dead to the events that stirred the globe's great populations, dead to the common interests of men, isolated and outcast from brotherhood with their kind. It was the most singular, and almost the most touching and melancholy, exile that fancy can imagine.

They were lovely fellows; charming comrades in every way and honest and honorable men; their credit was good for bacon and beans, and this was fortunate because their kind of mining was a peculiarly precarious one; it was called pocket-mining and so far as I have been able to discover, pocket-mining is confined and restricted on this planet to a very small region around about Jackass Gulch.

A "pocket" is a concentration of gold dust in one little spot on the mountainside; it is close to the surface; the rains wash its particles down the mountainside, and they spread, fan-shape, wider and wider as they go. The pocket-miner washes a pan of dirt, finds a speck or two of gold in it, makes a step to the right or the left, washes another pan, finds another speck or two, and goes on washing to the right and to the left until he knows when he has reached both limits of the fan by the best of circumstantial evidence, to wit—that his pan-washings furnish no longer the speck of gold. The rest of his work is easy—he washes along up the mountainside,

*The Jim Gillis cabin in the Jackass Gulch country near
Tuolumne, California.*

Courtesy of the Mark Twain Papers, The Bancroft Library

tracing the narrowing fan by his washings, and at last he reaches the gold deposit. It may contain only a few hundred dollars, which he can take out with a couple of dips of his shovel; also it may contain a concentrated treasure worth a fortune.

These friends of mine had been seeking that fortune daily for eighteen years; they had never found it but they were not at all discouraged; they were quite sure they would find it some day. During the three months that I was with them they found nothing, but we had a fascinating and delightful good time trying. Not long after I left, a Mexican came along and found a pocket with a hundred and twenty-five thousand dollars in it on a slope which our boys had never happened to explore. Such is luck!

Our clothes were pretty shabby but that was no matter; we were in the fashion; the rest of the slender population were dressed as we were. Our boys hadn't had a cent for several months and hadn't needed one. If there was any difference, Jim was the worst dressed of the three of us; if there was any discoverable difference in the matter of age, Jim's shreds were the oldest; but he was a gallant creature, and his style and bearing could make any costume regal. One day we were in the decayed and naked and rickety inn in Angel's Camp when a couple of musical tramps appeared; one of them played the banjo and the other danced unscientific clog-dances and sang comic songs that made a person sorry to be alive. They passed the hat and collected three or four dimes from the dozen bankrupt miners present. When the hat approached Jim he said to me, with his fine millionaire air, "Let me have a dollar."

I gave him a couple of halves. Instead of modestly dropping them into the hat, he pitched them into it at the distance of a yard, just as in the ancient novels milord the Duke doesn't hand the beggar a benefaction, but "tosses" it to him or flings it at his feet—and it is always a "purse of gold." In the novel, the witnesses are always impressed; Jim's great spirit was the spirit of the novel; to him the half-dollars were a purse of gold; like the Duke he was playing to the gallery, but the parallel ends there. In the Duke's case, the witnesses knew he could afford the purse of gold, and the largest part of their admiration consisted in envy of the man who could throw around purses of gold in that fine and careless way. The miners admired Jim's handsome liberality but they knew he couldn't afford what he had done, and that fact modified their admiration.

Often during a very rainy season, we sat around the stove in the Angel's Camp inn and swapped stories with other surface miners. One afternoon, Ben Coon, a former Illinois river pilot, spun a yarn about a frog—one that would become famous when not long after I published my version.

I heard the story told by a man who was not telling it to his hearers as a thing new to them, but as a thing which *they had witnessed and would remember*. He was a dull person, and ignorant; he had no gift as a storyteller, and no invention; in his mouth this episode was merely history—history and statistics; and the gravest sort of history, too; he was entirely serious, for he was dealing with what to him were austere facts, and they interested him solely because they *were* facts; he was drawing on his memory, not his mind; he saw no humor in his tale, neither did his listeners; neither he nor they ever smiled or laughed; in my time I have not attended a more solemn conference. To him and to his fellow gold miners there were just two things in the story that were worth considering. One was the smartness of the stranger in taking in its hero, Jim Smiley, with a loaded frog; and the other was the stranger's deep knowledge of a frog's nature—for he knew (as the narrator asserted and the listeners conceded) that a frog *likes shot* and is always ready to eat it. Those men discussed those two points, and those only. They were hearty in their admiration of them, and none of the party was aware that a first-rate story had been told in a first-rate way, and that it was brimful of a quality whose presence they never suspected—humor.

Here is "The Notorious Jumping Frog of Calaveras County" as told by "Mark Twain":

In compliance with the request of a friend of mine,[1] who wrote me from the East, I called on good-natured, garrulous old Simon Wheeler, and inquired after my friend's friend, Leonidas W. Smiley, as requested to do,

[1] Charles Farrar Browne (1834–1867), famous under the pseudonym of Artemus Ward, had met Clemens when visiting Virginia City to give a humorous lecture. He asked Twain to write a story for inclusion in the forthcoming *Artemus Ward: His Travels.* The story reached the pubisher too late for inclusion; it was passed along to the New York *Saturday Press* and published as a letter to "Mr. A. Ward" from Mark Twain on November 18, 1865. Extensively copied, it did much to spread its author's fame nationwide.

and I hereunto append the result. I have a lurking suspicion that *Leonidas W.* Smiley is a myth; that my friend never knew such a personage; and that he only conjectured that if I asked old Wheeler about him, it would remind him of his infamous *Jim* Smiley, and he would go to work and bore me to death with some exasperating reminiscence of him as long and as tedious as it should be useless to me. If that was the design, it succeeded.

I found Simon Wheeler dozing comfortably by the barroom stove of the dilapidated tavern in the decayed mining camp of Angel's, and I noticed that he was fat and bald-headed, and had an expression of winning gentleness and simplicity upon his tranquil countenance. He roused up, and gave me good day. I told him that a friend of mine had commissioned me to make some inquiries about a cherished companion of his boyhood named *Leonidas W.* Smiley—*Rev. Leonidas W.* Smiley, a young minister of the Gospel, who he had heard was at one time a resident of Angel's Camp. I added that if Mr. Wheeler could tell me anything about this Rev. Leonidas W. Smiley, I would feel under many obligations to him.

Simon Wheeler backed me into a corner and blockaded me there with his chair, and then sat down and reeled off the monotonous narrative which follows this paragraph. He never smiled, he never frowned, he never changed his voice from the gentle-flowing key to which he tuned his initial sentence, he never betrayed the slightest suspicion of enthusiasm; but all through the interminable narrative there ran a vein of impressive earnestness and sincerity, which showed me plainly that, so far from his imagining that there was anything ridiculous or funny about his story, he regarded it as a really important matter, and admired its two heroes as men of transcendent genius in *finesse*. I let him go on in his own way, and never interrupted him once.

"Rev. Leonidas W. H'm, Reverend Le—well, there was

a feller here once by the name of *Jim* Smiley, in the winter of '49—or maybe it was the spring of '50—I don't recollect exactly, somehow, though what makes me think it was one or the other is because I remember the big flume warn't finished when he first come to the camp; but anyway, he was the curiousest man about always betting on anything that turned up you ever see, if he could get anybody to bet on the other side; and if he couldn't he'd change sides. Any way that suited the other man would suit *him*—any way just so's he got a bet, *he* was satisfied. But still he was lucky, uncommon lucky; he most always come out winner. He was always ready and laying for a chance; there couldn't be no solit'ry thing mentioned but that feller'd offer to bet on it, and take ary side you please, as I was just telling you. If there was a horse race, you'd find him flush or you'd find him busted at the end of it; if there was a dog fight, he'd bet on it; if there was a cat fight, he'd bet on it; if there was a chicken fight, he'd bet on it; why, if there was two birds setting on a fence, he would bet you which one would fly first; or if there was a camp meeting, he would be there reg'lar to bet on Parson Walker, which he judged to be the best exhorter about here, and so he was too, and a good man. If he even see a straddle bug start to go anywheres, he would bet you how long it would take him to get to—to wherever he was going to, and if you took him up, he would foller that straddlebug to Mexico but what he would find out where he was bound for and how long he was on the road. Lots of boys here has seen that Smiley, and can tell you about him. Why, it never made no difference to *him*—he'd bet on *anything*—the dangdest feller. Parson Walker's wife laid very sick once, for a good while, and it seemed as if they warn't going to save her; but one morning he come in, and Smiley up and asked him how she was, and he said she was considerable better—thank the Lord for his inf'nite mercy—and coming on so smart that with the blessing of Prov'dence she'd get well yet; and Smiley, before he thought, says, 'Well, I'll resk two-and-a-half she don't anyway.'

"Thish-yer Smiley had a mare—the boys called her the fifteen-minute nag, but that was only in fun, you know, because of course she was faster than that—and he used to win money on that horse, for all she was so slow and always had the asthma, or the distemper, or the consumption, or something of that kind. They used to give her two or three hundred yards' start, and then pass her under way; but always at the fag end of the race she'd get excited and desperate like, and come cavorting and straddling up, and scattering her legs around limber, sometimes in the air, and sometimes out to one side among the fences, and kicking up m-o-r-e dust and raising m-o-r-e racket with her coughing and sneezing and blowing her nose—and *always* fetch up at the stand just about a neck ahead, as near as you could cipher it down.

"And he had a little small bull pup, that to look at him you'd think he warn't worth a cent but to set around and look ornery and lay for a chance to steal something. But as soon as money was up on him he was a different dog; his under jaw'd begin to stick out like the fo'castle of a steamboat, and his teeth would uncover and shine like the furnaces. And a dog might tackle him and bullyrag him, and bite him, and throw him over his shoulder two or three times, and Andrew Jackson—which was the name of the pup—Andrew Jackson would never let on but what *he* was satisfied, and hadn't expected nothing else—and the bets being doubled and doubled on the other side all the time, till the money was all up; and then all of a sudden he would grab that other dog jest by the j'int of his hind leg and freeze to it—not chaw, you understand, but only just grip and hang on till they throwed up the sponge, if it was a year. Smiley always come out winner on that pup, till he harnessed a dog once that didn't have

no hind legs, because they'd been sawed off in a circular
saw, and when the thing had gone along far enough, and
the money was all up, and he come to make a snatch for
his pet holt, he see in a minute how he'd been imposed
on, and how the other dog had him in the door, so to
speak, and he 'peared surprised, and then he looked sorter discouraged-like, and didn't try no more to win the
fight, and so he got shucked out bad. He give Smiley a
look, as much as to say his heart was broke, and it was *his*
fault, for putting up a dog that hadn't no hind legs for
him to take holt of, which was his main dependence in a
fight, and then he limped off a piece and laid down and
died. It was a good pup, was that Andrew Jackson, and
would have made a name for hisself if he'd lived, for the
stuff was in him and he had genius—I know it, because he
hadn't no opportunities to speak of, and it don't stand to
reason that a dog could make such a fight as he could
under them circumstances if he hadn't no talent. It always
makes me feel sorry when I think of that last fight of
his'n, and the way it turned out.

"Well, thish-yer Smiley had rat terriers, and chicken
cocks, and tomcats and all them kind of things, till you
couldn't rest, and you couldn't fetch nothing for him to
bet on but he'd match you. He ketched a frog one day,
and took him home, and said he cal'lated to educate him;
and so he never done nothing for three months but set in
his back yard and learn that frog to jump. And you bet
you he *did* learn him, too. He'd give him a little punch
behind, and the next minute you'd see that frog whirling
in the air like a doughnut—see him turn one summerset,
or maybe a couple, if he got a good start, and come down
flat-footed and all right, like a cat. He got him up so in
the matter of ketching flies, and kep' him in practice so
constant, that he'd nail a fly every time as fur as he could
see him. Smiley said all a frog wanted was education, and
he could do 'most anything—and I believe him. Why, I've

seen him set Dan'l Webster down here on this floor—
Dan'l Webster was the name of the frog—and sing out,
'Flies, Dan'l, flies!' and quicker'n you could wink he'd
spring straight up and snake a fly off'n the counter there,
and flop down on the floor again as solid as a gob of mud,
and fall to scratching the side of his head with his hind
foot as indifferent as if he hadn't no idea he'd been doin'
any more'n any frog might do. You never see a frog so
modest and straightfor'ard as he was, for all he was so
gifted. And when it come to fair and square jumping on a
dead level, he could get over more ground at one straddle
than any animal of his breed you ever see. Jumping on a
dead level was his strong suit, you understand; and when
it come to that, Smiley would ante up money on him as
long as he had a red. Smiley was monstrous proud of his
frog, and well he might be, for fellers that had traveled
and been everywheres all said he laid over any frog that
ever *they* see.

"Well, Smiley kep' the beast in a little lattice box, and
he used to fetch him downtown sometimes and lay for a
bet. One day a feller—a stranger in the camp, he was—
come acrost him with his box, and says:

'What might it be that you've got in the box?'

"And Smiley says, sorter indifferent-like, 'It might be a
parrot, or it might be a canary, maybe, but it ain't—it's
only just a frog.'

"And the feller took it, and looked at it careful, and
turned it round this way and that, and says, 'H'm—so 'tis.
Well, what's *he* good for?'

'Well,' Smiley says, easy and careless, 'he's good
enough for *one* thing, I should judge—he can outjump any
frog in Calaveras County.'

"The feller took the box again, and took another long,
particular look, and give it back to Smiley, and says, very
deliberate, 'Well,' he says, 'I don't see no p'ints about
that frog that's any better'n any other frog.'

*Artist's conception of "The Jumping Frog" from the
first edition of* Sketches, New and Old.

'Maybe you don't.' Smiley says. 'Maybe you understand frogs and maybe you don't understand 'em; maybe you've had experience, and maybe you ain't only a amature. Anyways, I've got *my* opinion, and I'll resk forty dollars that he can outjump any frog in Calaveras County.'

"And the feller studied a minute, and then says, kinder sad-like, 'Well, I'm only a stranger here, and I ain't got no frog; but if I had a frog, I'd bet you.'

"And then Smiley says, 'That's all right—that's all right—if you'll hold my box a minute, I'll go and get you a frog.' And so the feller took the box, and put up his forty dollars along with Smiley's, and set down to wait.

"So he set there a good while thinking and thinking to himself, and then he got the frog out and prized his mouth open and took a teaspoon and filled him full of quailshot—filled him pretty near up to his chin—and set him on the floor. Smiley, he went to the swamp and slopped around in the mud for a long time, and finally he ketched a frog, and fetched him in, and give him to this feller, and says:

'Now, if you're ready, set him alongside of Dan'l, with his fore paws just even with Dan'l's, and I'll give the word.' Then he says, 'One—two—three—*git*!' and him and the feller touched up the frogs from behind, and the new frog hopped off lively, but Dan'l give a heave, and hysted up his shoulders—so—like a Frenchman, but it warn't no use—he couldn't budge; he was planted as solid as a church, and he couldn't no more stir than if he was anchored out. Smiley was a good deal surprised, and he was disgusted too, but he didn't have no idea what the matter was, of course.

"The feller took the money and started away; and when he was going out at the door, he sorter jerked his thumb over his shoulder—so—at Dan'l, and says again, very deliberate, 'Well,' he says, '*I* don't see no p'ints about that frog that's any better'n any other frog.'

"Smiley he stood scratching his head and looking down at Dan'l a long time, and at last he says, 'I do wonder what in the nation that frog throw'd off for—I wonder if there ain't something the matter with him—he 'pears to look mighty baggy, somehow.' And he ketched Dan'l by the nap of the neck, and hefted him, and says, 'Why blame my cats if he don't weigh five pound!' and turned him upside down and he belched out a double handful of shot. And then he see how it was, and he was the maddest man—he set the frog down and took out after that feller, but he never ketched him. And _____ "

[Here Simon Wheeler heard his name called from the front yard, and got up to see what was wanted.] And turning to me as he moved away, he said: "Just set where you are stranger, and rest easy—I ain't going to be gone a second."

But, by your leave, I did not think that a continuation of the history of the enterprising vagabond *Jim* Smiley would be likely to afford me much information concerning the Rev. *Leonidas W.* Smiley, and so I started away.

At the door I met the sociable Wheeler returning, and he buttonholed me and recommenced:

"Well, thish-yer Smiley had a yaller one-eyed cow that didn't have no tail, only just a short stump like a bannanner, and _____ "

However, lacking both time and inclination, I did not wait to hear about the afflicted cow, but took my leave.

# XXI

## *Jim Gillis and an Imaginary Cat*

ABOUT once a year Jim Gillis would come down to San Francisco, discard his rough mining costume, buy a fifteen-dollar suit of ready-made slops, and stride up and down Montgomery Street with his hat tipped over one ear and looking as satisfied as a king. The sarcastic stares which the drifting stream of elegant fashion cast upon him did not trouble him; he seemed quite unaware. On one of these occasions Joe Goodman and I and one or two other intimates took Jim up into the Bank Exchange billiard room. It was the resort of the rich and fashionable young swells of San Francisco. The time was ten at night and the twenty tables were all in service, all occupied. We strolled up and down the place to let Jim have a full opportunity to contemplate and enjoy this notable feature of the city.

Every now and then a fashionable young buck dropped a sarcastic remark about Jim and his clothes. We heard these remarks, but hoped that Jim's large satisfaction with himself would prevent his discovering that he was the object of them; but that hope failed; Jim presently began to take notice; then he began to try to catch one of these men in the act of making a remark. He presently succeeded.

A large and handsomely dressed young gentleman was the utterer. Jim stepped toward him and came to a standstill, with his chin lifted and his haughty pride exhibiting itself in his attitude and bearing, and said, impressively, "That was for me. You must apologize, or fight."

Half a dozen of the neighboring players heard him say it, and they faced about and rested the butts of their cues on the floor and waited with amused interest for results. Jim's victim laughed ironically, and said, "Oh, is that so? What would happen if I declined?"

"You will get a flogging that will mend your manners."

"Oh, indeed! I wonder if that's so."

Jim's manner remained grave and unruffled. He said, "I challenge you. You must fight me."

"Oh, really! Will you please name the time?"

"*Now*."

"How prompt we are! Place?"

"*Here*."

"This is charming! Weapons?"

"Double-barreled shotguns loaded with slugs; distance, thirty feet."

It was high time to interfere. Goodman took the young fool aside and said, "You don't know your man and you are doing a most dangerous thing. You seem to think he is joking but he is not joking, he is not that kind; he's in earnest; if you decline the duel he will kill you where you stand; you must accept his terms, and you must do it right away for you have no time to waste; take the duel or apologize. You will apologize of course, for two reasons: you insulted him when he was not offending you; that is one reason, the other is that you naturally neither want to kill an unoffending man nor be killed yourself. You will apologize and you will have to let him word the apology; it will be more strong and more uncompromising than any apology that you, even with the most liberal intentions, would be likely to frame."

The man apologized, repeating the words as they fell from Jim's lips—the crowd massed around the pair and listening—and the character of the apology was in strict accordance with Goodman's prediction concerning it.

I mourn for Jim. He was a good and steadfast friend, a manly one; an honest and honorable man and endowed with a lovable nature. He instituted no quarrels himself but whenever a quarrel was put upon him he was on deck and ready.

I THINK Jim Gillis was a much more remarkable person than his family and his intimates ever suspected. He had a bright and smart imagination and it was of the kind that turns out impromptu work and does it well, does it with easy facility and without previous preparation, just builds a story as it goes along, careless of whither it is proceeding, enjoying each fresh fancy as it flashes from the brain and caring not at all whether the story shall ever end brilliantly and satisfactorily or shan't end at all. Jim was born a humorist and a very competent one. When I stop to think about how felicitous were his untrained efforts, I feel a conviction that he would have been a star performer if he had been discovered, and had been subjected to a few years of training with a pen. A genius is not very likely to ever discover himself; neither is he very likely to be discovered by his intimates; in fact I think I may put it in stronger words and say it is impossible that a genius—at least a literary genius—can ever be discovered by his intimates.

St. Peter's cannot be impressive for size to a person who has always seen it close at hand and has never been outside of Rome; it is only the stranger, approaching from far away in the Campagna, who sees Rome as an indistinct and characterless blur, with the mighty cathedral standing up out of it all lonely and unfellowed in its majesty. Thousands of geniuses live and die undiscovered—either by themselves or by others. But for the Civil War, Lincoln and Grant and Sherman and Sheridan would not have been discovered, nor have risen into notice. I have touched upon this matter in a small book which I wrote a generation ago and which I have not published as yet—*Captain Stormfield's Visit to Heaven*. When Stormfield arrived in heaven he was eager to get a sight of those unrivaled and incomparable military geniuses, Caesar, Alexander, and Napoleon, but was told by an old resident of heaven that they didn't amount to much there as military geniuses, that they ranked as obscure corporals only by comparison with a certain colossal military genius, a shoemaker by trade, who had lived and died unknown in a New England village and had never seen a battle in all his earthly life. He had not been discovered while he was on the earth, but heaven knew him as soon as he arrived there, and lavished upon him the honors which he would have received on the earth if the earth had known that he was the most prodigious military genius the planet had ever produced.

I spent three months in the log cabin home of Jim Gillis and his "pard," Dick Stoker, in Jackass Gulch, that serene and reposeful and dreamy and delicious sylvan paradise of which I have already spoken. Every now and then Jim would have an inspiration, and he would stand up before the great log fire, with his back to it and his hands crossed behind him, and deliver himself of an elaborate impromptu lie—a fairy tale, an extravagant romance—with Dick Stoker as the hero of it as a general thing. Jim always soberly pretended that what he was relating was strictly history, veracious history, not romance. Dick Stoker, gray-headed and good-natured, would sit smoking his pipe and listen with a gentle serenity to these monstrous fabrications and never utter a protest.

In one of my books—*Huckleberry Finn*, I think—I

have used one of Jim's impromptu tales, which he called "The Tragedy of the Burning Shame."[1] I had to modify it considerably to make it proper for print, and this was a great damage. As Jim told it, inventing it as he went along, I think it was one of the most outrageously funny things I have ever listened to. How mild it is in the book, and how pale and how gorgeous in its unprintable form!

I used another of Jim's inventions in *Roughing It*, the story of Jim Baker's cat, the remarkable Tom Quartz:

One of my comrades there—another of those victims of eighteen years of unrequited toil and blighted hopes—was one of the gentlest spirits that ever bore its patient cross in a weary exile: grave and simple Dick Baker, pocket-miner of Dead Horse Gulch. He was forty-six, gray as a rat, earnest, thoughtful, slenderly educated, slouchily dressed, and clay-soiled, but his heart was finer metal than any gold his shovel ever brought to light—than any, indeed, that ever was mined or minted.

Whenever he was out of luck and a little downhearted, he would fall to mourning over the loss of a wonderful cat

[1] In Chapter XXIII of *Adventures of Huckleberry Finn,* two confidence men whom he calls the King and the Duke stage "The Royal Nonesuch" (originally called in the manuscript "The Burning Shame") in Bricksville, Ark. The poster warns, "Ladies and Children Not Admitted." Huck says of a performance before a full house: ". . . the king come a-prancing out on all fours, naked; and he was painted all over, ring-streaked-and-striped, all sorts of colors . . . And—but never mind the rest of his outfit, it was just wild, but it was awful funny." Versions of the widely diffused oral tale upon which Jim's version almost certainly was based indicate that "the rest of his outfit" was indecent.

he used to own (for where women and children are not, men of kindly impulses take up with pets, for they must love something). And he always spoke of the strange sagacity of that cat with the air of a man who believed in his secret heart that there was something human about it— maybe even supernatural.

I heard him talking about this animal once. He said:

"Gentlemen, I used to have a cat here, by the name of Tom Quartz, which you'd 'a' took an interest in, I reckon—most anybody would. I had him here eight year—and he was the remarkablest cat *I* ever see. He was a large gray one of the Tom specie, an' he had more hard, natchral sense than any man in this camp—'n' a *power* of dignity— he wouldn't let the Gov'ner of Californy be familiar with him. He never ketched a rat in his life—'peared to be above it. He never cared for nothing but mining. He knowed more about mining, that cat did, than any man *I* ever, ever see. You couldn't tell *him* noth'n' 'bout placer-diggin's—'n' as for pocket-mining, why he was just born for it. He would dig out after me an' Jim when we went over the hills prospect'n', and he would trot along behind us for as much as five mile, if we went so fur. An' he had the best judgment about mining ground—why you never see anything like it. When we went to work, he'd scatter a glance around, 'n' if he didn't think much of the indications, he would give a look as much as to say, 'Well, I'll have to get you to excuse *me*,' 'n' without another word he'd hyste his nose into the air 'n' shove for home. But if the ground suited him, he would lay low 'n' keep dark till the first pan was washed, 'n' then he would sidle up 'n' take a look, an' if there was about six or seven grains of gold *he* was satisfied—he didn't want no better prospect 'n' that—'n' then he would lay down on our coats and snore like a steamboat till we'd struck the pocket, an' then get up 'n' superintend. He was nearly lightnin' on superintending.

"Well, by an' by, up comes this yer quartz excitement. Everybody was into it—everybody was pick'n' 'n' blast'n' instead of shovelin' dirt on the hillside—everybody was put'n' down a shaft instead of scrapin' on the surface. Noth'n' would do Jim, but *we* must tackle the ledges, too, 'n' so we did. We commenced putt'n' down a shaft, 'n' Tom Quartz he begin to wonder what in the Dickens it was all about. *He* hadn't ever seen any mining like that before, 'n' he was all upset, as you may say—he couldn't come to a right understanding of it no way—it was too many for *him*. He was down on it, too, you bet you—he was down on it powerful—'n' always appeared to consider it the cussedest foolishness out. But that cat, you know, was *always* agin new-fangled arrangements—somehow he never could abide 'em. *You* know how it is with old habits. But by an' by Tom Quartz begin to git sort of reconciled a little, though he never *could* altogether understand that eternal sinkin' of a shaft an' never pannin' out anything. At last he got to comin' down in the shaft, hisself, to try to cipher it out. An' when he'd git the blues, 'n' feel kind o' scruffy, 'n' aggravated 'n' disgusted—knowin' as he did, that the bills was runnin' up all the time an' we warn't makin' a cent—he would curl up on a gunnysack in the corner an' go to sleep. Well, one day when the shaft was down about eight foot, the rock got so hard that we had to put in a blast—the first blast'n' we'd ever done since Tom Quartz was born. An' then we lit the fuse 'n' clumb out 'n' got off 'bout fifty yards—'n' forgot 'n' left Tom Quartz sound asleep on the gunnysack. In 'bout a minute we seen a puff of smoke bust up out of the hole, 'n' then everything let go with an awful crash, 'n' about four million ton of rocks 'n' dirt 'n' smoke 'n' splinters shot up 'bout a mile an' a half into the air, an' by George, right in the dead center of it was old Tom Quartz a-goin' end over end, an' a-snortin' an' a-sneez'n', an' a-clawin' an' a-reachin' for things like all possessed. But it warn't no use, you know, it warn't no use. An' that was the last we see of *him* for about two minutes 'n' a half, an' then all of a sudden it begin to rain rocks and rubbage, an' directly he come down ker-whop about ten foot off f'm where we stood. Well, I reckon he was p'raps the orneriest lookin' beast you ever see. One ear was sot back on his neck, 'n' his tail was stove up, 'n' his eyewinkers was swinged off, 'n' he was all blacked up with powder an' smoke, an' all sloppy with mud 'n' slush f'm one end to the other. Well, sir, it warn't no use to try to apologize—we jest couldn't say a word. He took a sort of a disgusted look at hisself, 'n' then he looked at us—an' it was just exactly the same as if he had said—'Gents, maybe *you* think it's smart to take advantage of a cat that ain't had no experience of quartz minin', but *I* think *differrent*'—an' then he turned on his heel 'n' marched off home without ever saying another word.[2]

"That was jest his style. An' maybe you won't believe it, but after that you never see a cat so prejudiced agin quartz mining as what he was. An' by an' by when he *did* get to goin' down in the shaft ag'in, you'd 'a' been astonished at his sagacity. The minute we'd tetch off a blast 'n'

[2] Some of the phrases in the above are mining technicalities, purely, and may be a little obscure to the general reader. In "*placer-diggings*" the gold is scattered all through the surface dirt; in "*pocket-diggings*" it is concentrated in one little spot; in "*quartz*" the gold is in a solid, continuous vein of rock, inclosed between distinct walls of some other kind of stone—and this is the most laborious and expensive of all the different kinds of mining. "*Prospecting*" is hunting for a "*placer*"; "*indications*" are signs of its presence; "*panning out*" refers to the washing process by which the grains of gold are separated from the dirt; a "*prospect*" is what one finds in the first panful of dirt—and its value determines whether it is a good or bad prospect, and whether it is worth while to tarry there or seek further.—*Mark Twain's footnote.*

the fuse'd begin to sizzle, he'd give a look as much as to say, 'Well, I'll have to git you to excuse *me*,' an' it was surpris'n' the way he'd shin out of that hole 'n' go f'r a tree. Sagacity? It ain't no name for it. "Twas *inspiration*!"

I said, "Well, Mr. Baker, his prejudice against quartz mining *was* remarkable, considering how he came by it. Couldn't you ever cure him of it?"

"*Cure him*! No! When Tom Quartz was sot once, he was *always* sot—and you might 'a' blowed him up as much as three million times 'n' you'd never 'a' broken him of his cussed prejudice agin quartz mining."

The affection and pride that lit up Baker's face when he delivered this tribute to his humble friend of other days, will always be a vivid memory with me.

JIM BAKER was Dick Stoker, of course; Tom Quartz had never existed; there was no such cat, at least outside of Jim Gillis's imagination.

Once or twice Jim's energetic imagination got him into trouble. A squaw came along one day and tried to sell us some wild fruit that looked like large greengages. Dick Stoker had lived in that cabin eighteen years, and knew that that product was worthless and inedible; but heedlessly and without purpose, he remarked that he had never heard of it before. That was enough for Jim. He launched out with fervent praises of that devilish fruit, and the more he talked about it the warmer and stronger his admiration of it grew. He said that he had eaten it a thousand times; that all one needed to do was to boil it with a little sugar and there was nothing on the American continent that could compare with it for deliciousness. He was only talking to hear himself talk; and so he was brought up standing and for just one moment, or maybe two moments, smitten dumb when Dick interrupted him with the remark that if the fruit was so delicious why didn't he invest in it on the spot? Jim was caught but he wouldn't let on; he had gotten himself into a scrape but he was not the man to back down or confess; he pretended that he was only too happy to have this chance to enjoy once more this precious gift of God. Oh, he was a loyal man to his statements! I think he would have eaten that fruit if he had known it would kill him. He bought the lot, and said airily and complacently that he was glad enough to have that benefaction, and that if Dick and I didn't want to enjoy it with him we could let it alone.

Then there followed a couple of the most delightful hours I have ever spent. Jim took an empty kerosene can of about a three-gallon capacity; put it on the fire and filled it half full of water. Then he dumped into it a dozen of those devilish fruits; and as soon as the water came to a good boil he added a handful of brown sugar; as the boiling went on he tested the odious mess from time to time; the unholy vegetables grew softer and softer, pulpier and pulpier, and now he began to make tests with a tablespoon. He would dip out a spoonful and taste it, smack his lips with fictitious satisfaction, remark that perhaps it needed a little more sugar—so he would dump in a handful and let the boiling go on a while longer; handful after handful of sugar went in and still the tasting went on for two hours, Stoker and I laughing at him, ridiculing him, deriding him, blackguarding him all the while, and he retaining his serenity unruffled.

At last he said the manufacture had reached the right stage, the stage of perfection. He dipped his spoon, tasted, smacked his lips, and broke into enthusiasms of grateful joy; then he gave us a taste apiece. From all that we could discover, those tons of sugar had not affected that fruit's malignant sharpness in the least degree. Acid? It was all acid, vindictive acid, uncompromising acid, with not a trace of the modifying sweetness which the sugar ought to have communicated to it and would have communicated to it if that fruit had been invented anywhere outside of perdition. We stopped with that single taste, but that greathearted Jim, that dauntless martyr, went on sipping and sipping, and sipping, and praising and praising, and praising, and praising, until his teeth and tongue were raw, and Stoker and I nearly dead with gratitude and delight. During the next two days neither food nor drink passed Jim's teeth; so sore were they that they could not endure the touch of anything; even his breath passing over them made him wince; nevertheless he went steadily on voicing his adulations of that brutal mess and praising God. It was an astonishing exhibition of grit, but Jim was like all the other Gillises, he was made of grit.

# XXII

# *Baker's Bluejay Yarn*

I USED another of Jim's impromptus in a book of mine called *A Tramp Abroad*, a tale of how the poor innocent and ignorant woodpeckers[1] tried to fill up a house with acorns. It is a charming story, a delightful story, and full of happy fancies. Jim stood before the fire and reeled it off with the easiest facility, inventing its details as he went along and claiming as usual that it was all straight fact, unassailable fact, history pure and undefiled:

One never tires of poking about in the dense woods that clothe all these lofty Neckar hills to their tops.[2] The great deeps of a boundless forest have a beguiling and impressive charm in any country; but German legends and fairy tales have given these an added charm. They have peopled all that region with gnomes, and dwarfs, and all sorts of mysterious and uncanny features. At the time I am writing of, I had been reading so much of this literature that sometimes I was not sure but I was beginning to believe in the gnomes and fairies as realities.

[1] Describing the story long after it was first published, Mark Twain misremembered the kind of birds it celebrated.
[2] The framework introduction is part of Chapter 2, the quoted story all of Chapter 3 of the travel book. The whole is an interlude in an account of a stay in Heidelberg during which the author visits the Black Forest, where the Neckar River rises.

One afternoon I got lost in the woods about a mile from the hotel, and presently fell into a train of dreamy thought about animals which talk, and kobolds, and enchanted folk, and the rest of the pleasant legendary stuff; and so, by stimulating my fancy, I finally got to imagining I glimpsed small flitting shapes here and there down the columned aisles of the forest.

When I had stood ten minutes, thinking and imagining, and getting my spirit in tune with the place, and in the right mood to enjoy the supernatural, a raven suddenly uttered a hoarse croak over my head. It made me start; and then I was angry because I started. I looked up, and the creature was sitting on a limb right over me, looking down at me. I felt something of the same sense of humiliation and injury which one feels when he finds that a human stranger has been clandestinely inspecting him in his privacy and mentally commenting upon him. I eyed the raven, and the raven eyed me. Nothing was said during some seconds. Then the bird stepped a little way along his limb to get a better point of observation, lifted his wings, stuck his head far down below his shoulders toward me, and croaked again—a croak with a distinctly insulting expression about it. If he had spoken in English he could not have said any more plainly than he did say in raven, "Well, what do *you* want here?" I felt as foolish as if I had been caught in some mean act by a responsible being, and reproved for it. However, I made no reply; I would not bandy words with a raven. The adversary waited a while, with his shoulders still lifted, his head thrust down between them, and his keen bright eye fixed on me; then he threw out two or three more insults, which I could not understand, further than that I knew a portion of them consisted of language not used in church.

I still made no reply. Now the adversary raised his head and called. There was an answering croak from a little distance in the wood—evidently a croak of inquiry. The adversary explained with enthusiasm, and the other raven dropped everything and came. The two sat side by side on the limb and discussed me as freely and offensively as two great naturalists might discuss a new kind of bug. The thing became more and more embarrassing. They called in another friend. This was too much. I saw that they had the advantage of me, and so I concluded to get out of the scrape by walking out of it. They enjoyed my defeat as much as any low white people could have done. They craned their necks and laughed at me (for a raven *can* laugh, just like a man), they squalled insulting remarks after me as long as they could see me. They were nothing but ravens—I knew that—what they thought about me could be a matter of no consequence—and yet when even a raven shouts after you, "What a hat!" "Oh, pull down your vest!" and that sort of thing, it hurts you and humiliates you and there is no getting around it with fine reasoning and pretty arguments.

Animals talk to each other, of course. There can be no question about that; but I suppose there are very few people who can understand them. I never knew but one man who could. I knew he could, however, because he told me so himself. He was a middle-aged, simple-hearted miner who had lived in a lonely corner of California, among the woods and mountains, a good many years, and had studied the ways of his only neighbors, the beasts and the birds, until he believed he could accurately translate any remark which they made. This was Jim Baker. According to Jim Baker, some animals have only a limited education, and use only very simple words, and scarcely ever a comparison or a flowery figure; whereas, certain other animals have a large vocabulary, a fine command of language and a ready and fluent delivery; consequently these latter talk a great deal; they like it; they are conscious of their talent, and they enjoy "showing off." Baker said, that after long and careful observation, he had come to the conclusion that the bluejays were the best talkers he had found among birds and beasts. Said he:

"There's more *to* a bluejay than any other creature. He has got more moods, and more different kinds of feelings than other creatures; and, mind you, whatever a bluejay feels, he can put into language. And no mere commonplace language, either, but rattling, out-and-out booktalk—and bristling with metaphor, too—just bristling! And as for command of language—why *you* never see a bluejay get stuck for a word. No man ever did. They just boil out of him! And another thing: I've noticed a good deal, and there's no bird, or cow, or anything that uses as good grammar as a bluejay. You may say a cat uses good grammar. Well, a cat does—but you let a cat get excited once; you let a cat get to pulling fur with another cat on a shed, nights, and you'll hear grammar that will give you the lockjaw. Ignorant people think it's the *noise* which fighting cats make that is so aggravating, but it ain't so; it's the sickening grammar they use. Now I've never heard a jay use bad grammar but very seldom; and when they do, they are as ashamed as a human; they shut right down and leave.

"You may call a jay a bird. Well, so he is, in a measure—because he's got feathers on him, and don't belong to no church, perhaps; but otherwise he is just as much a human as you be. And I'll tell you for why. A jay's gifts, and instincts, and feelings, and interests, cover the whole ground. A jay hasn't got any more principle than a Congressman. A jay will lie, a jay will steal, a jay will deceive, a jay will betray; and four times out of five, a jay will go back on his solemnest promise. The sacredness of an obligation is a thing which you can't cram into no bluejay's head. Now, on top of all this, there's another thing; a jay can out-swear any gentleman in the mines. You think a cat can swear. Well, a cat can; but you give a bluejay a subject that calls for his reserve powers, and where is your cat? Don't talk to *me*—I know too much about this thing. And there's yet another thing; in the one little particular of scolding—just good, clean, out-and-out scolding—a bluejay can lay over anything, human or divine. Yes, sir, a jay is everything that a man is. A jay can cry, a jay can laugh, a jay can feel shame, a jay can reason and plan and discuss, a jay likes gossip and scandal, a jay has got a sense of humor, a jay knows when he is an ass just as well as you do—maybe better. If a jay ain't human, he better take in his sign, that's all. Now I'm going to tell you a perfectly true fact about some bluejays.

"When I first begun to understand jay language correctly, there was a little incident happened here. Seven years ago, the last man in this region but me moved away. There stands his house—been empty ever since; a log house, with a plank roof—just one big room, and no more; no ceiling—nothing between the rafters and the floor. Well, one Sunday morning I was sitting out here in front of my cabin, with my cat, taking the sun, and looking at the blue hills, and listening to the leaves rustling so lonely in the trees, and thinking of the home away yonder in the states, that I hadn't heard from in thirteen years, when a bluejay lit on that house, with an acorn in his mouth, and says, 'Hello, I reckon I've struck something.' When he spoke, the acorn dropped out of his mouth and rolled down the roof, of course, but he didn't care; his mind was all on the thing he had struck. It was a knothole in the roof. He cocked his head to one side, shut one eye and put the other one to the hole, like a 'possum looking down a jug; then he glanced up with his bright eyes, gave a wink or two with his wings—which signifies gratification, you understand—and says, 'It looks like a hole, it's located like a hole—blamed if I don't believe it *is* a hole!'

"Then he cocked his head down and took another

look; he glances up perfectly joyful, this time; winks his wings and his tail both, and says, 'Oh, no, this ain't no fat thing, I reckon! If I ain't in luck!—why it's a perfectly elegant hole!' So he flew down and got that acorn, and fetched it up and dropped it in, and was just tilting his head back, with the heavenliest smile on his face, when all of a sudden he was paralyzed into a listening attitude and that smile faded gradually out of his countenance like breath off'n a razor, and the queerest look of surprise took its place. Then he says, 'Why, I didn't hear it fall!' He cocked his eye at the hole again, and took a long look; raised up and shook his head; stepped around to the other side of the hole and took another look from that side; shook his head again. He studied a while, then he just went into the *de*tails—walked round and round the hole and spied into it from every point of the compass. No use. Now he took a thinking attitude on the comb of the roof and scratched the back of his head with his right foot a minute, and finally says, 'Well, it's too many for *me*, that's certain; must be a mighty long hole; however, I ain't got no time to fool around here, I got to 'tend to business; I reckon it's all right—chance it, anyway.'

"So he flew off and fetched another acorn and dropped it in, and tried to flirt his eye to the hole quick enough to see what become of it, but he was too late. He held his eye there as much as a minute; then he raised up and sighed, and says, 'Confound it, I don't seem to understand this thing, no way; however, I'll tackle her again.' He fetched another acorn, and done his level best to see what become of it, but he couldn't. He says, 'Well, *I* never struck no such a hole as this before; I'm of the opinion it's a totally new kind of a hole.' Then he begun to get mad. He held in for a spell, walking up and down the comb of the roof and shaking his head and muttering to himself; but his feelings got the upper hand of him, presently, and he broke loose and cussed himself black in the face. I never see a bird take on so about a little thing. When he got through he walks to the hole and looks in again for half a minute; then he says. 'Well, you're a long hole, and a deep hole, and a mighty singular hole altogether—but I've started in to fill you, and I'm d____d if I *don't* fill you, if it takes a hundred years!'

"And with that, away he went. You never see a bird work so since you was born. He laid into his work like a black man, and the way he hove acorns into that hole for about two hours and a half was one of the most exciting and astonishing spectacles I ever struck. He just never stopped to take a look any more—he just hove 'em in and went for more. Well, at last he could hardly flop his wings, he was so tuckered out. He comes a-drooping down, once more, sweating like an ice pitcher, drops his acorn in and says, *'Now* I guess I've got the bulge on you by this time!' So he bent down for a look. If you'll believe me, when his head come up again he was just pale with rage. He says, 'I've shoveled acorns enough in there to keep the family thirty years, and if I can see a sign of one of 'em I wish I may land in a museum with a belly full of sawdust in two minutes!'

"He just had strength enough to crawl up on to the comb and lean his back agin the chimbly, and then he collected his impressions and begun to free his mind. I see in a second that what I had mistook for profanity in the mines was only just the rudiments, as you may say.

"Another jay was going by, and heard him doing his devotions, and stops to inquire what was up. The sufferer told him the whole circumstance, and says, 'Now yonder's the hole, and if you don't believe me, go and look for yourself.' So this fellow went and looked, and comes back and says, 'How many did you say you put in there?' 'Not any less than two tons,' says the sufferer. The other jay went and looked again. He couldn't seem to make it out, so he raised a yell, and three more jays come. They all examined the hole, they all made the sufferer tell it over again, then they all discussed it, and got off as many leather-headed opinions about it as an average crowd of humans could have done.

"They called in more jays; then more and more, till pretty soon this whole region 'peared to have a blue flush about it. There must have been five thousand of them; and such another jawing and disputing and fipping and cussing, you never heard. Every jay in the whole lot put his eye to the hole and delivered a more chuckle-headed opinion about the mystery than the jay that went there before him. They examined the house all over, too. The door was standing half open, and at last one old jay happened to go and light on it and look in. Of course, that knocked the mystery galley-west in a second. There lay the acorns, scattered all over the floor. He flopped his wings and raised a whoop 'Come here!' he says, 'Come here, everybody; hang'd if this fool hasn't been trying to fill up a house with acorns!' They all came a-swooping down like a blue cloud, and as each fellow lit on the door and took a glance, the whole absurdity of the contract that that first jay had tackled hit him home and he fell over backwards suffocating with laughter, and the next jay took his place and done the same.

"Well, sir, they roosted around here on the housetop and the trees for an hour, and guffawed over that thing like human beings. It ain't any use to tell me a bluejay hasn't got a sense of humor, because I know better. And memory, too. They brought jays here from all over the United States to look down that hole, every summer for three years. Other birds, too. And they could all see the point, except an owl that come from Nova Scotia to visit the Yo Semite, and he took this thing in on his way back. He said he couldn't see anything funny in it. But then he was a good deal disappointed about Yo Semite, too."

# XXIII

## *Enchanted Islands*

A$_{\text{FTER}}$ a three months' absence, I found myself in
San Francisco again, without a cent. When my
credit was about exhausted (for I had become too
mean and lazy, now, to work on a morning paper,
and there were no vacancies on the evening journals), I was created San Francisco correspondent of
the *Enterprise*, and at the end of five months I was
out of debt, but my interest in my work was gone;
for, my correspondence being a daily one, without
rest or respite, I got unspeakably tired of it. I wanted another change. The vagabond instinct grew
strong upon me. Fortune favored, and I got a new
berth and a delightful one. It was to go down to the
Sandwich Islands[1] and write some letters for the
Sacramento *Union*, an excellent journal and liberal
with employees.

We sailed on the *Ajax*, in the middle of winter.
The almanac called it winter, distinctly enough, but
the weather was a compromise between spring and

[1]Captain James Cook, English navigator, named islands
he had discovered in 1778 the Sandwich Islands after his
patron, the earl of Sandwich: they now are called Hawaii. At
the time of Clemens's visit, Hawaii was a native kingdom,
but the expanding sugar industry was bringing increasing
United States involvement.

summer. Six days out, it became summer altogether.

On a certain bright morning the Islands hove in sight, lying low on the lonely sea, and everybody climbed to the upper deck to look. After two thousand miles of watery solitude the vision surely was a welcome one. As we neared the imposing promontory of Diamond Head rose up out of the ocean, its rugged front softened by the hazy distance, and presently the details of the land began to make themselves manifest; first the line of beach; then the plumed cocoanut trees of the tropics; then cabins of the natives; then the white town of Honolulu, said to contain between twelve and fifteen thousand inhabitants, spread over a dead level; with streets from twenty to thirty feet wide, solid and level as a floor, most of them straight as a line and a few as crooked as a corkscrew.

The further I traveled through the town the better I liked it. Every step revealed a new contrast— disclosed something that I was unaccustomed to. In place of the grand mud-colored brown fronts of San Francisco, I saw dwellings built of straw, adobes, and cream-colored pebble-and-shell-conglomerated coral, cut into oblong blocks and laid in cement; also a great number of neat white cottages, with green window shutters; in place of front yards like billiard tables with iron fences around them, I saw these homes surrounded by ample yards, thickly clad with green grass, and shaded by tall trees, through whose dense foliage the sun could scarcely

*Mark Twain at age 30, just before leaving for Hawaii.*
Courtesy of the Mark Twain Papers, The Bancroft Library

penetrate; in place of the customary geranium, calla lily, etc., languishing in dust and general debility, I saw luxurious banks and thickets of flowers, fresh as a meadow after a rain, and glowing with the richest dyes; in place of the dingy horrors of San Francisco's pleasure grove, the "Willows,"[2] I saw huge-bodied, and wide-spreading forest trees, with strange names and strange appearance—trees that cast a shadow like a thundercloud, and were able to stand alone without the indignity of being tied to long green poles.

I looked on a multitude of people, some white, in white coats, vests, and pantaloons, even white cloth shoes, made snowy with chalk duly laid on every morning; but the majority of the people were almost as dark as Negroes—women with comely features, fine black eyes, rounded forms, inclining to the voluptuous, clad in a single bright red or white garment that fell free and unconfined from shoulder to heel, long black hair falling loose, gypsy hats, encircled with wreaths of natural flowers of a brilliant carmine tint; plenty of dark men in various costumes, and some with nothing on but a battered stovepipe hat tilted on the nose, and a very scant breechclout; certain smoke-dried children were clothed in nothing but sunshine—a very neat fitting and picturesque apparel indeed.

[2]A privately operated park at the corner of Mission and 18th Street which housed a menagerie and featured singing and dancing.

In place of roughs and rowdies staring and black-guarding on the corners, I saw long-haired, saddle-colored Sandwich Island maidens sitting on the ground in the shade of corner houses, gazing indolently at whatever or whoever happened along; instead of wretched cobblestone pavements I walked on a firm foundation of coral, built up from the bottom of the sea, by the absurd but persevering insect of that name; in place of the hurry and bustle and noisy confusion of San Francisco, I moved in the midst of a summer calm as tranquil as dawn in the Garden of Eden; in place of the Golden City's skirting sandhills and the placid bay, I saw on the one side a framework of tall, precipitous mountains close at hand, clad in refreshing green, and cleft by deep, cool, chasm-like valleys—and in front the grand sweep of the ocean: a brilliant, transparent green near the shore, bound and bordered by a long white line of foamy spray dashing against the reef, and further out the dead blue water of the deep sea, flecked with "white caps," and in the far horizon a single, lonely sail—a mere accent mark to emphasize a slumberous calm and a solitude that were without sound or limit. When the sun sunk down—the one intruder from other realms and persistent in suggestions of them—it was tranced luxury to sit in the perfumed air and forget that there was any world but these enchanted islands.

Passing through the marketplace we saw that fine feature of Honolulu under its most favorable auspices—that is, in the full glory of Saturday afternoon, which is a festive day with the natives. The native girls, by twos and threes and parties of a dozen, and sometimes in whole platoons and companies, went cantering up and down the neighboring streets astride of fleet but homely horses, and with their gaudy riding habits streaming like banners behind them. Such a troop of free and easy riders, in their natural home, the saddle, makes for a gay and graceful spectacle. The riding habit I speak of is simply a long broad scarf, like a tavern tablecloth, brilliantly colored, wrapped around the loins once, then apparently passed between the limbs and each end thrown backward over the same, and floating and flapping behind on both sides beyond the horse's tail like a couple of fancy flags; then, slipping the stirrup irons between her toes, the girl throws her chest forward, sits like a major-general.

The girls put on all the finery they can on Saturday afternoon—fine black silk robes; flowing red ones that nearly put your eyes out; others as white as snow; still others that discount the rainbow; and they wear their hair in nets, and trim their jaunty hats with fresh flowers, and encircle their dusky throats with homemade necklaces of the brilliant vermilion-tinted blossom of the *ohia*;[3] and they fill the markets and the adjacent streets with their bright presences, and smell like a rag factory on fire with their offensive cocoanut oil.

[3] A species of apple tree.

Moving among the stirring crowds, you come to the poi merchants, squatting in the shade on their hams, in true native fashion, and surrounded by purchasers. (The Sandwich Islanders always squat on their hams, and who knows but they may be the original "ham sandwiches?" The thought is pregnant with interest.) The poi looks like common flour paste, and is kept in large bowls formed of a species of gourd, and capable of holding from one to three or four gallons. Poi is the chief article of food among the natives, and is prepared from the *taro* plant. The taro root looks like a thick, or, if you please, a corpulent sweet potato, in shape, but is of a light purple color when boiled. When boiled it answers as a passable substitute for bread. The buck Kanakas bake it underground, then mash it up with a heavy lava pestle, mix water with it until it becomes a paste, set it aside and let it ferment, and then it is poi—and an unseductive mixture it is, almost tasteless before it ferments and too sour for a luxury afterward. But nothing is more nutritious.

We found the fish market crowded; for the native is very fond of fish, and *eats the article raw and alive*! Let us change the subject.

In old times here, Saturday was a grand gala day indeed. All the native population of the town forsook their labors, and those of the surrounding country journeyed to the city. Then the white folks had to stay indoors, for every street was so packed with charging cavaliers and cavalieresses that it was next to impossible to thread one's way through the cavalcades without getting crippled.

At night they feasted and the girls danced the lascivious *hula hula*—a dance that is said to exhibit the very perfection of educated motion of limb and arm, hand, head, and body, and the exactest uniformity of movement and accuracy of "time." It was performed by a circle of girls with no raiment on them to speak of, who went through an infinite variety of motions and figures without prompting, and yet so true was their "time," and in such perfect concert did they move that when they were placed in a straight line, hands, arms, bodies, limbs, and heads waved, swayed, gesticulated, bowed, stooped, whirled, squirmed, twisted, and undulated as if they were part and parcel of a single individual.

Of late years, however, Saturday has lost most of its quondam gala features. This weekly stampede of the natives interfered too much with labor and the interests of the white folks, and by sticking in a law here, and preaching a sermon there, and by various other means, they gradually broke it up.

The demoralizing *hula hula* was forbidden to be performed, save at night, with closed doors, in presence of few spectators, and only by permission duly procured from the authorities and the payment of ten dollars for the same. There are few girls nowadays able to dance this ancient national dance in the highest perfection of the art.

The missionaries have christianized and educated

all the natives. They all belong to the church, and there is not one of them, above the age of eight, but can read and write with facility in the native tongue. It is the most universally educated race of people outside of China. They have any quantity of books, printed in the Kanaka language, and all the natives are fond of reading. They are inveterate churchgoers—nothing can keep them away.

I quote from my journal:

The natives had a romantic fashion of burying some of their children alive when the family became larger than necessary. The missionaries interfered in this matter too, and stopped it.

To this day the natives are able to *lie down and die whenever they want to*, whether there is anything the matter with them or not. If a Kanaka takes a notion to die, that is the end of him; nobody can persuade him to hold on; all the doctors in the world could not save him.

In the rural districts of any of the Islands, the traveler hourly comes upon parties of dusky maidens bathing in the streams or in the sea without any clothing on and exhibiting no very intemperate zeal in the matter of hiding their nakedness. When the missionaries first took up their residence in Honolulu, the native women would pay their families frequent friendly visits, day by day, not even clothed with a blush. It was found a hard matter to convince them that this was rather indelicate. Finally, the missionaries provided them with long, loose calico robes, and that ended the difficulty—for the women would troop through the town, stark naked, with their robes folded under their arms, march to the missionary houses and then proceed to dress! The natives soon manifested a strong proclivity for clothing, but it was shortly apparent that they only wanted it for grandeur. The missionaries imported a quantity of hats, bonnets, and other male and female wearing apparel, instituted a general distribution, and begged the people not to come to church naked, next Sunday, as usual. And they did not; but the national spirit of unselfishness led them to divide up with neighbors who were not at the distribution, and next Sabbath the preachers could hardly keep countenance before their vast congregations.

# XXIV

## *Other Notable Things*

BOUND for Hawaii[1] (a hundred and fifty miles distant), to visit the great volcano and behold the other notable things which distinguish that island above the remainder of the group, we sailed from Honolulu on a certain Saturday afternoon, in the good schooner *Boomerang*.

Monday morning we were close to the island of Hawaii. Two of its high mountains were in view—Mauna Loa and Hualalai.[2] The latter is an imposing peak, but being only ten thousand feet high is seldom mentioned or heard of. Mauna Loa is said to be sixteen thousand feet high. The rays of glittering snow and ice, that clasped its summit like a claw, looked refreshing when viewed from the blistering climate we were in. One could stand on that mountain (wrapped up in blankets and furs to keep warm), and while he nibbled a snowball or an icicle to quench his thirst he could look down the long sweep of its sides and see spots where plants are growing that grow only where the bitter cold of

[1] Hawaii, one of the eight major islands, is south of the isle of Oahu, where Honolulu is located.

[2] Modern measurements: Mt. Hualalai, 8,251 feet; Mt. Mauna Loa, 13,680 feet.

winter prevails; lower down he could see sections devoted to productions that thrive in the temperate zone alone; and at the bottom of the mountain he could see the home of the tufted cocoa palms and other species of vegetation that grow only in the sultry atmosphere of eternal summer. He could see all the climes of the world at a single glance of the eye, and that glance would only pass over a distance of four or five miles as the bird flies!

By and by we took boat and went ashore at Kailua, designing to ride horseback through the pleasant orange and coffee region of Kona, and rejoin the vessel at a point some leagues distant. This journey is well worth taking. The trail passes along on high ground—say a thousand feet above sea level—and usually about a mile distant from the ocean, which is always in sight, save that occasionally you find yourself buried in the forest in the midst of a rank tropical vegetation and a dense growth of trees, whose great boughs overarch the road and shut out sun and sea and everything, and leave you in a dim, shady tunnel, haunted with invisible singing birds and fragrant with the odor of flowers. It was pleasant to ride occasionally in the warm sun, and feast the eye upon the ever-changing panorama of the forest (beyond and below us), with its many tints, its softened lights and shadows, its billowy undulations sweeping gently down from the mountain to the sea. It was pleasant also, at intervals, to leave the sultry sun and pass into the cool, green depths of this forest and indulge in sentimental reflections under the inspiration of its brooding twilight and its whispering foliage.

We rode through one orange grove that had ten thousand trees in it! They were all laden with fruit.

At four o'clock in the afternoon we were winding down a mountain of dreary and desolate lava to the sea, and closing our pleasant land journey. This lava is the accumulation of ages; one torrent of fire after another has rolled down here in old times.

The last lava flow occurred here so long ago that there are none now living who witnessed it. In one place it inclosed and burned down a grove of cocoanut trees, and the holes in the lava where the trunks stood are still visible; their sides retain the impression of the bark; the trees fell upon the burning river, and becoming partly submerged, left in it the perfect counterpart of every knot and branch and leaf, and even nut, for curiosity seekers of a long-distant day to gaze upon and wonder at.

There were doubtless plenty of Kanaka sentinels on guard hereabouts at that time, but they did not leave casts of their figures in the lava as the Roman sentinels at Herculaneum and Pompeii did. It is a pity it is so, because such things are so interesting; but so it is. They probably went away—early, perhaps. Both had merits; the Romans exhibited pluck, but the Kanakas showed sounder judgment.

Shortly, we came in sight of that spot whose history is so familiar to every schoolboy in the wide world—Kealakekua Bay—the place where Captain Cook, the great circumnavigator, was killed by the natives, nearly a hundred years ago. The setting sun was flaming upon it, a summer shower was falling, and it was spanned by two magnificent rainbows.

As the bright sun looked across the placid ocean through the tall, clean stems of the cocoanut trees, like a blooming whisky bloat through the bars of a city prison, I went and stood in the edge of the water on the flat rock pressed by Captain Cook's feet when the blow was dealt which took away his life, and tried to picture in my mind the doomed man struggling in the midst of the multitude of exasperated savages; the men aboard the ship crowding to the vessel's side and gazing in anxious dismay toward the shore.

It was growing dark, the rain began to fall, we could see that the distant *Boomerang* was helplessly becalmed at sea, and so I adjourned to the cheerless little box of a warehouse and sat down to smoke and think, and wish the ship would make the land— for we had not eaten much for ten hours and were viciously hungry.

Toward midnight a fine breeze sprang up and the schooner soon worked herself into the bay and cast anchor. The boat came ashore for us, and in a little while the clouds and the rain were all gone. The moon was beaming tranquilly down upon the land and sea, and we were stretched upon the deck sleeping the refreshing sleep and dreaming the happy dreams that are only vouchsafed to the weary and the innocent.

In the breezy morning we went ashore and visited the ruined temple of the last god, Lono. Quite a broad tract of land near the temple, extending from the sea to the mountaintop, was sacred to the Lono in olden times—so sacred that if a common native set his sacrilegious foot upon it, it was judicious for him to make his will, because his time had come. He might go around it by water, but he could not cross it. It was well sprinkled with pagan temples and stocked with awkward, homely idols carved out of logs of wood. There was a temple devoted to prayers for rain—and with fine sagacity it was placed at a point so well up on the mountainside that if you prayed there twenty-four times a day for rain you would be likely to get it every time. You would seldom get to your Amen before you would have to hoist your umbrella.

At noon I observed a bevy of nude native young ladies bathing in the sea, and went and sat down on their clothes to keep them from being stolen. I begged them to come out, for the sea was rising, and I was satisfied that they were running some risk. But they were not afraid, and presently went on with their sport. They were finished swimmers and divers, and enjoyed themselves to the last degree. They swam races, splashed and ducked and tumbled each other about, and filled the air with their laughter. It is said that the first thing an Islander learns is how to swim; learning to walk, being a matter of smaller consequence, comes afterward. One hears tales of native men and women swimming ashore from vessels many miles at sea—more miles, indeed, than I dare vouch for or even mention. And they tell of a native diver who went down in thirty or forty-foot waters and brought up an anvil! I think he swallowed the anvil afterward, if my memory serves me. However, I will not urge this point.

At noon, we hired a Kanaka to take us down to the ancient ruins at Honaunau in his canoe—price two dollars—reasonable enough, for a sea voyage of eight miles, counting both ways.

At the end of an hour, we had made the four miles, and landed on a level point of land, upon which was a wide extent of old ruins, with many a tall cocoanut tree growing among them. Here was the ancient City of Refuge—a vast inclosure, whose stone walls were twenty feet thick at the base, and fifteen feet high; an oblong square, a thousand and forty feet one way and a fraction under seven hundred the other. Within this enclosure, in early times, have been three rude temples, each two hundred and ten feet long by one hundred wide, and thirteen high.

In those days, if a man killed another anywhere on the Island the relatives were privileged to take the murderer's life; and then a chase for life and liberty began—the outlawed criminal flying through pathless forests and over mountain and plain, with his hopes fixed upon the protecting walls of the City of Refuge, and the avenger of blood following hotly after him! Sometimes the race was kept up to the very gates of the temple, and the panting pair sped through lengthy files of excited natives, who watched the contest with flashing eye and dilated nostril, encouraging the hunted refugee with sharp, inspiriting ejaculations, and sending up a ringing shout of exultation when the saving gates closed upon him and the cheated pursuer sank exhausted at the threshold. But sometimes the flying criminal fell under the hand of the avenger at the very door, when one more brave stride, one more brief second of time would have brought his feet upon the sacred ground and barred him against all harm. Where did these isolated pagans get this idea of a City of Refuge—this ancient Oriental custom?

We got back to the schooner in good time, and then sailed down to Kau, where we disembarked and took our final leave of the vessel. Next day we bought horses and bent our way over the summer-clad mountain terraces, toward the great volcano of Kilauea. We made nearly a two days' journey of it, but that was on account of laziness. Toward sunset on the second day, we reached an elevation of some four thousand feet above sea level, and as we picked our careful way through billowy wastes of lava long generations ago stricken dead and cold in the climax of its tossing fury, we began to come upon signs of the near presence of the volcano—signs in the nature of ragged fissures that discharged jets of sulphurous vapor into the air, hot from the molten ocean down in the bowels of the mountain.

Shortly the crater came into view. I have seen Vesuvius since, but it was a mere toy, a child's volcano, a soup kettle, compared to this. Mount Vesuvius is a shapely cone thirty-six hundred feet high; its crater an inverted cone only three hundred feet deep, and not more than a thousand feet in diameter, if as much as that; its fires meager, modest, and docile. But here was a vast, perpendicular, walled cellar, nine hundred feet deep in some places, thirteen hundred in others, level-floored, and *ten miles in circumference*! Here was a huge yawning pit upon whose floor the armies of Russia could camp, and have room to spare.

A colossal column of cloud towered to a great height in the air immediately above the crater, and the outer swell of every one of its vast folds was dyed with a rich crimson luster, which was subdued to a pale rose tint in the depressions between. It glowed like a muffled torch and stretched upward to a dizzy height toward the zenith. I thought it just possible that its like had not been seen since the children of Israel wandered on their long march through the desert so many centuries ago over a path illuminated by the mysterious "pillar of fire." And I was sure that I now had a vivid conception of what the majestic "pillar of fire" was like, which almost amounted to a revelation.

We rode horseback around the island of Hawaii (the crooked road making the distance two hundred miles), and enjoyed the journey very much. We were more than a week making the trip, because our Kanaka horses would not go by a house or a hut without stopping—whip and spur could not alter their minds about it, and so we finally found that it economized time to let them have their way. Upon inquiry the mystery was explained; the natives are such thoroughgoing gossips that they never pass a house without stopping to swap news, and consequently their horses learn to regard that sort of thing as an essential part of the whole duty of man, and his salvation not to be compassed without it.

THE chief pride of Maui is her dead volcano of Haleakala—which means, translated, "the house of the sun." We climbed a thousand feet up the side of this isolated colossus one afternoon; then camped, and next day climbed the remaining nine thousand feet, and anchored on the summit, where we built a fire and froze and roasted by turns, all night. With the first pallor of dawn we got up and saw things that were new to us. Mounted on a commanding pinnacle, we watched Nature work her silent wonders. The sea was spread abroad on every hand, its tumbled surface seeming only wrinkled and dimpled in the distance. The valley below appeared like an ample checkerboard, its velvety green sugar plantations alternating with squares of barrenness and groves of trees that diminished to mossy tufts. Beyond the valley were mountains picturesquely grouped together.

Presently some vagrant white clouds came drifting along, high over the sea and the valley; then they came in couples and groups; then in imposing squadrons; gradually joining their forces, they banked themselves solidly together, a thousand feet under us, and *totally shut out land and ocean*—not a vestige of *anything* was left in view, but just a little of the rim of the crater, circling away from the pinnacle whereon we sat (for a ghostly procession of wanderers from the filmy hosts without had drifted through a chasm in the crater wall and filed round and round, and gathered and sunk and blended together till the abyss was stored to the brim with a fleecy fog). Thus banked, motion ceased, and silence reigned. Clear to the horizon, league upon league, the snowy floor stretched without a break— not level, but in rounded folds, with shallow creases between, and with here and there stately piles of vapory architecture lifting themselves aloft out of the common plain—some near at hand, some in the middle distances, and others relieving the monotony of the remote solitudes. There was little conversation, for the impressive scene overawed speech. I felt like the Last Man, neglected of the judgment, and left pinnacled in mid-heaven, a forgotten relic of a vanished world.

While the hush yet brooded, the messengers of

the coming resurrection appeared in the east. A growing warmth suffused the horizon, and soon the sun emerged and looked out over the cloud waste, flinging bars of ruddy light across it, staining its folds and billow caps with blushes, purpling the shaded troughs between, and glorifying the vapor palaces and cathedrals with a wasteful splendor of all blendings and combinations of rich coloring.

It was the sublimest spectacle I ever witnessed, and I think the memory of it will remain with me always.

I WROTE about these wanderings and others in letters to the *Sacramento Union*. The *Union* hadn't any use for them, but could afford to spend twenty dollars a week for nothing.

I had been in the islands several months when a great occasion to serve my journal [arose], and I not able to take advantage of it. I was in Honolulu [preparing to leave for home] when a boatload of skeletons arrived after forty-three days in an open boat on ten days' provisions—survivors of the clipper *Hornet*, which had perished by fire several thousand miles away. It was necessary for me to interview them for the *Union*. [But] I had been confined to my room a couple of weeks—by night to my bed, by day to a splint-bottom chair, deep sunk like a basket. There was another chair, but I preferred this one, because my malady was saddle boils.

By good luck his Excellency Anson Burlingame

was there at the time, on his way to take up his post in China, where he did such good work for the United States, and I had the honor and profit of his society daily and constantly during many days. He was a handsome and stately and courtly and graceful creature, in the prime of his perfect manhood, and it was a contenting pleasure to look at him. His outlook upon the world and its affairs was as wide as the horizon, and his speech was of a dignity and eloquence proper to it. It dealt in no commonplaces, for he had no commonplace thoughts. He was a kindly man, and most lovable. He was not a petty politician, but a great and magnanimous statesman. He did not serve his country alone, but China as well. He held the balances even. He wrought for justice and humanity. All his ways were clean; all his motives were high and fine.

He came and put me on a stretcher and had me carried to the hospital where the shipwrecked men were, and I never needed to ask a question. He attended to all of that himself, and I had nothing to do but make the notes. It was like him to take that trouble. He was a great man and a great American, and it was in his fine nature to come down from his high office and do a friendly turn whenever he could.

We got through with this work at six in the evening. I took no dinner, for there was no time to spare if I would beat the other correspondents. I spent four hours arranging the notes in their proper

## SACRAMENTO DAILY UNION.

### LETTER FROM HONOLULU.

[CORRESPONDENCE OF THE UNION.]

### BURNING OF THE CLIPPER SHIP HORNET AT SEA.

**Detailed Account of the Sufferings of Officers and Crew, as given by the Third Officer and Members of the Crew.**

HONOLULU, June 25, 1866.

In the postscript to a letter which I wrote two or three days ago, and sent by the ship Live Yankee, I gave you the substance of a letter received here from Hilo by Walker, Allen & Co., informing them that a boat containing fifteen men, in a helpless and starving condition, had drifted ashore at Laupohochoe, Island of Hawaii, and that they had belonged to the clipper ship Hornet, Mitchell master, and had been afloat on the ocean since the burning of that vessel, about one hundred miles north of the equator, on the 3d of May—forty-three days.

The third mate and ten of the seamen have arrived here and are now in the hospital, Captain Mitchell, one seaman named Antonio Passene, and two passengers (Samuel and Henry Ferguson, of New York city, young gentlemen, aged respectively 18 and 28) are still at Hilo, but are expected here within the week.

In the Captain's modest epitome of this terrible romance, which you have probably published, you detect the fine old hero through it. It reads like Grant.

#### The Third Mate.

I have talked with the seamen and with John S. Thomas, third mate, but their accounts are so nearly alike in all substantial points, that I will merely give the officer's statement and weave into it such matters as the men mentioned in the way of incidents, experiences, emotions, etc. Thomas is a very intelligent and very cool and self-possessed young man, and seems to have kept a pretty accurate log of his remarkable voyage in his head. He told his story, of three hours length, in a plain, straightforward way, and with no attempt at display and no straining after effect. Wherever any incident may be noted in this paper where any individual has betrayed any emotion, or enthusiasm, or has departed from strict, stoical self-possession, or had a solitary thought that was not an utterly unpoetical and essentially practical one, remember that Thomas, the third mate, was not that person. He has been eleven days on shore, and already looks sufficiently sound and healthy to pass almost anywhere without being taken for an invalid. He has the marks of a hard experience

easy, and we steered by the feel of the wind in our faces and the heave of the sea." Dark, and dismal, and lonesome work was that! Sometimes they got a fleeting glimpse of the sailor's friend, the north star, and then they lighted a match and hastened anxiously to see if their compass was faithful to them—for it had to be placed close to an iron ringbolt in the stern, and they were afraid, during those first nights, that this might cause it to vary. It proved true to them, however.

#### Sumptuous Fare.

On the fifth day a notable incident occurred. They caught a dolphin! and while their enthusiasm was still at its highest over this stroke of good fortune, they captured another. They made a trifling fire in a tin plate and warmed the prizes—to cook them was not possible—and divided them equitably among all hands and eat them.

On the sixth day two more dolphins were caught.

Two more were caught on the seventh day, and also a small bonita, and they began to believe they were always going to live in this extravagant way; but it was not to be; these were their last dolphins, and they never could get another bonita, though they saw them and longed for them often afterward.

#### Rations Reduced.

On the eighth day the rations were reduced about one-half. Thus—breakfast, one-fourth of a biscuit, an ounce of ham and a gill of water to each man; dinner, same quantity of bread and water, and four oysters or clams; supper, water and bread the same, and twelve large raisins or fourteen small ones, to a man. Also, during the first twelve or fifteen days, each man had one spoonful of brandy a day, then it gave out.

This day, as one of the men was gazing across the dull waste of waters as usual, he saw a small, dark object rising and falling upon the waves. He called attention to it, and in a moment every eye was bent upon it in intensest interest. When the boat had approached a little nearer, it was discovered that it was a small green turtle, fast asleep. Every noise was hushed as they crept upon the unconscious slumberer. Directions were given and hopes and fears expressed in guarded whispers. At the fateful moment—a moment of tremendous consequence to these famishing men—the expert selected for the high and responsible office stretched forth his hand, while his excited comrades bated their breath and trembled for the success of the enterprise, and seized the turtle by the hind leg and handed him aboard! His delicate flesh was carefully divided among the party and eagerly devoured—after being "warmed" like the dolphins which went before him.

#### The Boats Separate.

After the eighth day I have ten days unaccounted for—no notes of them save that the men say they had their two or three ounces of food and their gill of water three times a day—and then the same weary watching

order, then wrote all night and beyond it; with this result: that I had a very long and detailed account of the *Hornet* episode ready at nine in the morning, while the correspondents of the San Francisco journals had nothing but a brief outline report—for they didn't sit up. The now-and-then schooner was to sail for San Francisco about nine; when I reached the dock she was free forward and was just casting off her stern line. My fat envelope was thrown by a strong hand, and fell on board all right, and my victory was a safe thing. All in due time the ship reached San Francisco, but it was my complete report which made the stir and was telegraphed to the New York papers, by Mr. Cash; he was in charge of the Pacific bureau of the New York *Herald* at the time.

When I returned to California by and by, I went up to Sacramento and presented a bill for general correspondence at twenty dollars per week. It was paid. Then I presented a bill for "special" service on the *Hornet* matter of three columns of solid nonpareil *at a hundred dollars a column*. The cashier didn't faint, but he came rather near it. He sent for the proprietors, and they came and never uttered a protest. They only laughed in their jolly fashion, and said it was robbery, but no matter; it was a grand "scoop" (the bill or my *Hornet* report, I didn't know which); "pay it. It's all right." The best men that ever owned a newspaper.

I had published one little thing ("The Jumping

Frog") in an Eastern paper, but I did not consider that that counted. In my view, a person who published things in a mere newspaper could not properly claim recognition as a Literary Person: he must rise away above that; he must appear in a magazine. He would then be a Literary Person; also, he would be famous—right away. These two ambitions were strong upon me. I prepared my contribution (an article about the burning of the *Hornet*), and then looked around for the best magazine to go up to glory in. I selected the most important one in New York (*Harper's Magazine*). The contribution was accepted. I signed it "MARK TWAIN"; for that name had some currency on the Pacific coast, and it was my idea to spread it all over the world, now, at this one jump. The article appeared in the December number, and I sat up a month waiting for the January number; for that one would contain the year's list of contributors, my name would be in it, and I should be famous and could give the banquet I was meditating.

I did not give the banquet. I had not written the "MARK TWAIN" distinctly; it was a fresh name to Eastern printers, and they put it "Mike Swain" or "MacSwain," I do not remember which. At any rate, I was not celebrated, and I did not give the banquet. I was a Literary Person, but that was all—a buried one; buried alive.

# XXV

## End of a Seven-Year "Pleasure Trip"

AFTER half a year's luxurious vagrancy in the Islands,[1] I took shipping in a sailing vessel, and regretfully returned to San Francisco—a voyage in every way delightful, but without an incident; unless lying two long weeks in a dead calm, eighteen hundred miles from the nearest land, may rank as an incident. Schools of whales grew so tame that day after day they played about the ship among the porpoises and the sharks without the least apparent fear of us, and we pelted them with empty bottles for lack of better sport. Twenty-four hours afterward these bottles would be still lying on the glassy water under our noses, showing that the ship had not moved out of her place in all that time. The calm was absolutely breathless, and the surface of the sea absolutely without a wrinkle. For a whole day and part of a night we lay so close to another ship that had drifted to our vicinity, that we carried on conversations with her passengers, introduced each other by name, and became pretty intimately acquainted with people we had never heard of before, and have never heard of since. This was the only vessel we saw during the whole lonely voyage.

[1]Closer to five months—March 7–August 13, 1866.

We had fifteen passengers, and to show how hard pressed they were at last for occupation and amusement, I will mention that the gentlemen gave a good part of their time every day, during the calm, to trying to sit on an empty champagne bottle (lying on its side) and thread a needle without touching their heels to the deck, or falling over; and the ladies sat in the shade of the mainsail, and watched the enterprise with absorbing interest. We were at sea five Sundays; and yet, but for the almanac, we never would have known but that all the other days were Sundays too.

I returned home again, to San Francisco, without means and without employment. I tortured my brain for a saving scheme of some kind, and at last a public lecture occurred to me![2] I sat down and wrote one in a fever of hopeful anticipation. Then I showed it to several friends, but they all shook their heads. They said nobody would come to hear me, and I would make a humiliating failure of it. They said that as I had never spoken in public, I would break down in the delivery, anyhow. I was disconsolate now. But at last an editor slapped me on the back and told me to "go ahead." He said, "Take the largest house in town, and charge a dollar a ticket." The audacity of the proposition was charming; it

[2]Probably his memory of the success of Artemus Ward's comic lectures in the West in 1863 and of the favorable response to Twain's burlesque "Governor's Message to the Third House" in Carson City in 1864 helped him get the idea.

seemed fraught with practical worldly wisdom, however. The proprietor of the several theaters indorsed the advice, and said I might have his handsome new opera house at half price—fifty dollars. In sheer desperation I took it—on credit, for sufficient reasons. In three days I did a hundred and fifty dollars' worth of printing and advertising, and was the most distressed and frightened creature on the Pacific coast. I could not sleep—who could, under such circumstances? For other people there was facetiousness in the last line of my posters, but to me it was plaintive with a pang when I wrote it:

Doors open at $7\frac{1}{2}$. The trouble will begin at 8.

That line has done good service since. Showmen have borrowed it frequently, and I have even seen it appended to a newspaper advertisement reminding school pupils in vacation what time the next term would begin. As those three days of suspense dragged by, I grew more and more unhappy. I had sold two hundred tickets among my personal friends, but I feared they might not come. My lecture, which had seemed "humorous" to me, at first, grew steadily more and more dreary, till not a vestige of fun seemed left, and I grieved that I could not bring a coffin on the stage and turn the thing into a funeral. I was so panic-stricken, at last, that I went to three old friends, giants in stature, cordial by nature, and stormy-voiced, and said:

"This thing is going to be a failure; the jokes in it

are so dim that nobody will see them; I would ask you to sit in the parquette, and help me through."

They said they would. Then I went to the wife of a popular citizen,[3] and said that if she was willing to do me a very great kindness, I would be glad if she and her husband would sit prominently in the left-hand stage box, where the entire house could see them. I explained that if I should need help, I would turn toward her and smile, as a signal, when I had been delivered of an obscure joke—"then" I added, "don't wait to investigate, but *respond*!"

She promised. Down the street I met a man I never had seen before. He had been drinking, and was beaming with smiles and good nature. He said:

"My name's Sawyer. You don't know me, but that don't matter. I haven't got a cent, but if you knew how bad I wanted to laugh, you'd give me a ticket. Come, now, what do you say?"

"Is your laugh hung on a hair-trigger?—that is, is it critical, or can you get it off *easy*?"

My drawling infirmity of speech so affected him that he laughed a specimen or two that struck me as being about the article I wanted, and I gave him a ticket, and appointed him to sit in the second circle, in the center, and be responsible for that division of the house. I gave him minute instructions about how to detect indistinct jokes, and then went away, and left him chuckling placidly over the novelty of the idea.

[3]This helpful listener has not been identified.

I ate nothing on the last of the three eventful days—I only suffered. I had advertised that on this third day the box office would be opened for the sale of reserved seats. I crept down to the theater at four in the afternoon to see if any sales had been made. The ticket seller was gone, the box-office was locked up. I had to swallow suddenly, or my heart would have got out. "No sales," I said to myself; "I might have known it." I thought of suicide, pretended illness, flight. I thought of these things in earnest, for I was very miserable and scared. But of course I had to drive them away, and prepare to meet my fate. I could not wait for half past seven—I wanted to face the horror, and end it—the feeling of many a man doomed to hang, no doubt. I went down back streets at six o'clock, and entered the theater by the back door. I stumbled my way in the dark among the ranks of canvas scenery, and stood on the stage. The house was gloomy and silent, and its emptiness was depressing. I went into the dark among the scenes again, and for an hour and a half gave myself up to the horrors, wholly unconscious of everything else. Then I heard a murmur; it rose higher and higher, and ended in a crash, mingled with cheers. It made my hair raise, it was so close to me, and so loud. There was a pause, and then another; presently came a third, and before I well knew what I was about, I was in the middle of the stage, staring at a sea of faces, bewildered by the fierce glare of the lights, and quaking in every limb with a terror that seemed like to take my life away. The house was full, aisles and all!

The tumult in my heart and brain and legs continued a full minute before I could gain any command over myself. Then I recognized the charity and the friendliness in the faces before me, and little by little my fright melted away, and I began to talk. Within three or four minutes I was comfortable, and even content. My three chief allies, with three auxiliaries, were on hand, in the parquette, all sitting together, all armed with bludgeons, and all ready to make an onslaught upon the feeblest joke that might show its head. And whenever a joke did fall, their bludgeons came down and their faces seemed to split from ear to ear; Sawyer, whose hearty countenance was seen looming redly in the center of the second circle, took it up, and the house was carried handsomely. Inferior jokes never fared so royally before. Presently, I delivered a bit of serious matter with impressive unction (it was my pet), and the audience listened with an absorbed hush that gratified me more than any applause; and as I dropped the last word of the clause, I happened to turn and catch Mrs. _____'s intent and waiting eye; my conversation with her flashed upon me, and in spite of all I could do I smiled. She took it for the signal, and promptly delivered a mellow laugh that touched off the whole audience; and the explosion that followed was the triumph of the evening. I thought that that honest man Sawyer would choke himself; and as for the bludgeons, they performed like pile drivers. But my poor little morsel of pathos was ruined. It was taken in good faith as an intentional joke, and the prize one of the entertainment, and I wisely let it go at that.

All the papers were kind in the morning; my appetite returned; I had abundance of money. All's well that ends well.

I LAUNCHED out as a lecturer, now, with great boldness. I had the field all to myself, for public lectures were almost an unknown commodity in the Pacific market. They are not so rare, now, I suppose. I took an old personal friend along to play agent for me, and for two or three weeks we roamed through Nevada and California and had a very cheerful time of it.[4] Two days before I lectured in Virginia City, two stagecoaches were robbed within two miles of the town. The daring act was committed just at dawn, by six masked men, who sprang up alongside the coaches, presented revolvers at the heads of the drivers and passengers, and commanded a general dismount. Everybody climbed down, and the robbers took their watches and every cent they had.

[4]The San Francisco lecture was delivered on October 2, 1866. Since the first lecture on the tour was given in Sacramento on October 11, the likelihood is that the appearances were scheduled before the initial lecture's success. Seven lectures on the tour were given in October, and two in November, before he returned to San Francisco to give a second lecture there on November 16.

Then they took gunpowder and blew up the express specie boxes and got their contents. The leader of the robbers was a small, quick-spoken man, and the fame of his vigorous manner and his intrepidity was in everybody's mouth when we arrived.

The night after instructing Virginia, I walked over the desolate "divide" and down to Gold Hill, and lectured there. The lecture done, I stopped to talk with a friend, and did not start back till eleven. The "divide" was high, unoccupied ground, between the towns, the scene of twenty midnight murders and a hundred robberies. As we climbed up and stepped out on this eminence, the Gold Hill lights dropped out of sight at our backs, and the night closed down gloomy and dismal. A sharp wind swept the place, too, and chilled our perspiring bodies through.

"I tell you I don't like this place at night," said Mike, the agent.

"Well, don't speak so loud," I replied. "You needn't remind anybody that we are here."

Just then a dim figure approached me from the direction of Virginia—a man, evidently. He came straight at me, and I stepped aside to let him pass; he stepped in the way and confronted me again. Then I saw that he had a mask on and was holding something in my face—I heard a click-click and recognized a revolver in dim outline. I pushed the barrel aside with my hand and said:

"Don't!"

He ejaculated sharply:

"Your watch! Your money!"

I said:

"You can have them with pleasure—but take the pistol away from my face. It makes me shiver."

"No remarks! Hand out your money!"

"Certainly I "

"Put up your hands! Don't you go for a weapon! Put 'em up! Higher!"

I held them above my head.

A pause. Then:

"Are you going to hand out your money or not?"

I dropped my hands to my pockets and said:

"Certainly! I—"

"Put up your *hands*! Do you want your head blown off? Higher!"

I put them above my head again.

Another pause.

"*Are* you going to hand out your money or *not*? Ah-ah—again? Put up your hands! By George, you want the head shot off you awful bad!"

"Well, friend, I'm trying my best to please you. You tell me to give up my money, and when I reach for it you tell me to put up my hands. If you would only— Oh, now—don't! All six of you at me! That other man will get away while— Now, please take some of those revolvers out of my face. Each time one of them clicks my liver comes up into my throat! If you have a mother, or if any of you have ever *had* a mother—or a—grandmother—"

"Cheese it! *Will* you give up your money, or have we got to— There—there—none of that! Put up your *hands*!"

"Gentlemen. Yes I know you are gentlemen by your—"

"Silence! If you want to be facetious, young man, there are times and places more fitting. *This* is a serious business."

"You prick the marrow of my opinion. The funerals I have attended in my time were comedies compared to it. Now, *I* think—"

"Curse your palaver! Your money!—your money!—your money! Hold!—put up your hands!"

"Gentlemen, listen to reason. You *see* how I am situated—now *don't* put those pistols so close—I smell the powder. You see how I am situated. If I had four hands—so that I could hold up two and—"

"Throttle him! Gag him! Kill him!"

"Gentlemen, *don't*! Nobody's watching the other fellow. Why don't some of you— Ouch! Take it away, please! Gentlemen, you see that I've got to hold up my hands; and so I can't take out my money—but if you'll be so kind as to take it out for me, I will do as much for you some—"

"Search him, Beauregard—and stop his jaw with a bullet, quick, if he wags it again. Help, Beauregard, Stonewall."

Then three of them, with the small, spry leader, adjourned to Mike and fell to searching him. I was so excited that my lawless fancy tortured me to ask my two men all manner of facetious questions about their rebel brother-generals of the South, but, considering the order they had received, it was surely common prudence to keep still. When everything had been taken from me—watch, money, and a multitude of trifles of small value—I supposed I was free, and forthwith put my cold hands into my empty pockets and began an inoffensive jig to warm my feet and stir up some latent courage—but instantly all pistols were at my head, and the order came again:

"Be still! Put up your hands! And *keep* them up!"

They stood Mike up alongside of me, with strict orders to keep his hands above his head, too, and then the chief highwayman said:

"Beauregard, hide behind that boulder; Phil Sheridan, you hide behind that other one; Stonewall Jackson, put yourself behind that sage bush there. Keep your pistols bearing on these fellows, and if they take down their hands within ten minutes, or move a single peg, let them have it!"

Then three disappeared in the gloom toward the several ambushes, and the other three disappeared down the road toward Virginia.

It was depressingly still, and miserably cold. Now, this whole thing was a practical joke, and the robbers were personal friends of ours in disguise, and twenty more lay hidden within ten feet of us during the whole operation, listening. Mike knew all of this, and was in on the joke, but I suspected nothing of it. To me it was most uncomfortably genuine.

When we had stood there in the middle of the road five minutes, like a couple of idiots, with our hands aloft, freezing to death by inches, Mike's interest in the joke began to wane. He said:

"The time's up, now, ain't it?"

"No, you keep still. Do you want to take any chances with those bloody savages?"

Presently Mike said:

"*Now* the time's up, anyway. I'm freezing."

"Well, freeze. Better to freeze than carry your brains home in a basket. Maybe the time *is* up, but how do *we* know?—got no watch to tell by. I mean to give them good measure. I calculate to stand here fifteen minutes or die. Don't you move."

So, without knowing it, I was making one joker very sick of his contract. When we took our arms down at last, they were aching with cold and fatigue, and when we went sneaking off, the dread I was in that the time might not yet be up and that we would feel bullets in a moment, was not sufficient to draw all my attention from the misery that racked my stiffened body.

The joke of these highwayman friends of ours was mainly a joke upon themselves; for they had waited for me on the cold hilltop two full hours before I came, and there was very little fun in that; they were so chilled that it took them a couple of weeks to get warm again. Moreover, I never had any thought that they would kill me to get money which it was so perfectly easy to get without any such folly, and so they did not really frighten me bad enough to make their enjoyment worth the trouble they had taken. I was only afraid that their weapons would discharge accidentally. Their very numbers inspired me with confidence that no blood would be intentionally spilled. They were not smart; they ought to have sent only *one* highwayman, with a double-barreled shotgun, if they desired to see the author of this volume climb a tree.[5]

However, I suppose that in the long run I got the largest share of the joke at last; and in a shape not foreseen by the highwaymen; for the chilly exposure on the "divide" while I was in a perspiration gave me a cold which developed itself into a troublesome disease and kept my hands idle some three months, besides costing me quite a sum in doctors' bills. Since then I play no practical jokes on people and generally lose my temper when one is played upon me.

When I returned to San Francisco I projected a pleasure journey to Japan and thence westward around the world; but a strong desire to see home again changed my mind, and I took a berth in the steamship, bade goodby to the friendliest land and

[5]Evidently the author was much more irritated by the prank than his account indicates. He cancelled a second lecture scheduled in Virginia City for the following evening and left at once for San Francisco.

liveliest, heartiest community on our continent, and came by the way of the Isthmus to New York; a trip that was not much of a picnic excursion, for the cholera broke out among us on the passage, and we buried two or three bodies at sea every day. I found home a dreary place after my long absence; for half the children I had known were now wearing whiskers or waterfalls, and few of the grown people I had been acquainted with remained at their hearthstones prosperous and happy—some of them had wandered on to other scenes, some were in jail, and the rest had been hanged. These changes touched me deeply, and I went away and joined the famous Quaker City European Excursion and carried my tears to foreign lands.

Thus, after seven years of vicissitudes, ended a "pleasure trip" to the silver mines of Nevada which had originally been intended to occupy only three months. However, I usually miss my calculations further than that.

# Index

# INDEX

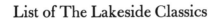

List of The Lakeside Classics

# The Lakeside Classics

447